Sell the Peaks and Buy the Dips

Understand the Crypto World and Thrive in the Most Lucrative Business of the Century

By

Jake Folger

© Copyright 2021by Jake Folger - All rights reserved.

This document is geared towards providing exact and reliable information regarding the topic and issue covered. The publication is sold with the idea that the publisher is not required to render accounting, officially permitted, or otherwise, qualified services. Suppose advice is necessary, legal, or professional. In that case, a practiced individual in the profession should be ordered from a Declaration of Principles, which was accepted and approved equally by a Committee of the American Bar Association and a Committee of Publishers and Associations. In no way is it legal to reproduce, duplicate, or transmit any part of this document in either electronic means or printed format. Recording of this publication is strictly prohibited, and any storage of this document is not allowed unless with written permission from the publisher. All rights reserved.

The information provided herein is stated to be truthful and consistent. In terms of inattention or otherwise, any liability, by any usage or abuse of any policies, processes, or directions contained within is the recipient reader's solitary and utter responsibility. Under no circumstances will any legal responsibility or blame be held against the publisher for reparation, damages, or monetary loss due to the information herein, either directly or indirectly.

Respective authors own all copyrights not held by the publisher.

The information herein is offered for informational purposes solely and is universal as such. The presentation of the information is without a contract or any guarantee assurance. The trademarks used are without any consent, and the publication of the trademark is without permission or backing by the trademark owner. All trademarks and brands within this book are for clarifying purposes only and are owned by the owners themselves, not affiliated with this document.

Table of Contents

Bubble or Revolution? The Basics of Bitcoin and Blockchain.

Chapter 1. What Is Bitcoin? 15

Chapter 2. What is Blockchain? 34

Chapter 3. Understanding the Crypto Market............................66

Chapter 4. Investing in Crypto Market 78

Chapter 5. The Beginner's Guide 94

The Cryptocurrency Investing | Advanced Guide

Chapter 1. Understanding cryptocurrency 122

Chapter 2. Mining of Cryptocurrency....................................161

Chapter 3. Before You Begin...191

Chapter 4. Are cryptocurrencies a good investment? 234

Dropshipping Business Model on a Budget

Introduction 248

Chapter 1. What is Dropshipping? 250

1.1 Benefits of dropshipping 251

Chapter 2. How Dropshipping Works 258

2.1 Awareness about the Supply Chain 259

2.2 The Supply Chain Process 259

2.3 What is Fulfillment? 261

2.4 The Steps to make Order Fulfillment 262

Chapter 3. Why dropshipping is one of the best way to make money in 2021. 264

3.1 Dropshipping Is The E-Commerce Future 265

Chapter 4. Niche And Product Selection 268

4.1 Steps how to search your right niche 269

4.2 Creating a good niche 273

Chapter 5. How to start dropshipping business in 2021 277

1. Commit yourself for starting a dropshipping business 278

2. Dropshipping business idea to chose 282

3. Do competitor research 283

4. Choose a dropshipping supplier 283

5. Build your ecommerce store 284

6. Market your dropshipping store 284

7. Analyze your offering 286

Chapter 6. How To identify Best Suppliers For Your New Dropshipping Business 288

6.1 The Importance of Selecting The Right Suppliers 289

6.2 Finding Your Dropshipping Suppliers 289

Chapter 7. Setting Up Your Dropshipping business On A Budget 297

1. Research Your Options 298

2. Create a Plan to Stick..298

3. Find Your Niche..299

4. Set Up Your eCommerce website 299

5. Make Meetings With Your Suppliers 300

6. Start Selling...301

7. Optimize Your Site 301

Chapter 8. Mistakes To Avoid When Developing Your Dropshipping Business..303

1. Worrying About Shipping Costs...305

2. Relying Much on Vendors..305

3. Expecting Easy Money...305

4. Making Order Difficult to Access. 306

5. Not Enough Brand Display...306

6. Return Complications. 306

7. Selling Trademarked Products 307

8. Picking the Wrong Field 308

9. Poor Relationship With Suppliers..308

10. Lowering Price To Extreme Levels 309

11. Poor Website Structure 309

Chapter 9. Smooth Running tips for Your Dropshipping Business 311

1. Add Value 312

2. Focus on SEO and marketing....................................313

3. Marketing Your Dropshipping Business 313

4. Social Media Source...314

5. Customer Ratings & Reviews 314

6. Email Marketing 315

7. Growth Hacking 315

Chapter 10. How To Maximize Your Chances Of Success?...........316

1. Things To Remember 317

Conclusion 320

<u>Short Stays Real Estate with No (or Low) Money Down</u>

Introduction...326

CHAPTER 1: Understand Income and Importance of Passive Income 330

1.1 Active Income..330

1.2 Portfolio Income...333

1.3 Passive Income 335

1.4 Taxing of passive income 339

1.5 Why Passive Income Beats Earned Income 340

1.6 Reasons Why Passive Income Is So Important 342

CHAPTER 2: Passive income ideas to help you make money in 2021........................349

2.1 How many streams of income should you have? 350

2.2 Passive income ideas for building wealth 351

2.3 Selling information products 351

2.4 Rental income 352

2.5 Affiliate marketing........................354

2.6 Flip retail products 356

2.7 Peer-to-peer lending 357

2.8 Dividend stocks........................359

2.9 Create an app........................360

2.10 REITs........................361

2.11 A bond ladder........................363

2.12 Invest in a high-yield CD or savings account 365

2.13 Buy Property........................366

2.14 Rent out your home short-term through Airbnb..................367

2.15 Air BnB Business as a Passive income Strategy 368

2.16 Advertise on your car........................373

2.17 Invest in Stocks........................374

2.18 Make Your Car Work for You 375

2.19 Sell your Videos 376

2.20 Create YouTube Videos 377

2.21 Write an eBook 377

2.22 Sell Digital Products 378

2.23 CPC Ads (Cost Per Click) 379

2.24 Minimize your taxes on passive income 380

CHAPTER 3:   Airbnb Offers The Best Passive Income
Generation Strategy 382

3.1 Understand the Vacation Rental Industry 383

3.2 Create a Maintenance Management System 384

3.3 Put Together a Vacation Rental Marketing Strategy 385

3.4 Invest in Property Management Tools 386

3.5 Outline Your Guest Management Strategy 388

3.6 Set a Reasonable (But Competitive) Price 389

3.7 How an Airbnb Business Works 390

3.8 The Bottom Line 402

Conclusion 404

The Complete Startup Crash Course

Introduction 408

CHAPTER 1: Lean Start-up..412

1.1 Learn to build a Lean Start-up...415

CHAPTER 2: Importance of Market Research.........................423

2.1 Develop an understanding of the Market Research.............424

2.2 Collection of information through Market Research 425

CHAPTER 3: Digital Entrepreneurship 432

CHAPTER 4: The Best Business 443

4.1 Start your own online Dropshipper business 444

4.2 How to Find and Work with Reliable Dropshipping Suppliers
....458

Conclusion 492

Deducting | The Right Way

Introduction..499

Chapter: 1 Online Business and its importance? 500

1.1 The importance of eCommerce..501

Chapter: 2 Accounting and Its Purpose 512

2.1 Why is Accounting Important? 512

2.2 What Is the Purpose of Accounting? 512

Chapter: 3 Why Is Accounting Useful for Small Business Owners? 517

Chapter: 4 Accounting basics How to Run a Successful Online Business 519

Chapter: 5 Common Accounting Mistakes and How to Avoid Them 532

Chapter: 6 Business Challenges & Solutions 536

Chapter: 7 Key Accounting Terms 552

Chapter: 8 Common Accounting Reports 555

8.1 Profit & Loss Statement 555

8.2 Balance Sheet 556

8.2 Cash Flow Statement 557

Chapter: 9 Taxation 559

9.1 What is Taxation 559

9.2 Purposes of Taxation 559

9.2 Classes of Taxes 560

Chapter: 10 Small Business Tax Return 567

Chapter: 11 How to Audit Your E-commerce Business 573

11.1 Review your current vision...573

11.2 Be critical 574

11.3 Use tools to source the accurate data you need 576

11.4 Get into auditing to maximize the value of your business .577

Chapter: 12 The impact of Covid-19 on eCommerce......................579

12.1 Six% eCommerce revenue decreased during the lockdown 580

12.2 Online profit margin increased by 38%...................581

12.3 The impact of Covid-19 on the workforce 582

12.4 Measurements for physical retailers...........................583

12.5 Shifted strategies 584

12.6 Financial consequences 585

Chapter: 13 What is the Future for Online Business? 586

Conclusion 590

Bubble or Revolution? The Basics of Bitcoin and Blockchain.

The Idiot-Proof Guide to Understand the Crypto Market and Become a Skilled Investor and Trader Starting from Scratch.

By

Jake Folger

Table of Contents

Chapter 1. What Is Bitcoin? 15

Chapter 2. What is Blockchain? 34

Chapter 3. Understanding the Crypto Market 66

Chapter 4. Investing in Crypto Market 78

Chapter 5. The Beginner's Guide 94

Chapter 1. What Is Bitcoin?

Bitcoin is advanced cash that was made in January 2009. It follows the thoughts set out in a white paper by the strange and pseudonymous Satoshi Nakamoto.The personality of the individual or people who made the innovation is as yet a secret. Bitcoin offers the guarantee of lower exchange charges than conventional online installment instruments, and, not at all like officially sanctioned monetary forms, it is worked by a decentralized position.

Bitcoin is a sort of cryptographic money. There are no physical bitcoins and just adjusts on a public record that everybody has straightforward admittance to. A monstrous measure of processing power checks all bitcoin exchanges. Bitcoins are not given or supported by any banks or governments, nor are individual bitcoins significant as a product. Notwithstanding it not being legitimate delicate, Bitcoin is well known and has set off many other digital forms of money, altogether alluded to as Altcoin. Bitcoin is normally condensed as "BTC."

Understanding Bitcoin

The bitcoin framework is an assortment of PCs (additionally alluded to as "hubs" or "diggers") that all run bitcoin's code and store its blockchain. Allegorically, a blockchain can be considered as an assortment of squares. In each square is an assortment of exchanges. Since every one of the PCs running the blockchain has similar rundown of squares and exchanges and can straightforwardly see these new squares being loaded up with new bitcoin exchanges, nobody can swindle the framework.

Regardless of whether they run a bitcoin "hub" or not, anybody can see these exchanges happening live. To accomplish a scandalous demonstration, a troublemaker would have to work 51% of the registering power that makes up bitcoin. Bitcoin has around 12,000 hubs as of January 2021, and this number is developing, making such an assault very unlikely.

In any case, if an assault were to occur, the bitcoin diggers, individuals who participate in the bitcoin network with their PC, would almost certainly fork to another blockchain putting forth the attempt the agitator set forth to accomplish the assault a waste.

Equilibriums of bitcoin tokens are kept utilizing public and hidden "keys," which are long series of numbers and letters connected through the numerical encryption calculation used to make them. The public key (similar to a financial balance number) fills in as the location distributed to the world and to which others may send bitcoins.

The private key (similar to an ATM PIN) is intended to be a watched secret and simply used to approve Bitcoin transmissions. Bitcoin keys ought not to be mistaken for a bitcoin wallet, a physical or computerized gadget that works with the exchanging of bitcoin and permits clients to follow responsibility for. The expression "wallet" is somewhat deceptive, as bitcoin's decentralized nature implies that it is rarely put away "in" a wallet but instead appropriately on a blockchain.

Peer-to-Peer Technology

Bitcoin is one of the main advanced monetary standards to utilize distributed innovation to work with moment installments. The autonomous people and organizations that own the overseeing figuring control and take an interest in the bitcoin network bitcoin "excavators" are accountable for handling the exchanges on the blockchain and are roused by remunerations (the arrival of new bitcoin) and exchange charges paid in bitcoin.

These excavators can be considered as the decentralized authority upholding the validity of the bitcoin network. New bitcoin is delivered to the diggers at a fixed yet intermittently declining rate. There is just 21 million bitcoin that can be mined altogether. As of January 30, 2021, there are around 18,614,806 bitcoin in presence and 2,385,193 bitcoin left to be mined.

Along these lines, bitcoin other digital forms of money work uniquely in contrast to fiat cash; in unified financial frameworks, the cash is delivered at a rate coordinating with the development in merchandise; this framework is proposed to keep up value steadiness. A decentralized framework, as bitcoin, sets the delivery rate early and as per a calculation.

Bitcoin Mining

Bitcoin mining is the interaction by which bitcoins are delivered into dissemination. By and large, mining requires settling computationally troublesome riddles to find another square, which is added to the blockchain.

Bitcoin mining adds and confirms exchange records across the organization. Excavators are compensated with a couple bitcoins; the prize is split each 210,000 squares. The square prize was 50 new bitcoins in 2009. On May 11, 2020, the third splitting happened, bringing the prize for each square revelation down to 6.25 bitcoins.

An assortment of equipment can be utilized to mine bitcoin. Nonetheless, some yield higher prizes than others. Certain CPUs, called Application-Specific Integrated Circuits (ASIC), and further developed handling units, similar to Graphic Processing Units (GPUs), can accomplish more rewards. These intricate mining processors are known as "mining rigs."

One bitcoin is detachable to eight decimal spots (100 millionths of one bitcoin), and this littlest unit is alluded to as a Satoshi if important. On the off chance that the taking interest diggers acknowledge the change, Bitcoin could at last be distinguishable to much more decimal spots.

History of Bitcoin

August 18, 2008

The area name bitcoin.org is enrolled. Today, this space is "WhoisGuard Protected," which means the personality of the individual who enrolled it isn't public data.

October 31, 2008

An individual or gathering utilizing the name Satoshi Nakamoto makes a declaration on The Cryptography Mailing list at metzdowd.com: "I've been chipping away at another electronic money framework that is completely distributed, with no confided in outsider. This now-acclaimed whitepaper distributed on bitcoin.org, named "Bitcoin: A Peer-to-Peer Electronic Cash System," would turn into the Magna Carta for how Bitcoin works today.

January 3, 2009

The principal Bitcoin block is mined Block 0. This progression is otherwise called the "beginning square" and contains the content: "The Times 03/Jan/2009 Chancellor near the very edge of second bailout for banks," maybe as evidence that the square was mined on or after that date, and maybe likewise as significant political commentary.

Jan. 8, 2009

The principal variant of the bitcoin programming is reported on The Cryptography Mailing list.

January 9, 2009

Square 1 is mined, and bitcoin mining begins vigorously.

Who Is Satoshi Nakamoto?

No one understands who made bitcoin, or if nothing else not conclusively. Satoshi Nakamoto is the name related with the individual or social event of people who conveyed the main Bitcoin white paper in 2008 and worked on the primary Bitcoin programming conveyed in 2009. Since that time, various individuals have either declared to be or have been proposed as the certifiable people behind the nom de plume. Regardless, as of January 2021, the certified character (or characters) behind Satoshi stays blurred.

Despite the fact that it is enticing to accept the media's twist that Satoshi Nakamoto is a lone, impractical virtuoso who made Bitcoin out of nowhere, such advancements don't ordinarily occur in a vacuum. Regardless of how unique appearing, all major logical revelations were based on beforehand existing exploration.

There are forerunners to Bitcoin: Adam Back's Hashcash, imagined in 1997,8 and thusly Wei Dai's b-cash, Nick Szabo's touch gold, and Hal Finney's Reusable Proof of Work. The bitcoin whitepaper itself refers to Hashcash and b-cash and different works traversing a few examination fields. Maybe obviously, a considerable lot of the people behind different ventures named above have been estimated to have likewise had a section in making bitcoin.

There are a couple of potential inspirations for bitcoin's creators choosing to stay quiet. One is protection: As bitcoin has acquired in notoriety — turning out to be something of an overall wonder — Satoshi Nakamoto would almost certainly collect a ton of consideration from the media and governments...

Another explanation could be the potential for bitcoin to cause a significant interruption in the current banking and financial frameworks. On the off chance that bitcoin were to acquire mass selection, the framework could outperform countries' sovereign fiat monetary standards. This danger to existing cash could propel governments to need to make a lawful move against bitcoin's maker.

The other explanation is wellbeing. 32,489 squares were mined; at the award pace of 50 bitcoin per block, the absolute payout in 2009 was 1,624,500 bitcoin. One may reason that solitary Satoshi and maybe a couple of others were mining through 2009 and have a dominant part of that reserve of bitcoin.

Somebody possessing that much bitcoin could turn into an objective of crooks, particularly since bitcoins are less similar to stocks and more like money. The private keys expected to approve spending could be printed out and held under a sleeping pad. The designer of Bitcoin would avoid potential risk to make any blackmail prompted moves discernible; staying mysterious is a decent path for Satoshi to restrict openness.

Special Considerations
Bitcoin as a Form of Payment

Bitcoins can be acknowledged as methods for installment for items sold or benefits gave. Physical stores can show a sign saying "Bitcoin Accepted Here"; the exchanges can be taken care of with the imperative equipment terminal or wallet address through QR codes and contact screen applications. An online business can undoubtedly acknowledge bitcoins by adding this installment alternative to its other online installment choices: Mastercards, PayPal, and so on

Bitcoin Employment Opportunities

The individuals who are independently employed can find paid for a line of work identified with bitcoin. There are a few different ways to accomplish this, for example, making any web access and adding your bitcoin wallet address to the website as a type of installment. There are additionally a few sites and occupation sheets that are committed to computerized monetary standards:

- Cryptogrind unites work searchers and imminent managers through its site.
- Coinality highlights occupations — independent, low maintenance and full-time — that offer installment in bitcoins, just as other digital currencies like Dogecoin and Litecoin
- Jobs4Bitcoins, part of reddit.com
- BitGigs
- Bitwage offers an approach to pick a level of your work check to be changed over into bitcoin and shipped off your bitcoin address.

Putting resources into Bitcoins

Numerous Bitcoin allies accept that advanced cash is what's to come. Numerous people who underwrite bitcoin accept that it works with a lot quicker, low-expense installment framework for exchanges around the world. Albeit any administration or national bank doesn't back it, bitcoin can be traded for conventional monetary forms; truth be told, its conversion scale against the dollar draws in expected financial backers and brokers intrigued by cash plays. For sure, one of the essential purposes behind the development of computerized monetary standards like bitcoin is that they can go about as an option in contrast to public fiat cash and conventional wares like gold.

In March 2014, the IRS expressed that every virtual cash, including bitcoins, would be burdened as property instead of money. Gains or misfortunes from bitcoins held as capital will be acknowledged as capital increases or misfortunes, while bitcoins held as stock will cause normal additions or misfortunes. The offer of bitcoins that you mined or bought from another gathering, or the utilization of bitcoins to pay for merchandise or administrations, is instances of exchanges that can be burdened.

Like some other resource, the standard of purchasing low and selling high applies to bitcoins. The most famous method of storing up the money is through purchasing on a bitcoin trade, however there are numerous alternate approaches to procure and claim bitcoins.

Types of Risks Associated With Bitcoin Investing

In spite of the fact that Bitcoin was not planned as an ordinary value venture (no offers have been given), some theoretical financial backers were attracted to the computerized cash after it appreciated quickly in May 2011 and again in November 2013. Subsequently, numerous individuals buy bitcoin for its speculation esteem as opposed to its capacity to go about as a mode of trade.

Nonetheless, the absence of ensured worth and its advanced nature implies the buy and utilization of bitcoins conveys a few inalienable dangers. Numerous financial backer cautions have been given by the Securities and Exchange Commission (SEC), the Financial Industry Regulatory Authority (FINRA), the Consumer Financial Protection Bureau (CFPB), and different organizations.

The idea of virtual cash is as yet novel and, contrasted with conventional speculations; bitcoin doesn't have a very remarkable longterm history or history of validity to back it. With their expanding prominence, bitcoins are turning out to be fewer tests each day; after just 10 years, all advanced monetary forms stay in an improvement stage. "It is essentially the most noteworthy danger, best yield venture that you can make," says Barry Silbert, CEO of Digital Currency Group, which fabricates and puts resources into Bitcoin and blockchain organizations.

Administrative Risk

Putting cash into bitcoin in any of its numerous pretenses isn't for the danger loath. Bitcoins are an adversary to government cash and might be utilized for underground market exchanges, illegal tax avoidance, criminal operations, or tax avoidance. Therefore, governments may look to manage, confine, or boycott the utilization and offer of bitcoins (and some as of now have). Others are thinking of different standards.

For instance, in 2015, the New York State Department of Financial Services settled guidelines that would require organizations managing the purchase, sell, move, or capacity of bitcoins to record the personality of clients, have a consistence official, and keep up capital stores. The exchanges worth $10,000 or more should be recorded and detailed.

The absence of uniform guidelines about bitcoins (and other virtual money) brings up issues over their life span, liquidity, and all-inclusiveness.

Security Risk

Most people who own and use bitcoin have not procured their tokens through mining activities. Maybe, they purchase and sell bitcoin and other computerized monetary standards on some famous online business sectors, known as bitcoin trades.

Bitcoin trades are completely computerized and, similarly as with any virtual framework, are in danger from programmers, malware, and operational glitches. In the event that a criminal accesses a Bitcoin proprietor's PC hard drive and takes their private encryption key, they could move the taken bitcoin to another record. (Clients can forestall this just if bitcoins are put away on a

PC that isn't associated with the Internet, or, more than likely by deciding to utilize a paper wallet printing out the bitcoin private keys and addresses and not keeping them on a PC by any means.)

Programmers can likewise target Bitcoin trades, accessing a great many records and advanced wallets where bitcoins are put away. One particularly famous hacking episode occurred in 2014, when Mt. Gox, a bitcoin trade in Japan, had to shut down after large number of dollars' worth of bitcoins was taken.

This is especially hazardous, given that all Bitcoin exchanges are lasting and irreversible. It resembles managing cash: Any exchange did with bitcoins must be turned around if the individual who has gotten them discounts them. There is no outsider or an installment processor, as on account of a charge or MasterCard—thus, no wellspring of assurance or allure if there is an issue.

Protection Risk

A few ventures are safeguarded through the Securities Investor Protection Corporation. Typical financial balances are guaranteed through the Federal Deposit Insurance Corporation (FDIC) up to a specific sum contingent upon the purview.

As a rule, bitcoin trades and bitcoin accounts are not protected by any bureaucratic or government program. In 2019, the great seller and exchanging stage SFOX reported it would furnish bitcoin financial backers with FDIC protection, however just for the part of exchanges including cash.13

Extortion Risk

While bitcoin utilizes private key encryption to check proprietors and register exchanges, fraudsters and tricksters may endeavor to sell bogus bitcoins. For example, in July 2013, the SEC brought lawful activity against an administrator of a bitcoin-related Ponzi conspire. There have likewise been recorded instances of bitcoin value control, another basic type of misrepresentation.

Market Risk

Like with any speculation, Bitcoin esteems can vary. Undoubtedly, the money's worth has seen wild swings in cost over its short presence. Subject to high volume purchasing and selling on trades, it has a high affectability to any newsworthy occasions. As per the CFPB, the cost of bitcoins fell by 61% in a solitary day in 2013, while the one-day value drop record in 2014 was just about as large as 80%.

In the event that fewer individuals start to acknowledge bitcoin as money, these computerized units may lose esteem and could get useless. Without a doubt, there was theory that the "bitcoin bubble" had blasted when the cost declined from its untouched high during the cryptographic money surge in late 2017 and mid-2018.

There is as of now a lot of rivalry. In spite of the fact that Bitcoin has a colossal lead over the many other advanced monetary standards that have jumped up on account of its image acknowledgment and investment cash, a mechanical leap forward as a superior virtual coin is consistently a danger.

Splits in the Cryptocurrency Community

In the years since Bitcoin dispatched, there have been various examples in which conflicts between groups of excavators and engineers incited huge scope parts of the digital currency local area. In a portion of these cases, gatherings of Bitcoin clients and diggers have changed the bitcoin network convention itself.

This cycle is known as "forking" and it as a rule brings about making another sort of bitcoin with another name. This split can be a "hard fork," in which another coin imparts exchange history to bitcoin until a definitive split point, so, all in all another token is made. Instances of cryptographic forms of money that have been made because of hard forks incorporate bitcoin cash (made in August 2017), bitcoin gold (made in October 2017), and Bitcoin SV (made in November 2017).

A "delicate fork" is a change to the convention that is as yet viable with the past framework rules. For instance, bitcoin delicate forks have expanded the complete size of squares.

Chapter 2. What is Blockchain?

Blockchain appears to be convoluted, and it unquestionably can be, yet its center idea is very basic. A blockchain is a sort of data set. Understanding blockchain assists first with understanding what an information base is.

A data set is an assortment of data that is put away electronically on a PC framework. In data sets, data or information is regularly organized in table arrangement to take into consideration simpler looking and separating of explicit data. What is the contrast between utilizing a bookkeeping page to store data instead of an information base?

Bookkeeping pages are intended for one individual, or a little gathering of individuals, to store and access restricted measures of data. Conversely, a data set is intended to house altogether bigger measures of data that can be gotten to, separated, and controlled rapidly and effectively by quite a few clients on the double.

Enormous data sets accomplish this by lodging information on workers made of amazing PCs. These workers can some of the time be constructed utilizing hundreds or thousands of PCs to have the computational force and capacity limit important for some clients to get to the information base at the same time. While a bookkeeping page or information base might be open to numerous individuals, it is regularly possessed by a business and overseen by a selected person who has unlimited oversight over how it functions and the information inside it.

Storage Structure

One key distinction between a normal data set and a blockchain is the manner by which the information is organized. A blockchain gathers data together in gatherings, otherwise called blocks that hold sets of data. Squares have certain capacity limits and, when filled, are affixed onto the recently filled square, framing a chain of information known as the "blockchain." All new data that follows that newly added block is arranged into a recently shaped square that will at that point likewise be added to the chain once filled.

A data set designs its information into tables, while a blockchain, similar to its name suggests, structures its information into pieces (blocks) affixed together. This makes it with the goal that all blockchains are data sets, however not all data sets are blockchains. This framework likewise naturally makes an irreversible timetable of information when executed in a decentralized nature. At the point when a square is filled, it is unchangeable and turns into a piece of this course of events. Each square in the chain is given a precise timestamp when added to the chain.

Decentralization

For comprehension blockchain, it is informative to see it with regards to how Bitcoin has carried out it. Like an information base, Bitcoin needs an assortment of PCs to store its blockchain. For Bitcoin, this blockchain is only a particular kind of information base that stores each Bitcoin exchange at any point made. For Bitcoin's situation, and not at all like most information bases, these PCs are not all under one rooftop. Every PC or gathering of PCs is worked by an exceptional individual or gathering of people.

Envision that an organization claims a worker included 10,000 PCs with a data set holding the entirety of its customer's record data. This organization has a stockroom containing these PCs under one rooftop and has full control of every one of these PCs and all the data contained inside them. Likewise, Bitcoin comprises of thousands of PCs. All things considered, every PC or gathering of PCs that hold its blockchain is in an alternate geographic area, and they are completely worked by independent people or gatherings of individuals. These PCs that make up Bitcoin's Network are called hubs.

In this model, Bitcoin's blockchain is utilized in a decentralized way. Nonetheless, private, concentrated blockchains, where the PCs that make up its organization are possessed and worked by a solitary substance, exist.

In a blockchain, every hub has a full record of the information that has been put away on the blockchain since its commencement. For Bitcoin, the information is the whole history of all Bitcoin exchanges. In the event that one hub has a mistake in its information, it can utilize the huge number of different hubs as a kind of perspective highlight right itself. Thusly, nobody hub inside the organization can adjust data held inside it. Along these lines, the historical backdrop of exchanges in each square that make up Bitcoin's blockchain is irreversible.

In the event that one client alters Bitcoin's record of exchanges, any remaining hubs would cross-reference one another and effectively pinpoint the hub with the mistaken data. This framework assists with setting up a definite and straightforward request of occasions. For Bitcoin, this data is a rundown of exchanges. In any case, it is likewise feasible for a blockchain to hold different data like lawful agreements, state distinguishing pieces of proof, or an organization's item stock.

To change how that framework functions or the data put away inside it, the vast majority of the decentralized organization's registering force would have to concur on said changes. This guarantees that whatever changes happen are in the greater part's wellbeing.

Transparency

On account of the decentralized idea of Bitcoin's blockchain, everything exchanges can be straightforwardly seen by either having an individual hub or by utilizing blockchain wayfarer that permits anybody to see exchanges happening live. Every hub has its duplicate of the chain that gets refreshed as new squares are affirmed and added. This implies that you could follow Bitcoin any place it goes in the event that you needed to.

For instance, trades have been hacked in the past were the individuals who held Bitcoin on the trade lost everything. While the programmer might be altogether unknown, the Bitcoins they separated are effectively detectable. On the off chance that the Bitcoins taken in a portion of these hacks were to be moved or spent some place, it would be known.

Is Blockchain Secure?

Blockchain innovation represents the issues of safety and trust severally. To start with, new squares are constantly put away directly and sequentially. They are constantly added to the "end" of the blockchain. In the event that you take a gander at Bitcoin's blockchain, you'll see that each square has a situation on the chain, called a "tallness." As of November 2020, the square's stature had arrived at 656,197 squares up until now.

After a square has been added to the furthest limit of the blockchain, it is hard to return and change the substance of the square except if the larger part arrived at an agreement to do as such. That is on the grounds that each square contains its hash, alongside the hash of the square before it, just as the recently referenced time stamp. Hash codes are made by a numerical capacity that transforms advanced data into a series of numbers and letters. On the off chance that that data is altered in any capacity, the hash code changes.

Here's the reason that is critical to security. Suppose a programmer needs to modify the blockchain and take Bitcoin from every other person. If they somehow happened to change their single duplicate, it would presently don't line up with every other person's duplicate. At the point when every other person cross-references their duplicates against one another, they would see this one duplicate stick out, and that programmer's rendition of the chain would be given away a role as ill-conceived.

Prevailing with such a hack would necessitate that the programmer at the same time control and change 51% of the duplicates of the blockchain so their new duplicate turns into the dominant part duplicate and, along these lines, the settled upon chain. Such an assault would likewise require a tremendous measure of cash and assets as they would have to re-try the entirety of the squares since they would now have distinctive timestamps and hash codes.

Because of the size of Bitcoin's Network and how quick it is developing, the expense to pull off such an accomplishment would most likely be inconceivable. In addition to the fact that this would be amazingly costly, yet it would likewise likely be vain. Doing something like this would not go undetected, as organization individuals would see such radical changes to the blockchain. The organization individuals would then fork off to another rendition of the chain that has not been influenced.

This would make the assaulted form of Bitcoin fall in esteem, making the assault at last trivial as the troublemaker controls a useless resource. The equivalent would happen if the agitator assaulted the new fork of Bitcoin. It is constructed this way so that participating in the organization is definitely more financially boosted than assaulting it.

Bitcoin vs. Blockchain

The objective of blockchain is to permit advanced data to be recorded and appropriated yet not altered. Blockchain innovation was first laid out in 1991 by Stuart Haber and W. Scott Stornetta, two analysts who needed to carry out a framework where archive timestamps couldn't be messed with. In any case, it wasn't until right around twenty years after the fact, with the dispatch of Bitcoin in January 2009, that blockchain had its first genuine application.

The Bitcoin convention is based on a blockchain. In an exploration paper presenting the computerized money, Bitcoin's pseudonymous maker, Satoshi Nakamoto, alluded to it as "another electronic money framework that is completely shared, with no confided in outsider."

The critical thing to comprehend here is that Bitcoin simply utilizes blockchain to record a record of installments straightforwardly. In any case, in principle, blockchain can be utilized to record quite a few information focuses changelessly. As talked about over, this could be as exchanges, votes in a political decision, item inventories, state IDs, deeds to homes, and considerably more.

There is a wide assortment of blockchain-based activities hoping to carry out blockchain in approaches to help society other than recording exchanges. One genuine model is that of blockchain being utilized to cast a ballot in just decisions. The idea of blockchain's changelessness implies that deceitful democratic would get undeniably harder to happen.

For instance, a democratic framework could work to such an extent that every resident of a nation would be given a solitary digital currency or token. Every competitor would then be given a particular wallet address, and the electors would send their token or crypto to whichever up-and-comer's location they wish to decide in favor of. The straightforward and recognizable nature of blockchain would take out the requirement for human vote checking and the capacity of agitators to mess with actual polling forms.

Blockchain versus Banks

Banks and decentralized blockchains are inconceivably extraordinary. To perceive how a bank contrasts from blockchain, we should contrast the financial framework with Bitcoin's blockchain execution.

How is Blockchain Used?

As we currently know, blocks on Bitcoin's blockchain store information about money related exchanges. Yet, incidentally, blockchain is a solid method of putting away information about different sorts of exchanges.

A few organizations that have effectively joined blockchain incorporate Wal-Mart, Pfizer, AIG, Siemens, Unilever, and a large group of others. For instance, IBM has made its Food Trust blockchain to follow the excursion that food items take to get to their areas.

For what reason do this? The food business has seen endless flare-ups of e Coli, salmonella, listeria, and unsafe materials being unintentionally acquainted with food varieties. It has required a long time to discover the wellspring of these episodes or the reason for infection from what individuals are eating before.

Utilizing blockchain enables brands to follow a food item's course from its root, through each stop it makes, lastly, it is conveyance. In the event that a food is discovered to be sullied, it very well may be followed back through each stop to its root. That, however these organizations can likewise now see all the other things they may have interacted with, permitting the recognizable proof of the issue to happen far sooner, conceivably saving lives. This is one illustration of blockchains practically speaking yet numerous other blockchain execution structures.

Banking and Finance

Maybe no industry stands to profit by coordinating blockchain into its business activities more than banking. Monetary foundations just work during business hours, five days every week. That implies in the event that you attempt to store a keep an eye on Friday at 6 p.m., you will probably need to stand by until Monday morning to see that cash hit your record. Regardless of whether you set aside your installment during business hours, the exchange can in any case take one to three days to check because of the sheer volume of exchanges that banks need to settle. Blockchain, then again, never dozes.

By coordinating blockchain into banks, shoppers can see their exchanges prepared in just 10 minutes. The time it takes to add a square to the blockchain, paying little heed to occasions or the hour of day or week. With blockchain, banks additionally can trade assets between establishments all the more rapidly and safely. For instance, in the stock exchanging business, the repayment and clearing cycle can require as long as three days (or more, if exchanging universally), implying that the cash and offers are frozen for that period.

Given the size of the whole in question, even the couple of days that the cash is on the way can convey significant expenses and dangers for banks. European bank Santander and its exploration accomplices put the possible investment funds at $15 billion to $20 billion per year. Cap Gemini, a French consultancy, appraises that buyers could set aside to $16 billion in banking and protection charges every year through blockchain-based applications.

Money

Blockchain structures the bedrock for digital currencies like Bitcoin. The Federal Reserve controls the US dollar. Under this focal power framework, a client's information and money are in fact at the impulse of their bank or government. In the event that a client's bank is hacked, the customer's private data is in danger. On the off chance that the customer's bank breakdowns or they live in a country with a precarious government, the worth of their money might be in danger. In 2008, a portion of the banks that ran out of cash were rescued in part utilizing citizen cash. These are the concerns out of which Bitcoin was first imagined and created.

By spreading its activities across an organization of PCs, blockchain permits Bitcoin and other digital currencies to work without the requirement for a focal power. This lessens hazard and disposes of a large number of the preparing and exchange expenses. It can likewise give those in nations with insecure monetary standards or monetary frameworks a more steady cash with more applications and a more extensive organization of people and establishments they can work with, both locally and universally.

Utilizing digital money wallets for investment accounts or as methods for installment is particularly significant for the individuals who have no state recognizable proof. A few nations might be war-torn or have governments that do not have any genuine foundation to give ID. Such nations might not approach reserve funds or money market funds and, hence, no real way to store abundance securely.

Medical care

Medical care suppliers can use blockchain to store their patients' clinical records safely. At the point when a clinical record is created and marked, it tends to be composed into the blockchain, which gives patients the evidence and certainty that the record can't be changed. These individual wellbeing records could be encoded and put away on the blockchain with a private key so they are just open by specific people, accordingly guaranteeing security.

Records of Property

On the off chance that you have at any point invested energy in your nearby Recorder's Office, you will realize that the way toward recording property rights is both difficult and wasteful. Today, an actual deed should be conveyed to an administration representative at the neighborhood recording office, where it is physically gone into the region's focal data set and general list. On account of a property debate, cases to the property should be accommodated with the overall file.

This interaction isn't simply expensive and tedious; it is additionally filled with human mistake, where every error makes following property proprietorship less productive. Blockchain can possibly kill the requirement for filtering archives and finding actual documents in a nearby account office. On the off chance that property proprietorship is put away and checked on the blockchain, proprietors can believe that their deed is precise and forever recorded.

In war-torn nations or zones with practically zero government or monetary foundation and absolutely no "Recorder's Office," it very well may be almost difficult to demonstrate responsibility for property. On the off chance that a gathering of individuals living in such a region can use blockchain, straightforward and clear timetables of land owners could be set up.

Shrewd Contract

A savvy contract is a PC code incorporated into the blockchain to work with, confirm, or arrange an agreement understanding. Savvy contracts work under a bunch of conditions that clients consent to. At the point when those conditions are met, the provisions of the understanding are naturally done.

Say, for instance, a potential occupant might want to rent a loft utilizing a keen agreement. The landowner consents to give the inhabitant the entryway code to the condo when the occupant pays the security store. Both the inhabitant and the property manager would send their particular bits of the arrangement to the savvy contract, which would clutch and naturally trade the entryway code for the security store on the date the rent starts. On the off chance that the property manager doesn't supply the entryway code by the rent date, the shrewd agreement discounts the security store. This would wipe out the expenses and cycles normally connected with utilizing a legal official, outsider arbiter, or lawyers.

Supply Chains

As in the IBM Food Trust model, providers can utilize blockchain to record the roots of their bought materials. This would permit organizations to confirm the credibility of their items, alongside such basic marks as "Natural," "Neighborhood," and "Reasonable Trade."

As revealed by Forbes, the food business is progressively receiving blockchain to follow the way and security of food all through the homestead to-client venture.

Casting a ballot

As referenced, blockchain could be utilized to work with a cutting edge casting a ballot framework. Casting a ballot with blockchain conveys the possibility to wipe out political race misrepresentation and lift elector turnout, as was tried in the November 2018 midterm decisions in West Virginia. Utilizing blockchain in this manner would make cast a ballot almost difficult to alter. The blockchain convention would likewise keep up straightforwardness in the appointive interaction, lessening the faculty expected to lead a political decision and giving authorities almost moment results. This would dispose of the requirement for describes or any genuine worry that misrepresentation may compromise the political race.

Advantages and Disadvantages of Blockchain

For the entirety of its intricacy, blockchain's potential as a decentralized type of record-keeping is practically limitless. From more prominent client protection and increased security to bring down preparing expenses and less mistakes, blockchain innovation may well see applications past those laid out above. However, there are additionally a few burdens.

Pros

- Improved exactness by eliminating human contribution in check
- Cost decreases by disposing of outsider check
- Decentralization makes it harder to mess with
- Transactions are secure, private, and effective
- Transparent innovation
- Provides a financial other option and approach to protect individual data for residents of nations with precarious or immature governments

Cons

- Significant innovation cost related with mining bitcoin
- Low exchanges each second
- History of utilization in unlawful exercises
- Regulation

Here are the selling points of blockchain for organizations available today in more detail.

Benefits of Blockchain

Exactness of the Chain

An organization endorses exchanges on the blockchain organization of thousands of PCs. This eliminates practically all human inclusion in the check cycle, bringing about less human blunder and an exact record of data. Regardless of whether a PC on the organization were to commit a computational error, the blunder would just be made to one duplicate of the blockchain. For that mistake to spread to the remainder of the blockchain, at any rate 51% of the organization's PCs would should be made — a close to difficulty for an enormous and developing organization the size of Bitcoin's.

Cost Reductions

Ordinarily, buyers pay a bank to confirm an exchange, a public accountant to sign a record, or a priest to play out a marriage. Blockchain wipes out the requirement for outsider confirmation and, with it, their related expenses. Entrepreneurs cause a little expense at whatever point they acknowledge installments utilizing Visas, for instance, since banks and installment preparing organizations need to deal with those exchanges. Then again, Bitcoin doesn't have a focal position and has restricted exchange charges.

Decentralization

Blockchain doesn't store any of its data in a focal area. All things being equal, the blockchain is replicated and spread across an organization of PCs. At whatever point another square is added to the blockchain, each PC on the organization refreshes its blockchain to mirror the change. By spreading that data across an organization, blockchain turns out to be harder to mess with as opposed to putting away it in one focal data set. In the event that a duplicate of the blockchain fell under the control of a programmer, just a solitary duplicate of the data, as opposed to the whole organization, would be undermined.

Productive Transactions

Exchanges put through a focal authority can take up to a couple of days to settle. On the off chance that you endeavor to store a mind Friday evening, for instance, you may not see assets in your record until Monday morning. While monetary establishments work during business hours, five days every week, blockchain is working 24 hours per day, seven days per week, and 365 days per year. Exchanges can be finished in just ten minutes and can be viewed as secure after only a couple hours. This is especially valuable for cross-line exchanges, which generally take any longer on account of time-region issues and that all gatherings should affirm installment preparing.

Private Transactions

Numerous blockchain networks work as open information bases, implying that anybody with a web association can see an organization's exchange history list. Despite the fact that clients can get to insights regarding exchanges, they can't get to recognizing data about the clients making those exchanges. It is a typical misperception that blockchain networks like bitcoin are unknown when they are just secret.

At the point when a client unveils exchanges, their special code called a public key is recorded on the blockchain as opposed to their own data. In the event that an individual has made a Bitcoin buy on a trade that requires recognizable proof, at that point the individual's character is as yet connected to their blockchain address. In any case, in any event, when attached to an individual's name, an exchange doesn't uncover any close to home data.

Secure Transactions

When an exchange is recorded, its credibility should be checked by the blockchain network. A great many PCs on the blockchain hurry to affirm that the buy subtleties are right. After a PC has approved the exchange, it is added to the blockchain block. Each square on the blockchain contains its exceptional hash, alongside the novel hash of the square before it. At the point when the data on a square is altered in any capacity, that square's hash code changes; nonetheless, the hash code on the square after it would not. This inconsistency makes it incredibly hard for data on the blockchain to be changed without notice.

Straightforwardness

Most blockchains are altogether open-source programming. This implies that anybody and everybody can see its code. This enables inspectors to audit digital forms of money like Bitcoin for security. This additionally implies no genuine expert on who controls Bitcoin's code or how it is altered. Along these lines, anybody can recommend changes or moves up to the framework. In the event that most organization clients concur that the new form of the code with the overhaul is sound and beneficial, at that point Bitcoin can be refreshed.

Banking the Unbanked

Maybe the most significant aspect of blockchain and Bitcoin is the capacity for anybody, paying little heed to nationality, sex, or social foundation, to utilize it. As indicated by the World Bank, almost 2 billion grown-ups don't have ledgers or any methods for putting away their cash or abundance. Virtually these people live in non-industrial nations where the economy is outset and totally reliant upon cash.

These individuals frequently bring in little cash that is paid in actual money. They at that point need to store this actual money in secret areas in their homes or places of living, leaving them subject to burglary or superfluous viciousness. Keys in a bitcoin wallet can be put away on a piece of paper, a modest cell, or even remembered whether essential. For a great many people likely, these alternatives are more effortlessly covered up than a little heap of money under a sleeping pad.

Blockchains of things to come are likewise searching for answers for be a unit of record for abundance stockpiling and store clinical records, property rights, and an assortment of other legitimate agreements.

Disadvantages of Blockchain

While there are huge potential gains to the blockchain, there are additionally critical difficulties to its appropriation. The barricades to the utilization of blockchain innovation today are not simply specialized. The genuine difficulties are political and administrative, generally, to avoid mentioning the great many hours (read: cash) of custom programming plan and back-end programming needed to coordinate blockchain into current business organizations. Here are a portion of the difficulties holding up traffic of far reaching blockchain appropriation.

Innovation Cost

Despite the fact that blockchain can get a good deal on exchange charges, the innovation is a long way from free. The "evidence of work" framework that bitcoin uses to approve exchanges, for instance, burns-through huge measures of computational force. In reality, the force from the large numbers of PCs on the bitcoin network is near what Denmark burns-through yearly. Accepting power expenses of $0.03~$0.05 each kilowatt-hour, mining costs elite of equipment costs are about $5,000~$7,000 per coin.

In spite of the expenses of mining bitcoin, clients keep on driving up their power bills to approve exchanges on the blockchain. That is on the grounds that when diggers add a square to the bitcoin blockchain, they are remunerated with enough bitcoin to make their time and energy advantageous. In any case, with regards to blockchains that don't utilize cryptographic money, excavators should be paid or in any case boosted to approve exchanges.

A few answers for these issues are starting to emerge. For instance, bitcoin mining ranches have been set up to utilize sun oriented force, overabundance petroleum gas from deep oil drilling destinations, or force from wind ranches.

Speed Inefficiency

Bitcoin is an ideal contextual analysis for the potential failures of blockchain. Bitcoin's "confirmation of work" framework requires around ten minutes to add another square to the blockchain. At that rate, it's assessed that the blockchain organization can just oversee around seven exchanges each second (TPS). Albeit other digital currencies, for example, Ethereum perform better compared to bitcoin, they are as yet restricted by blockchain. Inheritance brand Visa, for setting, can deal with 24,000 TPS.

Answers for this issue have been being developed for quite a long time. There are presently blockchains that are gloating more than 30,000 exchanges each second.

Criminal behavior

While classification on the blockchain network shields clients from hacks and jelly protection, it additionally takes into account illicit exchanging and movement on the blockchain network. The most referred to illustration of blockchain being utilized for illegal exchanges is likely the Silk Road, an online "dim web" drug commercial center working from February 2011 until October 2013, when the FBI shut it down.

The site permitted clients to peruse the site without being followed utilizing the Tor program and make illicit buys in Bitcoin or other cryptographic forms of money. Current U.S. guidelines require monetary specialist co-ops to acquire data about their clients when they open a record, check the character of every client, and affirm that clients don't show up on any rundown of known or suspected psychological militant associations. This framework can be viewed as both an expert and a con. It gives anybody admittance to monetary records and permits hoodlums to execute all the more without any problem. Many have contended that the great employments of crypto, such as banking the unbanked world, exceed the awful employments of cryptographic money, particularly when most criminal behavior is as yet achieved through untraceable money.

Guideline

Numerous in the crypto space have communicated worries about unofficial law over cryptographic forms of money. While it is getting progressively troublesome and close to difficult to end something like Bitcoin as its decentralized organization develops, governments could hypothetically make it illicit to claim digital currencies or partake in their organizations.

Over the long run this worry has developed more modest as enormous organizations like PayPal start to permit the possession and utilization of cryptographic forms of money on their foundation.

What's Next for Blockchain?

First proposed as an examination project in 1991, blockchain is serenely sinking into its late twenties. Like most recent college grads its age, blockchain has seen something reasonable of public examination in the course of the most recent twenty years, with organizations overall hypothesizing about what the innovation is able to do and where it's going in the years to come.

With numerous commonsense applications for the innovation previously being carried out and investigated, blockchain at long last becomes well known at age 27, in no little part in view of bitcoin and cryptographic money. As a popular expression on the tongue of each financial backer in the country, blockchain stands to make business and government activities more precise, productive, secure, and modest with fewer delegates.

As we get ready to head into the third decade of blockchain, it's not, at this point an issue of "if" heritage organizations will get on to the innovation; it's an issue of "when."

Chapter 3. Understanding the Crypto Market

There are a few things that each trying Bitcoin financial backer necessities. A digital currency trade account, individual ID reports on the off chance that you are utilizing a Know Your Customer (KYC) stage, a safe association with the Internet, and an installment strategy. It is additionally suggested that you have your wallet outside of the trade account. Legitimate techniques for installment utilizing this way incorporate ledgers, charge cards, and Mastercards. It is likewise conceivable to get Bitcoin at particular ATMs and by means of P2P trades. Notwithstanding, know that Bitcoin ATMs progressively required government provided IDs as of mid-2020.

Protection and security are significant issues for Bitcoin financial backers. Despite the fact that there are no actual Bitcoins, it is normally an impractical notion to gloat about enormous possessions. Any individual who acquires the private key to a public location on the Bitcoin blockchain can approve exchanges. Private keys ought to be kept mystery; hoodlums may endeavor to take them on the off chance that they learn huge possessions. Know that anybody can see the equilibrium of a public location you use. That makes it a smart thought to keep critical speculations at public tends to that are not straightforwardly associated with ones that are utilized for exchanges.

Anybody can see a past filled with exchanges made on the blockchain, even you. Yet, while exchanges are openly recorded on the blockchain, distinguishing client data isn't. Just a client's public key shows up close to an exchange on the Bitcoin blockchain, making exchanges secret yet not unknown. One might say, Bitcoin exchanges are more straightforward and detectable than cash; however the cryptographic money can likewise be utilized namelessly.

Following are a few stages you need to follow in the event that you need to put resources into digital currency:

1. Choose an Exchange

Pursuing a digital money trade will permit you to purchase, sell, and hold digital money. It is by and large best practice to utilize a trade that permits clients to likewise pull out their crypto to their online wallet for more secure keeping. This element may not make any difference for those hoping to exchange Bitcoin or other digital forms of money.

There are numerous kinds of digital money trades. Since the Bitcoin ethos is about decentralization and individual sway, a few trades permit clients to stay unknown and don't expect clients to enter individual data. Such trades work self-governing and, commonly, are decentralized, which implies they don't have an essential issue of control.

While such frameworks can be utilized for odious exercises, they are additionally used to offer types of assistance for the world's unbanked populace. For specific classes of individuals – displaced people or those living in nations with practically no administration credit or banking framework – unknown trades can help carry them into the standard economy.

Be that as it may, the most mainstream trades are not decentralized and do require KYC. In the United States, these trades incorporate Coinbase, Kraken, Gemini, and Binance U.S., to give some examples. These trades have filled altogether in the quantity of highlights they offer.

Coinbase, Kraken, and Gemini offer Bitcoin and a developing number of altcoins. These three are presumably the simplest entrance to crypto in the whole business. Binance takes into account a further developed broker, offering more genuine exchanging usefulness and a superior assortment of altcoins to browse.

Something critical to note while making a digital currency trade account is to utilize safe web rehearses. This incorporates utilizing two-factor confirmation and utilizing an extraordinary and long secret phrase, including an assortment of lower-case letters, uppercase letters, exceptional characters, and numbers.

2.   Connect Your Exchange to a Payment Option

Whenever you have picked a trade, you presently need to accumulate your reports. Contingent upon the trade, these may incorporate photos of a driver's permit, government managed retirement number, just as data about your boss and wellspring of assets. The data you may need can rely upon the area you live in and its laws. The cycle is to a great extent equivalent to setting up an average investment fund.

After the trade has guaranteed your character and authenticity, you may now interface an installment alternative. At most trades, you can associate your ledger straightforwardly, or you can interface with a charge or Mastercard. While you can utilize a Visa to buy cryptographic money, it is by and large something that ought to be kept away from because of the instability that digital currencies can insight.

While Bitcoin is legitimate in the United States, a few banks don't take excessively benevolent to the thought and may address or even stop stores to crypto-related locales or trades. It is a smart thought to check to guarantee that your bank permits stores at your picked trade.

There are differing expenses for stores by means of a financial balance, charge, or Visa. Coinbase is a strong trade for fledglings and has a 1.49% expense for ledgers, with a 3.99% charge for charge and Mastercards. It is critical to investigate the charges related with every installment choice to help pick a trade or pick which installment alternative works best.

Trades additionally charge expenses per exchange. This charge can either be a level expense (if the exchanging sum is low) or a level of the exchanging sum. Visas cause a handling charge notwithstanding the exchange expenses.

3.   Place an Order

Whenever you have picked trade and associated an installment alternative, you would now be able to purchase Bitcoin and other digital forms of money. Lately, cryptographic money trades have gradually become standard. They have filled altogether regarding liquidity and their broadness of highlights. The operational changes at cryptographic money trades equal the adjustment of impression of digital currencies. An industry that was once considered as a trick or one with problematic practices is gradually transforming into a genuine one that has attracted interest from every one of the enormous players the monetary administrations industry.

Presently, cryptographic money trades have arrived at a point where they have almost similar degree of highlights as their stock financier partners. Whenever you have discovered a trade and associated an installment strategy, you are all set.

Crypto trades today offer a few request types and approaches to contribute. Practically all crypto trades offer both market and breaking point requests, and some likewise offer stop-misfortune orders. Of the trades referenced above, Kraken offers the most request types. Kraken takes into account, as far as possible, stop-misfortune, stop-limit, take-benefit, and take-benefit limit orders.

Beside different request types, trades likewise offer approaches to set up repeating speculations permitting customers to dollar cost normal into their ventures of decision. Coinbase, for instance, allows clients to set repeating buys for consistently, week, or month.

4.   Safe Storage

Bitcoin and cryptographic money wallets are a spot to store computerized resources all the more safely. Having your crypto outside of the trade and in your wallet guarantees that lone you have authority over the private key to your assets. It additionally enables you to store finances from a trade and keep away from the danger of your trade getting hacked and losing your assets.

A few wallets have a larger number of highlights than others. Some are Bitcoin just, and some offer the capacity to store various altcoins. A few wallets likewise offer the capacity to trade one token for another.

With regards to picking a Bitcoin wallet, you have a few choices. The main thing you should comprehend about crypto wallets is hot wallets (online wallets) and cold wallets (paper or equipment wallets).

5.   Hot Wallets

Online wallets are otherwise called "hot" wallets. Hot wallets will be wallets that sudden spike in demand for web associated gadgets like PCs, telephones, or tablets. This can make weakness in light of the fact that these wallets produce the private keys to your coins on these web associated gadgets. While a hot wallet can be advantageous in the manner you can access and make exchanges with your resources rapidly, putting away your private key on a web associated gadget makes it more helpless to a hack.

This may sound unrealistic; however individuals who are not utilizing sufficient security when utilizing these hot wallets can have their assets taken. This is certainly not an inconsistent event, and it can happen by one way or another. For instance, gloating on a public discussion like Reddit about the amount Bitcoin you hold while you are utilizing almost no security and putting away it in a hot wallet would not be savvy. All things considered, these wallets can be made to be secure insofar as insurances are taken. Solid passwords, two-factor verification, and safe web perusing ought to be viewed as least prerequisites.

These wallets are best utilized for modest quantities of digital currency or cryptographic money that you are effectively exchanging on a trade. You could compare a hot wallet to a financial records. Ordinary monetary shrewdness would say to hold just going through cash in a financial records while the heft of your cash is in bank accounts or other speculation accounts. The equivalent could be said for hot wallets. Hot wallets incorporate versatile, work area, web, and trade account guardianship wallets.

As referenced beforehand, trade wallets are custodial records given by the trade. The client of this wallet type isn't the private key holder to the digital currency held in this wallet. On the off chance that an occasion was to happen where the trade is hacked, or your record becomes bargained, your assets would be lost. The expression "not your key, not your coin" is intensely rehashed inside digital money gatherings and networks.

6. Cold Wallets

The easiest portrayal of a cool wallet is a wallet that isn't associated with the Internet and stands at a far lesser danger of being undermined. These wallets can likewise be alluded to as disconnected wallets or equipment wallets.

These wallets store a client's private key on something that isn't associated with the Internet and can accompany programming that works in equal so the client can see their portfolio without putting their private key in danger.

Maybe the most secure approach to store cryptographic money disconnected is by means of a paper wallet. A paper wallet is a wallet that you can create off specific sites. It at that point produces both public and private keys that you print out on a piece of paper. Getting to digital money in these locations is just conceivable in the event that you have that piece of paper with the private key. Numerous individuals cover these paper wallets and store them in wellbeing store boxes at their bank or even protected in their homes. These wallets are intended for high security and long haul ventures since you can't rapidly sell or exchange Bitcoin put away thusly.

An all the more generally utilized kind of chilly wallet is an equipment wallet. An equipment wallet is normally a USB drive gadget that stores a client's private keys safely disconnected. Such wallets have genuine benefits over hot wallets as they are unaffected by infections on one's PC. Private keys never interact with your organization associated PC or possibly weak programming with equipment wallets. These gadgets are likewise normally open-source, permitting the local area to decide its wellbeing through code reviews as opposed to an organization announcing that it is protected to utilize.

Cold wallets are the most secure approach to store your Bitcoin or other cryptographic forms of money. Generally, be that as it may, they require somewhat more information to set up.

Chapter 4. Investing in Crypto Market

Putting resources into cryptographic money has advanced a ton since the pinnacle of 2017, when anybody could rapidly bounce in, get some Bitcoin on their nearby trade, and make a benefit. What the market has instructed us is actually similar to the financial exchange, a more key and thoroughly examined approach should be taken. This eBook contains the nuts and bolts of beginning in this market for the individuals who have no past experience putting resources into cryptographic forms of money. The part that follows, "The One Strategy," that anybody can apply to take their crypto contributing to the following level.

1.   Safety First

Before you jump online to begin constructing your pinnacle of crypto power, we should ensure your establishment is strong. This implies that before you start exchanging, your PC, apparatuses, and association should all be just about as free from any and all harm as could really be expected. In the crypto world, there is no bank to run crying to in the event that somebody takes your charge card and purchases 1000 dollars of treats. On the off chance that you get hacked, and your coins are taken, they are GONE. So offer yourself a tremendous kindness and find the accompanying ways to get your venture cash.

Secure Device

A simple spot to begin is to ensure you are utilizing a PC that is tidy and has forward-thinking security programming introduced. Preferably, it's likewise acceptable to exchange from a gadget exclusively utilized for crypto and not one that you additionally use to ride every one of the dull corners of the Internet. Secure organization As hip as it very well may be to purchase Ethereum from your smooth PC in your nearby coffeehouse with an almond milk latte in your grasp, don't exchange utilizing a public organization. No libraries, no eateries, and no malevolent companions' homes. Utilize your organization that is set up to be scrambled and secure.

Great Password Habits

An apparatus we firmly suggest is a secret key supervisor. You've likely caught wind of how significant a solid secret phrase is for limiting your danger of getting hacked (at least fifteen characters, including upper and lower-case letters, numbers, distinctive accentuation marks, and so forth) however, you actually use "timmy123" for the entirety of your records. We get it- - how are you going to recall each one of those diverse convoluted passwords? A secret key director is a piece of programming you can download that allows you to deal with every one of your passwords effectively and successfully, and you can get a beautiful darn great one free of charge

2.   Fiat to Crypto

You've currently done, at any rate, what we've requested that you do to put resources into crypto with some degree of safety (perhaps somewhat more since you're that committed to the wellbeing of your future resources.) Now you're prepared to get rolling...

Register at an Exchange

To begin transforming your money into Bitcoin or some other coin (otherwise known as Altcoin), you need to set up a record on a trade. CoinBase is presumably the most notable, yet there are a couple of others, all of which offer fluctuated charge designs and coin contributions. Joining incorporates making a record with various layers of safety and interfacing an installment strategy, which are all clarified bit by bit in the trade's arrangement cycle. Whenever you are done, you are allowed to buy Bitcoin and a few other "fundamental" altcoins, including Ethereum, Bitcoin Cash, and Litecoin.

3. Buying Different Coins

In the event that you will probably go farther than purchase and hold a portion of the principle coins, you'll need to get familiar with purchasing altcoins. Albeit new coins and organizations are promising incredible computerized arrangements springing up consistently, most won't ever proceed to become wildly successful. However, in case you're one of the first to contribute, easily, in another coin that succeeds, you could wind up winning the big stake. To purchase altcoins, you first need to discover which trades offer the Altcoin you might want to put resources into.

Enlisting at one of these trades will be basically the same as the enrollment cycle for your underlying trade. On the off chance that you did it the first occasion when, I have confidence that you can do it a second.

When set up, you should move crypto from your first trade to your new trade. This can be perhaps the most difficult advances in the event that you have never done anything identified with crypto. Basically, this is finished by reordering a location or code for the area you will send your assets to. For a nitty gritty model, we will utilize the guidelines for moving cash out of CoinBase.

Web

- Navigate to the "accounts" interface on the fundamental route bar.

- Select the "send" button for the computerized cash wallet that you'd prefer to send from.
- In the send discourse, select "wallet address" in case you're shipping off a computerized cash wallet outside to CoinBase or "email address" in case you're sending through email.
- Enter the measure of advanced money you'd prefer to send in the "sum" field.
- Alternatively, you can determine the sum you might want to send in your nearby money. Note that the finances will consistently be sent as advanced money, not your nearby cash.
- Click "proceed".
- Confirm the subtleties of the exchange and complete the send.

iOS (For CoinBase portable application)

- Tap the menu symbol close to the upper left of the screen to open the Navbar.
- Select the wallet you wish to send from, situated in the Navbar.
- Tap the paper plane symbol in the upper right hand of the screen.
- Enter the sum you wish to send
- Tap the up/down bolts to switch between monetary forms. • Press "send."
- Enter the email or wallet address and any notes you wish to incorporate.

- Review the subtleties of your exchange and select "send" in the upper right corner of the screen.
-

On the off chance that you have been given a QR code

- Tap the QR symbol in the upper right.
- Take an image of the QR code
- Enter the ideal sum and press "proceed."
- Review the subtleties of your exchange and select "send" in the upper right corner of the screen. Android (For the CoinBase versatile application)
- Tap the menu symbol close to the upper left of the screen to open the Navbar.
- Select the wallet you wish to send from, situated in the Navbar.
- Tap the "+" symbol close to the lower right hand of the screen.
- Select "send."
- Enter the sum you wish to send.
- Use the up/down bolts to switch between kinds of money.
- Enter the email or wallet address and any notes you wish to incorporate.
- Review the subtleties of your exchange and tap the "forward" bolt in the upper right corner of the screen.

Android (For the CoinBase portable application)

- Tap the menu symbol close to the upper left of the screen to open the Navbar
- Select the wallet you wish to send from, situated in the Navbar.

- Tap the "+" symbol close to the lower right hand of the screen
- Select "send."
- Enter the sum you wish to send.
- Use the up/down bolts to switch between sorts of money.
- Enter the email or wallet address and any notes you wish to incorporate.
- Review the subtleties of your exchange and tap the "forward" bolt in the upper right corner

Or then again in the event that you have been given a QR code

- Tap the QR symbol in the upper right.
- Take an image of the QR code
- Enter the ideal sum and press "proceed."
- Review the subtleties of your exchange and tap the "forward" bolt in the upper right corner of the screen. Since you've become a crypto reorder star, you are prepared to purchase altcoins and prepared to proceed onward to figuring out how to utilize a wallet for care.

4.   Using a Crypto Wallet

A crypto wallet isn't exactly similar to the ordinary wallet, which you push into your jeans pocket for putting away your fiat cash. Without getting a lot into the hidden innovation (in light of the fact that those of you who need to comprehend everything about everything can Google it for more data), a wallet is a product program that stores public and private "keys" so that individuals can send and get crypto and screen their equilibrium, which is recorded and scrambled on the blockchain.

At the point when somebody sends you cryptographic money, it's simply a trade of responsibility for cash to your wallet's location. To get this going, the private "key" put away in your wallet should relate to the public location the money is appointed to. In the event that people in general and private keys match, the exchange is finished, and you can give a major moan of alleviation that you didn't unintentionally glue in the URL of a dumb feline video on YouTube that you shipped off a companion an hour sooner. There are a few various types of wallets.

Portable

Wallet applications for your cell phone are helpful to get to and can even be utilized in certain stores however are generally not as refined and can't store as much information like different sorts because of a telephone's restricted stockpiling limit.

On the web

These wallets run on the cloud and are available from any gadget, anyplace. This makes it simple for you to get to your crypto. Lamentably, it additionally makes it simple for anybody hacking the outsider organization dealing with your wallet to take your crypto. Pick your wallet organization carefully in the event that you go this course.

Work area

These wallets are downloaded onto a solitary PC or PC and are just open from that point and no other gadget. This makes it less open, and somehow or another more secure, than an online wallet. In any case, if your gadget is hacked, gets an infection, or unintentionally drops off a bluff into the sea, you could wind up without something other than an unrepairable PC.

Paper

This is a technique for printing your public and private keys onto actual duplicate, which would then be able to be (and ought to be) securely put away. This is protected in light of the fact that it is put away disconnected however can at times be troublesome to get to.

Equipment

Regularly as a thumb-drive-type gadget, an equipment wallet gives an incredible harmony between disconnected wellbeing and simple access. With a speedy addition into a USB port, you can approach, send, and get digital currency.

Whichever structure you pick, it is critical to ensure that you duplicate your resources into a wallet when you are finished exchanging on a trade. On the off chance that your crypto is sitting in a trade and the site gets hacked, your coins are effectively available for the taking, and you'll most likely never get them back.

5.   Basic Strategies

It's absolutely impossible we can make somebody with next to zero insight into a specialist crypto financial backer by perusing a couple of pages of text, however we can attempt to point you the correct way with the accompanying essential standards.

To be predictable with the general effortlessness of this guide, we'll give you three:

Purchase Low, Sell High

"Much obliged, Captain Obvious," you may be thinking, however in the event that this were so self-evident, for what reason do such countless individuals lose cash in contributing? It is the key law of contributing, yet to do this successfully, you should be straightforward with yourself about what sort of broker you are, just as what amount of cash, what amount hazard, and how long you can stand to contribute? The less you know your capacities, the less you will realize whose counsel to follow, which can eventually lead you to exchange a counterproductive way.

Examination, Research, Research

Simply doing what every other person is doing is a profoundly powerful method of getting messy seconds. Don't simply find out about market patterns. Become familiar with the organizations behind both new and existing coins. Who is an individual from their administration and specialized groups, and what is their central goal for what's to come? These basic advances can frequently remove a large number of the coins bound to come up short from the beginning.

Keep it Simple

From the start, simply contribute a limited quantity to get the hang of the "how to." Don't get extravagant. Get a portion of the top coins and sit on them. In the event that there is one thing that is steady about the unbelievably conflicting crypto market, genuine development requires years, not days. This way to sit and hold and don't get excessively combative and be a wild crypto pirate except if you realize that you understand what you're doing.

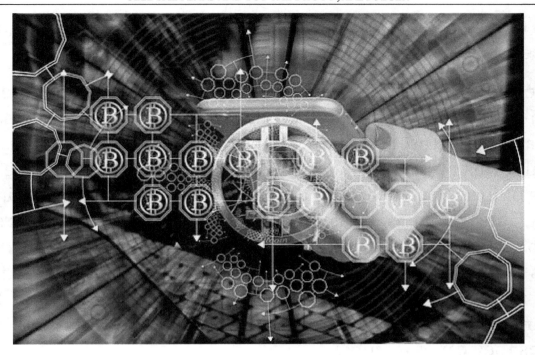

The One Strategy

Since you comprehend the fundamentals of putting resources into digital currency, it's an ideal opportunity to examine procedure. While a few specialists may trust it's beneficial to show many years' worth of contributing and exchanging mastery, we comprehend that this isn't commonsense for the vast majority. What number of us has the opportunity to learn everything about the unpredictable innovation of the blockchain world and how it means the organizations and tokens available? What numbers of us need to focus on turning into a specialist in the complexities of resource exchanging? What number of us can sit throughout the day before the PC watching the ongoing patterns on the lookout?

The appropriate response is, a great many people don't. Therefore, we need to discuss approaches to reasonably contribute, expand, and follow proficient techniques without taking up a great deal of your everyday life or turning into a full-time master dealer yourself.

Before most financial backers move into another market, there's a warm-up period that includes understanding a specific resource class and how it may find a way into your monetary picture. With digital forms of money and blockchain instruments, there are extra layers of intricacy, including the thought of cryptography, diggers, blockchains, tokens, hashing, and verifications. There's an extraordinary level of newness and intricacy related with digital forms of money for the unenlightened. However, the ordinary financial backer is relied upon to bounce onto a trade and begin exchanging, particularly in the event that exchanged nothing as long as they can remember.

Expansion is Key

Hand-picking digital currency ventures is a test. Cryptographic money markets are profoundly unpredictable, and surprisingly the most established are still truly in their outset stage. The choice cycle for token postings changes broadly among trades and is as of now not very much managed. Choosing champs from washouts or attempting to time the market has demonstrated to be amazingly troublesome. An investigation by Bitwise highlighted the worth of expansion on account of the limit changeability in the profits of even the best ten coins.

List Style Investing

In 2007, world-well known financial backer, Warren Buffett, bet 1,000,000 dollars that a record asset would outflank an assortment of multifaceted investments more than ten years. He won that bet and pointed out the viability of deliberately enhanced and sporadically rebalanced portfolios. There are numerous crypto portfolios available, however approaching one curated by a real expert, not a self-announced master on YouTube, is another story. These records are simply open to licensed financial backers (those with a total assets of in any event $1,000,000, barring the worth of one's main living place, or have a pay off at any rate $200,000 every year throughout the previous two years) however what numerous individuals don't know is that they all put their portfolio allotment online for people in general! Just by following the allotment rates of every token, you can take your venture and expand it very much like these selective and expertly oversaw reserves do.

Despite the fact that it will require some investment to do the exploration and choose which list reserve you might want to reflect, just as to figure and buy every token independently, fortunately these portfolios commonly just rebalance about once per month, so you will not need to do this regularly. Thus, the writing is on the wall, a manner by which, even with simply the most essential information, you can put resources into crypto with enhancement, adequacy, and expert ability.

Chapter 5. The Beginner's Guide

Exchanging cryptographic money can make a tremendous benefit. Notwithstanding, it's likewise profoundly hazardous. You can win and lose a lot of cash rapidly. This implies crypto exchanging is energizing, and it tends to be hard to hold significant serenity under hefty tension. There are numerous approaches to bring in cash in the digital currency markets, however not the entirety of the ways are viable and safe. I will investigate some demonstrated methods of putting resources into cryptographic money. Here are the main 10.

1.   Trade digital money CFDs

Any item with value vacillations can be exchanged a Contract For Difference. CFD is a T+0 edge exchanging device, which permits you to exchange a bigger situation with a couple of capitals. For instance, you can exchange just 0.1 parcel bitcoin with a little store as an underlying edge.

The benefit of utilizing CFD is you can go long or go short regardless of the market moves; you will have the chances for dangerous gets back from business sectors fluctuating. Additionally, exchanging Bitcoin CFD is more adaptable, and you can exchange 24 hours and seven days.

It's likewise famous to utilize CFDs to support actual portfolios for financial backers, particularly in unstable business sectors.

As an ASIC-directed (AFSL398528) forex agent, Mitra de offers 100+ mainstream worldwide instruments, including forex, products, records, US stocks, and digital currencies. Mitra de offers you the chance to BUY (go long) or Sell (go short) on all Bitcoin exchanges, so you can utilize your favored methodology paying little mind to what direction the money is moving.

Pros:

- Speculate on crypto cost without possessing the crypto
- No compelling reason to manage crypto trades or open a crypto stockpiling wallet
- Low store, Higher influence
- The capacity to open long/short positions
- T+0 exchanging is more adaptable

Cons:

- The principle hazard related with CFD exchanging implies influence.
- Not reasonable for standing firm on a foothold in long haul

Presently, Mitrade gives advancements to new clients; You can apply for a 50USD free Trail Bonus to exchange any monetary resources with no dangers, which is useful for novices and amateurs.

2. Day Trading

Assume you are keen on bringing in cash with digital money in a quicker way. Around there, you can attempt crypto day exchanging, which is an exchanging methodology where financial backers purchase and sell orders on different occasions in a single day.

The high instability of Bitcoin and digital forms of money makes the crypto market like a thrill ride, which is ideal for day exchanging, as during the day, you will have enough good and bad times to get a decent benefit.

Preferably, you'll search for a low-evaluated freedom to purchase in and afterward sell it at a more exorbitant cost. In spite of the fact that this might be a little pay, this can acquire extensive benefits to financial backers the since a long time ago run.

Day exchanging is an expertise, very much like whatever else. On the off chance that you set aside more effort to see how it functions, it very well might be a full-time experience. Obviously, nobody will win in each exchanging, yet the objective of day exchanging is just to win more occasions.

So day exchanging requires financial backers more information and abilities. You can attempt to rehearse with a demo account on Mitrade, which gives a 50000 USD practice account. When you have a lot exchanging experience, you can choose to exchange a genuine record.

Pros:

- Relatively minimal effort
- Trading bitcoin on value changes

Cons:

- Need more abilities
- Much time and energy

3. Bitcoin Mining

Mining digital forms of money is not quite the same as the over two different ways of exchanging. Mining might be more troublesome than different ways, yet it very well might be more productive when you mine effectively. Albeit the mining cycle should be possible from a PC, you actually need essential programming, explicit equipment, crypto wallets, and much power. For the vast majority, mining is an exceptionally specific industry that isn't reasonable for singular financial backers. Most Bitcoin mining is done in an enormous distribution center with modest power.

In some cases, the equipment is additionally costly. For instance, during the positively trending market in 2017, the cost of GPU raised steeply, while as the market breakdowns, you can purchase great mining hardware with less expense.

In the early years, bitcoin excavators could acquire coins moderately rapidly. However, by 2019, cryptographic money mining is more convoluted. Numerous expert diggers have fabricated enormous exhibits to mine, making it harder for more modest excavators. Obviously, you can join a bitcoin mining pool to be more successful, however that accompanies a charge. I likewise discover some crypto excavator application in the crypto business professing to help you mine crypto coins. It's more similar to diversion mining. Try not to depend on the application to bring in extraordinary cash for you.

Pros:

- Earning possibilities is higher

Cons:

- High cost to begin

- relatively troublesome

4.   Long Term Investing

This is the simplest method to bring in cash with digital currency. Numerous individuals choose not to exchange cryptographic forms of money but rather purchase a specific number of coins and afterward put them in their wallets until the value ascends to make benefits. The reason of long haul contributing is that you have investigated and accept the digital currencies you put resources into will get more piece of the pie after some time.

In spite of the fact that there are a wide range of advanced coins, we suggest that you pick safe and profoundly fluid monetary forms, like BTC, LTC, and XRP. These coins have been famous available. In the event that you put resources into another crypto coin, it very well might be modest, however the coin is probably going to vanish after the market preliminary. Presently, numerous individuals acquire a major benefit from Bitcoin on the grounds that they purchased Bitcoin in the year 2011 or 2012, and they hold these computerized coins for quite a while regardless of whether the cost of bitcoin had ascended to 18,000 USD.

Pros:

- Easy to begin
- Beginner-accommodating

Cons:

- Take quite a while

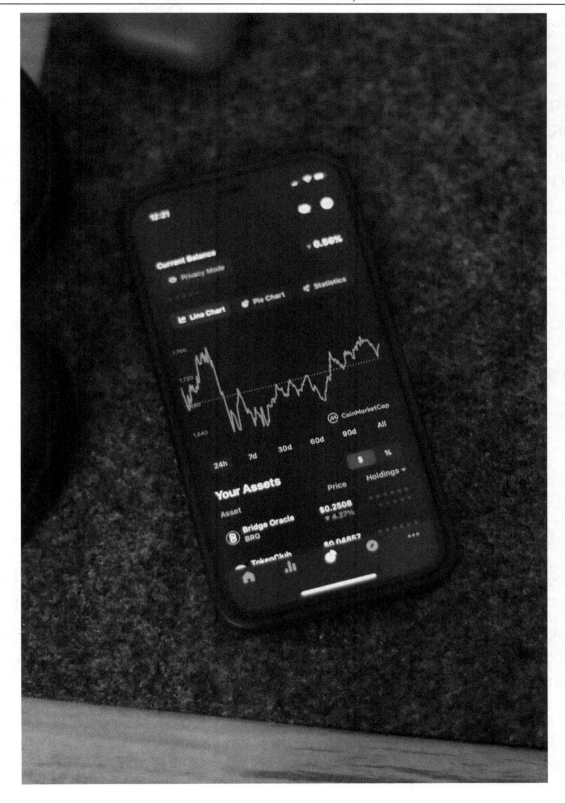

5.   Arbitrage

A few financial backers additionally utilize the method of exchange to bring in cash with digital forms of money. This implies when you purchase a computerized coin in crypto trade and afterward sell it on another crypto trade. Yet, truly, crypto exchange is uncommon that likely will not cause you to get rich rapidly.

Pros:

- Instant benefit
- Low prerequisites for section

Cons:

- Good openings are uncommon
- High hazard of losing benefits because of the great unpredictability in the digital currency markets

6.   Cryptocurrency spigot

In the event that you are tracking down a compelling method to benefit from modest quantities of digital forms of money, at that point a Crypto fixture might be one decision. A Crypto spigot resembles a trickling fixture. It is a site delivering very limited quantities of digital currencies, like Bitcoin, like clockwork. You need to do a few assignments as per the site necessities.

The crypto spigot site will bring in cash with publicizing and traffic. At the point when you're looking out for the page, there will be promotion arrangements.

Pros:

- Easy to utilize
- Easy to procure coins

Cons:

- Quite a limited quantity of coins
- Need to invest a lot of energy
- It can't cause you to get rich

7. ICO

ICO implies Initial Coin Offerings, which are like crowd funding. ICO permits business visionaries to raise assets by making and selling their virtual money without hazard capital. It can make an enormous profit from your venture, however it likewise brings tremendous instability and dangers. ICO has a ton of traps. You must be cautious about picking the privilege ICO. In the event that the ICO coin isn't entirely significant, you may hazard losing cash. In this way, you would do well to contribute when you think the undertaking is sufficient and just put resources into what misfortunes you can bear.

Pros:

- Opportunity to put resources into point of view ventures at a beginning phase
- Low section limit

Cons:
- Many tricks
- Hacker assaults
- High chances

8. Crypto gaming

This is additionally a genuinely regular approach to acquire Bitcoin, messing around to get BTC; it is like joining the Bitcoin taps above. There will be new titles delivered, and they need to have more individuals download and mess around to make the game better known. These games will grant BTC prizes to clients. Your work is basically to have a telephone, download these games, and afterward sit and play. Subsequent to finishing the game, you will get a specific measure of BTC.

Pros:
- Easy to acquire Bitcoin

Cons:

- Have to invest a lot of energy
- Quite a modest quantity

9.   Be a blockchain engineer.

Blockchain improvement isn't very different from normal web advancement. Numerous designers have built up their own dispersed applications (DAPP) on certain stages, like Ethureum and NEO. At that point, you can bring in cash by showing advertisements, buys, memberships, and so forth, inside the application. Nonetheless, making and keeping a typical blockchain isn't simple. Above all else, the code is public and apparent to everybody. Anybody can see the code and check for blunders and weaknesses. This permits any software engineer to attack.

Pros:
- High pay
- Safe approach to acquire coins

Cons:

- You should think about coding

10. By advertising crypto with affiliate marketing

In the event that you own a site or blog for crypto, this might be a decent method to acquire an optional pay. The cryptographic money industry, particularly Bitcoin, is developing, however the substance around Bitcoin on the Internet is still "scant." You can accept this open door to make a site work in posting news, tips, and directions for Bitcoin exchanging.

Pros:

- Low speculation costs
- Passive pay
- Flexible working timetable

Cons:

- You should have a site
- You don't control partner promoting programs
- Freelance occupations are not for everybody

What's preventing fledglings from making a steady pay from exchanging cryptographic money?

- **Make cash with digital currency will take a great deal of time and steady exertion**.

In contrast to proficient financial backers, most fledgling brokers figuring out how to exchange aren't full-time dealers to drench themselves in the business sectors.

That implies they need more an ideal opportunity to get themselves to the level where they can exchange like a star.

- **You have no unmistakable exchanging methodology.**

Ask yourself an inquiry: "What is my exchanging procedure?" If you replied: "System? Indeed, I just purchased and held up in trust, so was that viewed as a system? ". Presently we need to talk. On the off chance that you don't have a reasonable exchanging methodology, regardless of whether it depends on specialized pointers or essential information on crypto resources, or dependent on innovation (algorithmic exchanging), at that point surely there is very There are numerous potential issues that you may experience.

Notwithstanding, first, you need to get yourself and your exchanging style better. Advanced resources are quite possibly the most unpredictable resources nowadays, and yet, fundamental blockchain innovation sets out a freedom to get more extravagant later on.

- **You indiscriminately desire to recuperate.**

The visually impaired any expectation of a bounce back or Bull Run is something each broker has encountered in any event once. That is the reason you will see rehashed updates in speculation archives that, "What occurred in the past isn't a pointer of future value developments." Indeed, there is a contrast between specialized examination and gazing at the screen and reciting "Bitcoin will arrive at 21,000" until that occurs.

- **You are averaging your situation during the downtrend.**

Another difficult you may discover in the bear market is the normal of the downtrend, or all in all, to inundate you on the lookout. Some altcoins are viewed as promising or genuine prospects, however pause and wonder why you continue to stay nearby this coin and can't get out. Purchasing when the market is falling is a decent method to purchase low, however you likewise need to sell when it feels right, or perhaps you should see the cash's decrease significantly more profound before it shows any benefit.

You likely realize that a few group can purchase A for 100, the value tumbles to 80 and still doesn't cut misfortunes as recently suspected, and afterward to 60 individuals who trust that the market will return, go through cash, purchase in to trust you're not kidding "normal" position and diminish misfortunes. At that point it goes down once more, and you become terrified.

- **You totally disregarded danger the board.**

Without addressing why an altcoin (or even Bitcoin) is so unpredictable will lead us to the following justification responding to the inquiry, "for what reason are you losing cash in the bear market?" If you don't focus on hazard the board, you are putting yourself at a misfortune. Ask yourself your present normal danger level by resources and trades? Will I get an opportunity to recuperate on the off chance that one of the coins is delisted or the trade is hacked? In the event that you don't have clear responses to these inquiries - you might be strolling in a minefield.

- **You don't gain from your own mix-ups.**

The last explanation is presumably the most significant. Nearly everybody has begun a couple of times at the screen and asked for an expansion in venture. Or then again a few groups keep on purchasing a sinking crypto resource that is probably not going to recuperate. Yet, they have taken in a couple of things. In case you're committing an error from this bear market, focus on them. It is the expense of instruction, albeit the misfortune isn't fun; in the event that you don't make the most of that chance and gain from botches, particularly because of unnecessary expectation or restricted information, you will lose more expectation.

How to become a professional crypto trader?

The principal thing we will begin with is a clarification of who is a "proficient cryptographic money dealer" and what is "exchanging": In basic words, exchanging implies trading or selling activities between two market members, where exchanging resources change hands.

Digital currency exchanging is a trade exchange between crypto-to-crypto or digital currencies to-fiat cash. Purchasing digital money like Bitcoin for US dollars is a trade activity, which implies you trade your money for crypto.

Being a merchant is something other than a diversion. It is a genuine energy or calling, which requires a ton of time and no less specialized information just; for this situation, exchanging will bring standard benefit.

A digital money merchant is a client of a cryptographic money stage or trade following up on its drive by exchanging advanced resources (cryptographic forms of money and fiat cash) to benefit from the exchanging interaction itself (purchasing and selling reserves). The motivation behind exchanging is to get cash for proficiently performed tasks (shut with benefit).

Cryptographic money exchanging is getting increasingly mainstream. Consistently an ever increasing number of individuals might want to attempt themselves as dealers. There are numerous fantasies around this calling, and most accept that to turn into a broker, you need higher monetary schooling or have an over-created instinct, over-reason, be an expert from God, and so forth Indeed, this would be a huge reward, yet in no way, shape or form an essential. What's more, today, we will demonstrate it!

Would i be able to see myself as a broker after a few effective exchanges?

The notable principle of "novice's karma" applies here too. You can benefit once or even a few times from opening exchanging positions indiscriminately, at the same time, tragically, it works in an unexpected way. For fruitful and successful digital money exchanging, you need to comprehend a few perspectives:

- Current market circumstance.
- How exchanging instruments work (what sorts of requests are accessible, and so forth);
- Understand how to understand graphs. For instance, you need to realize how to check the ethereum cost in pounds on the off chance that you are keen on exchanging this cash pair.
- Most critically, examine exchanging examples and developments on the outline to fabricate the correct exchanging procedure.

A broker's demonstrable skill lies he would say on the lookout, how he responds in upsetting circumstances, the amount he thinks out his exchanging steps, and "fallback alternatives."

Despite the exchanging system sought after, the primary exchanging objective remaining parts unaltered. To be specific, "Purchase less expensive – sell more costly" – the lone justification any exchanging activity is to benefit.

What information do I have to improve my exchanging abilities?

Market examination is the establishment of a fruitful exchanging methodology and makes a benefit. Not a solitary exchanging system, even Buy&HODL, is effective without seeing how market developments work and the primary exchanging candle designs.

Try not to BE SCARED

You don't need to be an expert to begin exchanging! Indeed, even a novice can bring in cash by purchasing/selling digital currencies with the privilege and insightful advances. Experience characterizes an expert, and experience is the thing that you need to procure. Hence, go through this way of turning out to be from an odd one out to a swan! For our situation, from amateur to proficient ;).

From the very beginning, it is critical to comprehend the kinds of orders gave on the stage utilized and what "pictures on the diagram" mean, how to put orders and what instruments are accessible on the stage. Interestingly, this will be all that anyone could need!

We can draw a similarity with power – to turn on a TV, forced air system, or night light – you don't really have to know how they work in the engine. It's sufficient to figure out how to work them. A similar rationale applies here!

Is there a simple success exchanging strategy to bring in cash on cryptographic forms of money?

Slight an interesting inquiry in light of the fact that the appropriate response is both "yes" and "no" all the while.

The truth of the matter is that the cryptographic money market is unstable; hence, it generally gives a chance to bring in cash for the individuals who follow the market "at the current second" and ability to utilize exchanging devices effectively.

"Purchase less expensive sell more costly" that is the proverb of any exchanging methodology.

The Buy&HODL system can be viewed as winning under specific conditions. Its substance is to purchase a resource and stand by till it develops. The primary concern isn't to miss the second and sell on schedule. Subsequently, when purchasing a specific exchanging resource for hold it, you need to make a primer investigation and get a few signs that the resources cost being referred to will probably flood. Something else, there is a danger of misfortunes.

How to pick a stage for crypto exchanging on the off chance that I am a novice?

Check the state's public assessment and notoriety. Security is critical! The stage should agree with the most elevated security norms to ensure your information and assets. Discover the rundown of the upheld nations: not all administrations cover clients' entrance all throughout the planet. Check if occupants of your nation can be the stage's clients. It is additionally critical to have client assistance nonstop. You need to ensure you can find support from the client care whenever you need it.

Benefits of the cryptographic money market:

Market instability no monetary market can contrast with the changes in digital money rates. Today, it is the most adaptable approach to bring in cash on exchanging; the cost of certain resources can make x100 in a real sense in a day. Despite the fact that note, they can likewise drop as quickly as they develop.

Cryptographic money accessibility advanced monetary forms are accessible whenever. The digital currency market works day in and day out, and you can exchange, store, or your crypto resources when you need. Namelessness regardless of whether the exchange can be followed – you'll see the wallet address, not the ID information of the proprietor. Unwavering quality cryptographic forms of money are protected. Be that as it may! Just on the off chance that you utilize a demonstrated and secure assistance. Slender discharge is useful for cryptographic money tokens. The less coins were given, the more interest for them.

Cryptographic money is decentralized cash; no single element or middle person controls the exchanges. Low exchange expenses the commission for moving assets is a lot of lower than the bank moves, for instance.

Why stopping? Go, pick the stage, make a record, and begin exchanging. Simply remember one principle consistently do your exploration first!

The Cryptocurrency Investing | Advanced Guide

Study, Anticipate the Crypto Market and Raise the first Million Dollar from Bitcoin, Ethereum, Cardano and other unknown Altcoins that costs less than 1$

By

Jake Folger

Table of Contents

Chapter 1. Understanding cryptocurrency 122

Chapter 2. Mining of Cryptocurrency 161

Chapter 3. Before You Begin...191

Chapter 4. Are cryptocurrencies a good investment? 234

Chapter 1. Understanding cryptocurrency

A cryptocurrency ("crypto") is a digital currency that may be used to shop for items and offerings but makes use of an online ledger with robust cryptography to relaxed online transactions. Much of the hobby in these unregulated currencies is to trade for profit, ith speculators at times driving prices skyward. A cryptocurrency is a form of payment that can be exchanged online for goods and offerings. Many organizations have issued their own currencies, often called tokens, and those can be traded especially for the best or provider that the employer gives. Think of them as you will arcade tokens or casino chips. You'll want to alternate real forex for the cryptocurrency to get entry to the best or carrier.

Why Cryptocurrency Is So Popular

Cryptocurrencies have gone from a difficult to understand part of finance to centre-level over the past 12 months. In the space of twelve months, bitcoin has exploded from buying and selling at $8,166 on 8 March 2020 to hit all-time highs of over $58,000 in February 2021 and now trading at $54,011 as of 9:31 am GMT on 9th March.

Their meteoric upward push has been observed by means of elevated institutional interest, consisting of big names like HSBC, Goldman Sachs, BNY Mellon and JPMorgan.

There are hundreds of cryptocurrencies around the sector but the core group of 20 coins constitutes around 99% of the marketplace through quantity, according to crypto internet site CoinDesk.

In the primary week of March — the quietest week for the reason that early January — inflows into digital asset investment products had been $108m, in step with James Butterfill, an investment strategist at CoinShares. Of these inflows, 90% had been bitcoin, with $4m invested in ethereum. Trading volumes for bitcoin, but, remained high, with each day average of $11.8bn for 2021 in comparison to $2.2bn in 2020.

As cryptocurrencies hold their rollercoaster rally into 2021 and hitting record highs in February and March, Financial News has compiled a list of the ten largest cryptocurrencies by using market capitalization.

Following are some reasons why cryptocurrency is popular for:

Low Fees

One of the reasons why cryptocurrency is famous around the world is that there are very few fees associated with using it. When you're using alternative options of online payment options, you're often going to incur massive costs. The very low charges that you have to deal with while the use of numerous cryptocurrencies will be a far higher deal for you. It makes the experience for many people to use cryptocurrencies to pay for items online and people also find it to be safe.

No Associatation of Cryptocurrencies with World Governments

Another reason why people have placed faith in cryptocurrencies is that those currencies aren't associated with world governments. This means that cryptocurrencies have the capacity to remain strong even if there is turmoil in a particular country. Some investors see cryptocurrencies as a terrific way to guard their wealth and that is one motive why cryptocurrency has persevered to upward push over time. The capacity that cryptocurrencies will be safer than some government currencies makes them extra appealing.

It's Getting Easier to Use Cryptocurrency

Using cryptocurrency is getting less complicated all of the time, thanks to greater online companies adopting it. You'll find that more web sites are beginning to accept cryptocurrencies as a fee and this could simplest emerge as more widely widespread in the future. It's also thrilling to notice that there are now things that include cryptocurrency debit cards popping up in certain locations.

This won't be widespread right now however it's far something that is very much occurring.

As cryptocurrency keeps turning out to be greater, not unusual, it's going to reach increasingly more people. This leads to a growth in consciousness and a common surge in popularity. More people remember the fact that that is an alternative now and some of the questions about what cryptocurrency is are being answered. Lots of people have at least a bit of understanding approximately what things such as Bitcoin are and this makes it extra ideal.

There Is Potential for Profit

Of course, the potential for profit is another huge reason why people get involved with cryptocurrencies. If you buy Bitcoin while it's at a low price, then you can potentially profit when that price rises. Lots of people who invested in cryptocurrencies before they got super hot wound up making huge profits. Investors are still making money from cryptocurrencies because the market has not cooled in recent years.

Overall Security Is Important

Protecting your identity and your money is important, and you know how hard cybersecurity has become in modern times. Using cryptocurrency to pay for things online is actually a lot safer than many other traditional payment options. If you're at all worried about cybersecurity issues, then deciding to use cryptocurrency might be a good idea. The security of cryptocurrency is one of the things that has helped it to become so popular over time.

It's Easy to Get

Getting cryptocurrency isn't some difficult thing that you're going to have to jump through a lot of hoops to do. It's actually possible to get the cryptocurrency that you want from reputable sources and the ease of getting cryptocurrency has helped it to grow in popularity. In the past, people might have thought of cryptocurrency as some type of shady and unknown entity but it's become a common thing in many circles now. If you have yet to purchase cryptocurrency, then you'll find that the process is decidedly simple and customer-friendly.

It's Seen as the Future

Finally, you could say that cryptocurrencies are seen as the future of money by many individuals. People who adopt cryptocurrency now are also adopting major technological innovations such as blockchain. This allows you to be on the cutting edge and it makes sense for many to get ahead of the curve. Blockchain technology is supposed to change the world in many ways and it's going to make trading a much more transparent process.

Types of Cryptocurrency

The first blockchain-based totally cryptocurrency became Bitcoin, which still remains the most popular and most valuable. Today, there are lots of alternate cryptocurrencies with diverse features and specs. Some of those are clones or forks of Bitcoin, while others are new currencies that were built from scratch.

Bitcoin was released in 2009 by an individual or group known by the pseudonym "Satoshi Nakamoto.1 As of March 2021, there had been over 18.6 million bitcoins in flow with a complete marketplace cap of around $927 billion.

Some of the competing cryptocurrencies spawned by means of Bitcoin's fulfilment, known as "altcoins," encompass Litecoin, Peercoin, and Namecoin, in addition to Ethereum, Cardano, and EOS. Today, the mixture price of all of the cryptocurrencies in life is round $1.5 trillion—Bitcoin currently represents more than 60% of the total value.

Advantages and Disadvantages of Cryptocurrency

Advantages

Cryptocurrencies preserve the promise of creating it less difficult to switch funds immediately among two parties, without the need for reliance on a third party like a financial institution or credit card enterprise. These transfers are alternatively secured through using public keys and private keys and distinctive kinds of incentive structures, like Proof of Work or Proof of Stake.

In modern cryptocurrency systems, a consumer's "wallet," or account address, has a public key, at the same time as the private key known only to the owner and is used to sign transactions. Fund transfers are finished with minimal processing expenses, allowing customers to keep away from the steep costs charged via banks and financial establishments for wire transfers.

Disadvantages

The semi-anonymous nature of cryptocurrency transactions makes them well-suited for a host of illegal activities, such as money laundering and tax evasion. However, cryptocurrency advocates often highly value their anonymity, citing benefits of privacy like protection for whistleblowers or activists living under repressive governments. Some cryptocurrencies are more private than others.

Bitcoin, for instance, is a relatively poor choice for conducting illegal business online, since the forensic analysis of the Bitcoin blockchain has helped authorities arrest and prosecute criminals. More privacy-oriented coins do exist, however, such as Dash, Monero, or ZCash, which are far more difficult to trace.

Special Considerations

Central to the appeal and functionality of Bitcoin and other cryptocurrencies is blockchain technology, which is used to keep an online ledger of all the transactions that have ever been conducted, thus providing a data structure for this ledger that is quite secure and is shared and agreed upon by the entire network of an individual node, or computer maintaining a copy of the ledger. Every new block generated must be verified by each node before being confirmed, making it almost impossible to forge transaction histories.

Many experts see blockchain technology as having serious potential for uses like online voting and crowdfunding, and major financial institutions such as JPMorgan Chase (JPM) see the potential to lower transaction costs by streamlining payment processing.4 However, because cryptocurrencies are virtual and are not stored on a central database, a digital cryptocurrency balance can be wiped out by the loss or destruction of a hard drive if a backup copy of the private key does not exist. At the same time, there is no central authority, government, or corporation that has access to your funds or your personal information.

Criticism of Cryptocurrency

Since market prices for cryptocurrencies are based on supply and demand, the rate at which a cryptocurrency can be exchanged for another currency can fluctuate widely, since the design of many cryptocurrencies ensures a high degree of scarcity.

Bitcoin has experienced some rapid surges and collapses in value, climbing as high as $19,000 per Bitcoin in Dec. of 2017 before dropping to around $7,000 in the following months.2 Cryptocurrencies are thus considered by some economists to be a short-lived fad or speculative bubble.

There is concern that cryptocurrencies like Bitcoin are not rooted in any material goods. Some research, however, has identified that the cost of producing a Bitcoin, which requires an increasingly large amount of energy, is directly related to its market price.

Cryptocurrency blockchains are highly secure, but other aspects of a cryptocurrency ecosystem, including exchanges and wallets, are not immune to the threat of hacking. In Bitcoin's 10-year history, <u>several online exchanges</u> have been the subject of hacking and theft, sometimes with millions of dollars' worth of "coins" stolen.

Nonetheless, many observers see potential advantages in cryptocurrencies, like the possibility of preserving value against inflation and facilitating exchange while being easier to transport and divide than precious metals and existing outside the influence of central banks and governments.

What Is Bitcoin?

Bitcoin is a digital currency that was created in January 2009. It follows the ideas set out in a white paper by the mysterious and pseudonymous Satoshi Nakamoto. The identity of the person or persons who created the technology is still a mystery. Bitcoin offers the promise of lower transaction fees than traditional online payment mechanisms and, unlike government-issued currencies, it is operated by a decentralized authority.

Bitcoin is a type of cryptocurrency. There are no physical bitcoins, only balances kept on a public ledger that everyone has transparent access to.

All bitcoin transactions are verified by a massive amount of computing power. Bitcoins are not issued or backed by any banks or governments, nor are individual bitcoins valuable as a commodity. Despite it not being legal tender Bitcoin is very popular and has triggered the launch of hundreds of other cryptocurrencies, collectively referred to as alcoin. Bitcoin is commonly abbreviated as "BTC."

Peer-to-Peer Technology

Bitcoin is one of the first digital currencies to use peer-to-peer technology to facilitate instant payments. The independent individuals and companies who own the governing computing power and participate in the bitcoin network—bitcoin "miners"—are in charge of processing the transactions on the blockchain and are motivated by rewards (the release of new bitcoin) and transaction fees paid in bitcoin.

These miners can be thought of as the decentralized authority enforcing the credibility of the bitcoin network. New bitcoin is released to the miners at a fixed, but periodically declining rate. There are only 21 million bitcoin that can be mined in total. As of January 30, 2021, there are approximately 18,614,806 bitcoin in existence and 2,385,193 bitcoin left to be mined.3

In this way, bitcoin other cryptocurrencies operate differently from fiat currency; in centralized banking systems, currency is released at a rate matching the growth in goods; this system is intended to maintain price stability. A decentralized system, like bitcoin, sets the release rate ahead of time and according to an algorithm.

What is Blockchain?

Blockchain seems complicated, and it definitely can be, but its core concept is really quite simple. A blockchain is a type of database. To be able to understand blockchain, it helps to first understand what a database actually is.

A database is a collection of information that is stored electronically on a computer system. Information, or data, in databases is typically structured in table format to allow for easier searching and filtering for specific information. What is the difference between someone using a spreadsheet to store information rather than a database?

Spreadsheets are designed for one person, or a small group of people, to store and access limited amounts of information. In contrast, a database is designed to house significantly larger amounts of information that can be accessed, filtered, and manipulated quickly and easily by any number of users at once.

Large databases achieve this by housing data on servers that are made of powerful computers. These servers can sometimes be built using hundreds or thousands of computers in order to have the computational power and storage capacity necessary for many users to access the database simultaneously. While a spreadsheet or database may be accessible to any number of people, it is often owned by a business and managed by an appointed individual that has complete control over how it works and the data within it.

So how does a blockchain differ from a database?

Storage Structure

One key difference between a typical database and a blockchain is the way the data is structured. A blockchain collects information together in groups, also known as blocks that hold sets of information. Blocks have certain storage capacities and, when filled, are chained onto the previously filled block, forming a chain of data known as the "blockchain." All new information that follows that freshly added block is compiled into a newly formed block that will then also be added to the chain once filled.

A database structures its data into tables whereas a blockchain, like its name implies, structures its data into chunks (blocks) that are chained together. This makes it so that all blockchains are databases but not all databases are blockchains. This system also inherently makes an irreversible timeline of data when implemented in a decentralized nature. When a block is filled it is set in stone and becomes a part of this timeline. Each block in the chain is given an exact timestamp when it is added to the chain.

Decentralization

For the purpose of understanding blockchain, it is instructive to view it in the context of how it has been implemented by Bitcoin. Like a database, Bitcoin needs a collection of computers to store its blockchain. For Bitcoin, this blockchain is just a specific type of database that stores every Bitcoin transaction ever made. In Bitcoin's case, and unlike most databases, these computers are not all under one roof, and each computer or group of computers is operated by a unique individual or group of individuals.

Imagine that a company owns a server comprised of 10,000 computers with a database holding all of its client's account information. This company has a warehouse containing all of these computers under one roof and has full control of each of these computers and all the information contained within them. Similarly, Bitcoin consists of thousands of computers, but each computer or group of computers that hold its blockchain is in a different geographic location and they are all operated by separate individuals or groups of people. These computers that makeup Bitcoin's network are called nodes.

In this model, Bitcoin's blockchain is used in a decentralized way. However, private, centralized blockchains, where the computers that make up its network are owned and operated by a single entity, do exist.

In a blockchain, each node has a full record of the data that has been stored on the blockchain since its inception. For Bitcoin, the data is the entire history of all Bitcoin transactions. If one node has an error in its data it can use the thousands of other nodes as a reference point to correct itself. This way, no one node within the network can alter information held within it. Because of this, the history of transactions in each block that make up Bitcoin's blockchain is irreversible.

If one user tampers with Bitcoin's record of transactions, all other nodes would cross-reference each other and easily pinpoint the node with the incorrect information. This system helps to establish an exact and transparent order of events. For Bitcoin, this information is a list of transactions, but it also is possible for a blockchain to hold a variety of information like legal contracts, state identifications, or a company's product inventory.

In order to change how that system works, or the information stored within it, a majority of the decentralized network's computing power would need to agree on said changes. This ensures that whatever changes do occur are in the best interests of the majority.

Transparency

Because of the decentralized nature of Bitcoin's blockchain, all transactions can be transparently viewed by either having a personal node or by using blockchain explorer that allow anyone to see transactions occurring live. Each node has its own copy of the chain that gets updated as fresh blocks are confirmed and added. This means that if you wanted to, you could track Bitcoin wherever it goes.

For example, exchanges have been hacked in the past where those who held Bitcoin on the exchange lost everything. While the hacker may be entirely anonymous, the Bitcoins that they extracted are easily traceable. If the Bitcoins that were stolen in some of these hacks were to be moved or spent somewhere, it would be known.

Is Blockchain Secure?

Blockchain technology accounts for the issues of security and trust in several ways. First, new blocks are always stored linearly and chronologically. That is, they are always added to the "end" of the blockchain. If you take a look at Bitcoin's blockchain, you'll see that each block has a position on the chain, called a "height." As of November 2020, the block's height had reached 656,197 blocks so far.

After a block has been added to the end of the blockchain, it is very difficult to go back and alter the contents of the block unless the majority reached a consensus to do so. That's because each block contains its own hash, along with the hash of the block before it, as well as the previously mentioned time stamp. Hash codes are created by a math function that turns digital information into a string of numbers and letters. If that information is edited in any way, the hash code changes as well.

Here's why that's important to security. Let's say a hacker wants to alter the blockchain and steal Bitcoin from everyone else. If they were to alter their own single copy, it would no longer align with everyone else's copy. When everyone else cross-references their copies against each other, they would see this one copy stand out and that hacker's version of the chain would be cast away as illegitimate.

Succeeding with such a hack would require that the hacker simultaneously control and alter 51% of the copies of the blockchain so that their new copy becomes the majority copy and thus, the agreed-upon chain. Such an attack would also require an immense amount of money and resources as they would need to redo all of the blocks because they would now have different timestamps and hash codes.

Due to the size of Bitcoin's network and how fast it is growing, the cost to pull off such a feat would probably be insurmountable. Not only would this be extremely expensive, but it would also likely be fruitless. Doing such a thing would not go unnoticed, as network members would see such drastic alterations to the blockchain. The network members would then fork off to a new version of the chain that has not been affected.

This would cause the attacked version of Bitcoin to plummet in value, making the attack ultimately pointless as the bad actor has control of a worthless asset. The same would occur if the bad actor were to attack the new fork of Bitcoin. It is built this way so that taking part in the network is far more economically incentivized than attacking it.

How is Blockchain Used?

As we now know, blocks on Bitcoin's blockchain store data about monetary transactions. But it turns out that blockchain is actually a reliable way of storing data about other types of transactions, as well.

Some companies that have already incorporated blockchain include Walmart, Pfizer, AIG, Siemens, Unilever, and a host of others. For example, IBM has created its Food Trust blockchain1 to trace the journey that food products take to get to its locations.

Why do this? The food industry has seen countless outbreaks of e Coli, salmonella, listeria, as well as hazardous materials being accidentally introduced to foods. In the past, it has taken weeks to find the source of these outbreaks or the cause of sickness from what people are eating.

Using blockchain gives brands the ability to track a food product's route from its origin, through each stop it makes, and finally its delivery. If a food is found to be contaminated then it can be traced all the way back through each stop to its origin. Not only that, but these companies can also now see everything else it may have come in contact with, allowing the identification of the problem to occur far sooner, potentially saving lives. This is one example of blockchains in practice, but there are many other forms of blockchain implementation.

Banking and Finance

Perhaps no industry stands to benefit from integrating blockchain into its business operations more than banking. Financial institutions only operate during business hours, five days a week. That means if you try to deposit a check on Friday at 6 p.m., you will likely have to wait until Monday morning to see that money hit your account. Even if you do make your deposit during business hours, the transaction can still take one to three days to verify due to the sheer volume of transactions that banks need to settle. Blockchain, on the other hand, never sleeps.

By integrating blockchain into banks, consumers can see their transactions processed in as little as 10 minutes,2 basically the time it takes to add a block to the blockchain, regardless of holidays or the time of day or week. With blockchain, banks also have the opportunity to exchange funds between institutions more quickly and securely. In the stock trading business, for example, the settlement and clearing process can take up to three days (or longer, if trading internationally), meaning that the money and shares are frozen for that period of time.

Given the size of the sums involved, even the few days that the money is in transit can carry significant costs and risks for banks. European bank Santander and its research partners put the potential savings at $15 billion to $20 billion a year.3 Capgemini, a French consultancy, estimates that consumers could save up to $16 billion in banking and insurance fees each year4 through blockchain-based applications.

Currency

Blockchain forms the bedrock for cryptocurrencies like Bitcoin. The U.S. dollar is controlled by the Federal Reserve. Under this central authority system, a user's data and currency are technically at the whim of their bank or government. If a user's bank is hacked, the client's private information is at risk. If the client's bank collapses or they live in a country with an unstable government, the value of their currency may be at risk. In 2008, some of the banks that ran out of money were bailed out partially using taxpayer money. These are the worries out of which Bitcoin was first conceived and developed.

By spreading its operations across a network of computers, blockchain allows Bitcoin and other cryptocurrencies to operate without the need for a central authority. This not only reduces risk but also eliminates many of the processing and transaction fees. It can also give those in countries with unstable currencies or financial infrastructures a more stable currency with more applications and a wider network of individuals and institutions they can do business with, both domestically and internationally.

Using cryptocurrency wallets for savings accounts or as a means of payment is especially profound for those who have no state identification. Some countries may be war-torn or have governments that lack any real infrastructure to provide identification. Citizens of such countries may not have access to savings or brokerage accounts and therefore, no way to safely store wealth.

Healthcare

Health care providers can leverage blockchain to securely store their patients' medical records. When a medical record is generated and signed, it can be written into the blockchain, which provides patients with the proof and confidence that the record cannot be changed. These personal health records could be encoded and stored on the blockchain with a private key, so that they are only accessible by certain individuals, thereby ensuring privacy.

Records of Property

If you have ever spent time in your local Recorder's Office, you will know that the process of recording property rights is both burdensome and inefficient. Today, a physical deed must be delivered to a government employee at the local recording office, where it is manually entered into the county's central database and public index. In the case of a property dispute, claims to the property must be reconciled with the public index.

This process is not just costly and time-consuming it is also riddled with human error, where each inaccuracy makes tracking property ownership less efficient. Blockchain has the potential to eliminate the need for scanning documents and tracking down physical files in a local recording office. If property ownership is stored and verified on the blockchain, owners can trust that their deed is accurate and permanently recorded.

In war-torn countries or areas that have little to no government or financial infrastructure, and certainly no "Recorder's Office," it can be nearly impossible to prove ownership of a property. If a group of people living in such an area is able to leverage blockchain, transparent and clear timelines of property ownership could be established.

Smart Contracts

A smart contract is a computer code that can be built into the blockchain to facilitate, verify, or negotiate a contract agreement. Smart contracts operate under a set of conditions that users agree to. When those conditions are met, the terms of the agreement are automatically carried out.

Say, for example, a potential tenant would like to lease an apartment using a smart contract. The landlord agrees to give the tenant the door code to the apartment as soon as the tenant pays the security deposit. Both the tenant and the landlord would send their respective portions of the deal to the smart contract, which would hold onto and automatically exchange the door code for the security deposit on the date the lease begins. If the landlord doesn't supply the door code by the lease date, the smart contract refunds the security deposit. This would eliminate the fees and processes typically associated with the use of a notary, third-party mediator, or attornies.

Supply Chains

As in the IBM Food Trust example, suppliers can use blockchain to record the origins of materials that they have purchased. This would allow companies to verify the authenticity of their products, along with such common labels as "Organic," "Local," and "Fair Trade."

As reported by Forbes, the food industry is increasingly adopting the use of blockchain to track the path and safety of food throughout the farm-to-user journey.

Voting

As mentioned, blockchain could be used to facilitate a modern voting system. Voting with blockchain carries the potential to eliminate election fraud and boost voter turnout, as was tested in the November 2018 midterm elections in West Virginia. Using blockchain in this way would make votes nearly impossible to tamper with. The blockchain protocol would also maintain transparency in the electoral process, reducing the personnel needed to conduct an election and providing officials with nearly instant results. This would eliminate the need for recounts or any real concern that fraud might threaten the election.

Advantages and Disadvantages of Blockchain

For all of its complexity, blockchain's potential as a decentralized form of record-keeping is almost without limit. From greater user privacy and heightened security to lower processing fees and fewer errors, blockchain technology may very well see applications beyond those outlined above. But there are also some disadvantages.

Pros

· Improved accuracy by removing human involvement in verification

· Cost reductions by eliminating third-party verification

· Decentralization makes it harder to tamper with

· Transactions are secure, private, and efficient

· Transparent technology

· Provides a banking alternative and way to secure personal information for citizens of countries with unstable or underdeveloped governments

Cons

· Significant technology cost associated with mining bitcoin

· Low transactions per second

· History of use in illicit activities

· Regulation

Here are the selling points of blockchain for businesses on the market today in more detail.

Chapter 2. Mining of Cryptocurrency

Mining is how new units of cryptocurrency are released into the world, generally in exchange for validating transactions. While it's theoretically possible for the average person to mine cryptocurrency, it's increasingly difficult in proof of work systems, like Bitcoin.

"As the Bitcoin network grows, it gets more complicated, and more processing power is required," says Spencer Montgomery, founder of Uinta Crypto Consulting. "The average consumer used to be able to do this, but now it's just too expensive. There are too many people who have optimized their equipment and technology to outcompete."

And remember: Proof of work cryptocurrencies require huge amounts of energy to mine. It's estimated that 0.21% of all of the world's electricity goes to powering Bitcoin farms. That's roughly the same amount of power Switzerland uses in a year. It's estimated most Bitcoin miners end up using 60% to 80% of what they earn from mining to cover electricity costs.

While it's impractical for the average person to earn crypto by mining in a proof of work system, the proof of stake model requires less in the way of high-powered computing as validators are chosen at random based on the amount they stake. It does, however, require that you already own a cryptocurrency to participate. (If you have no crypto, you have nothing to stake.)

History of Cryptocurrency

In 1983, the American developed a cryptographic system referred to as eCash. Twelve years later, they developed every system DigiCash, that used cryptography to make economic transactions personal.

However, the first time the concept or time period "cryptocurrency" turned into coined changed into in 1998. That year, Wei Dai began to consider developing a brand new payment method that used a cryptographic system and whose important feature was decentralization. In 2008, a funding crisis affecting everybody, together with America's superpower, changed into booming. The effects of such a large economic disaster were dormant and the coins were losing value faster and faster.

In 2009, the so-called Satoshi Nakamoto someone whose identity still remains secret, no person knows who invented bitcoin, or at the least no longer conclusively. Satoshi Nakamoto is the call associated with the person or organization of people who released the authentic bitcoin white paper in 2008 and worked at the authentic bitcoin software program that was launched in 2009. As you have already read, he was not the first person who came up with the idea to create it. In the years since that time, many individuals have either claimed to be or have been suggested as the real-life people behind the pseudonym, but as of January 2021, the authentic identity (or identities) in the back of Satoshi remains obscured. Although it's far tempting to agree with the media's spin that Satoshi Nakamoto is a solitary, quixotic genius who created

Bitcoin out of thin air, such improvements do now not normally appear in a vacuum. All foremost medical discoveries, no matter how original-seeming, have been constructed on previously present research.

There are precursors to bitcoin: Adam Back's Hashcash, invented in 1997, and finally Wei Dai's b-money, Nick Szabo's bit gold, and Hal Finney's Reusable Proof of Work. The bitcoin whitepaper itself cites Hashcash and b-cash, as well as diverse different works spanning numerous studies fields. Perhaps unsurprisingly, most of the individuals behind the other initiatives named above had been imagined to have additionally had a component in creating bitcoin.

There are a few feasible motivations for bitcoin's inventor deciding to preserve their identity mystery. One is privacy: As bitcoin has gained in recognition—becoming some thing of a worldwide phenomenon—Satoshi Nakamoto would likely garner a number of attention from the media and from governments.

Another motive will be the ability for bitcoin to purpose a major disruption inside the contemporary banking and financial systems. If bitcoin have been to advantage mass adoption, the device should surpass nations' sovereign fiat currencies. This chance to existing forex should inspire governments to need to take legal movement in opposition to bitcoin's creator.

The different motive is safety. Looking at 2009 by myself, 32,489 blocks were mined; at the praise fee of 50 bitcoin according to block, the total payout in 2009 become 1,624,500 bitcoin. One may additionally finish that best Satoshi and perhaps a few different human beings had been mining via 2009 and that they possess a majority of that stash of bitcoin.

Someone in ownership of that lots bitcoin should turn out to be a target of criminals, especially since bitcoins are much less like shares and more like coins, in which the personal keys needed to authorize spending may be published out and actually kept underneath a mattress. While it is likely the inventor of bitcoin could take precautions to make any extortion-brought on transfers traceable, closing anonymous is a superb way for Satoshi to restrict publicity.

Why you should consider investing in Cryptocurrency?

Investing in currencies such as Bitcoin and Ethereum is considered a "high-risk" investment. The price of cryptocurrencies is generally volatile; some can go wrong, others could turn out to be scams, while others may increase in value and produce a great return for the investors. If you are considering investing in Cryptocurrency, you need to find a trusted and reliable trading platform such as Bitfinex. You can read about the <u>trusted Bitfinex review</u>.

To some people, Cryptocurrency could remain niche or vanish just like that. But Cryptocurrency should be considered a high-risk investment just like any other investment. With more and more businesses accepting crypto, it is now evident that Cryptocurrency is here to stay and it will not disappear any time soon.

Some of the big brands that have accepted crypto include Starbucks, Tesla, and other top casinos. This proves that crypto will soon find its way into so many big brands, making it a worthy investment. But just like any other investment, before you invest in crypto, you need to do extensive diligence and don't pin your hopes on one Cryptocurrency or one company. The best decision is to spread your money across so that you can spread the risk. Again, remember to invest only what you can afford to lose.

Types of Risks Associated with Cryptocurrency Investing

Although Bitcoin was not designed as a normal equity investment (no shares have been issued), some speculative investors were drawn to the digital currency after it appreciated rapidly in May 2011 and again in November 2013. Thus, many people purchase bitcoin for its investment value rather than its ability to act as a medium of exchange.

However, the lack of guaranteed value and its digital nature means the purchase and use of bitcoins carries several inherent risks. Many investor alerts have been issued by the Securities and Exchange Commission (SEC), the Financia Industry Regulatory Authority (FINRA), the Consumer Financial Protection Bureau (CFPB), and other agencies.

The concept of a virtual currency is still novel and, compared to traditional investments; bitcoin doesn't have much of a long-term track record or history of credibility to back it. With their increasing popularity, bitcoins are becoming less experimental every day; still, after only a decade, all digital currencies still remain in a development phase. "It is pretty much the highest-risk, highest-return investment that you can possibly make," says Barry Silbert, CEO of Digital Currency Group, which builds and invests in Bitcoin and blockchain companies.10

Regulatory Risk

Investing money into bitcoin in any of its many guises is not for the risk-averse. Bitcoins are a rival to government currency and may be used for black market transactions, money laundering, illegal activities, or tax evasion. As a result, governments may seek to regulate, restrict, or ban the use and sale of bitcoins (and some already have). Others are coming up with various rules.

For example, in 2015, the New York State Department of Financial Services finalized regulations that would require companies dealing with the buy, sell, transfer, or storage of bitcoins to record the identity of customers, have a compliance officer, and maintain capital reserves. The transactions worth $10,000 or more will have to be recorded and reported.

The lack of uniform regulations about bitcoins (and other virtual currency) raises questions over their longevity, liquidity, and universality.

Security Risk

Most individuals who own and use bitcoin have not acquired their tokens through mining operations. Rather, they buy and sell bitcoin and other digital currencies on any of a number of popular online markets, known as bitcoin exchanges.

Bitcoin exchanges are entirely digital and, as with any virtual system, are at risk from hackers, malware, and operational glitches. If a thief gains access to a bitcoin owner's computer hard drive and steals their private encryption key, they could transfer the stolen bitcoin to another account. (Users can prevent this only if bitcoins are stored on a computer that is not connected to the internet, or else by choosing to use a paper wallet printing out the bitcoin private keys and addresses, and not keeping them on a computer at all.)

Hackers can also target bitcoin exchanges, gaining access to thousands of accounts and digital wallets where bitcoins are stored. One especially notorious hacking incident took place in 2014, when Mt. Gox, a bitcoin exchange in Japan, was forced to close down after millions of dollars' worth of bitcoins were stolen.

This is particularly problematic given that all Bitcoin transactions are permanent and irreversible. It's like dealing with cash: Any transaction carried out with bitcoins can only be reversed if the person who has received them refunds them. There is no third party or a payment processor, as in the case of a debit or credit card—hence, no source of protection or appeal if there is a problem.

Insurance Risk

Some investments are insured through the Securities Investor Protection Corporation. Normal bank accounts are insured through the Federal Deposit Insurance Corporation (FDIC) up to a certain amount depending on the jurisdiction.

Generally speaking, bitcoin exchanges and bitcoin accounts are not insured by any type of federal or government program. In 2019, prime dealer and trading platform SFOX announced it would be able to provide bitcoin investors with FDIC insurance, but only for the portion of transactions involving cash.13

Fraud Risk

While bitcoin uses private key encryption to verify owners and register transactions, fraudsters and scammers may attempt to sell false bitcoins. For instance, in July 2013, the SEC brought legal action against an operator of a bitcoin-related Ponzi scheme. There have also been documented cases of bitcoin price manipulation, another common form of fraud.

Market Risk

Like with any investment, bitcoin values can fluctuate. Indeed, the value of the currency has seen wild swings in price over its short existence. Subject to high volume buying and selling on exchanges, it has a high sensitivity to any newsworthy events. According to the CFPB, the price of bitcoins fell by 61% in a single day in 2013, while the one-day price drop record in 2014 was as big as 80%.

If fewer people begin to accept bitcoin as a currency, these digital units may lose value and could become worthless. Indeed, there was speculation that the "bitcoin bubble" had burst when the price declined from its all-time high during the cryptocurrency rush in late 2017 and early 2018.

There is already plenty of competition, and although bitcoin has a huge lead over the hundreds of other digital currencies that have sprung up because of its brand recognition and venture capital money, a technological break-through in the form of a better virtual coin is always a threat.

Imposter Websites

You may be following a solid tip from someone with a lot of expertise but still become a victim by accidently visiting a fake website. There's a surprising number of websites that have been set up to resemble original, valid startup companies. If there isn't a small lock icon indicating security near the URL bar and no "https" in the site address think twice.

Even if the site looks identical to the one you think you're visiting, you may find yourself directed to another platform for payment. For example, you click on a link that looks like a legitimate site, but attackers have created a fake URL with a zero in it instead of a letter 'o'. That platform, of course, isn't taking you to the cryptocurrency investment that you've already researched. To avoid this, carefully type the exact URL into your browser. Double check it, too.

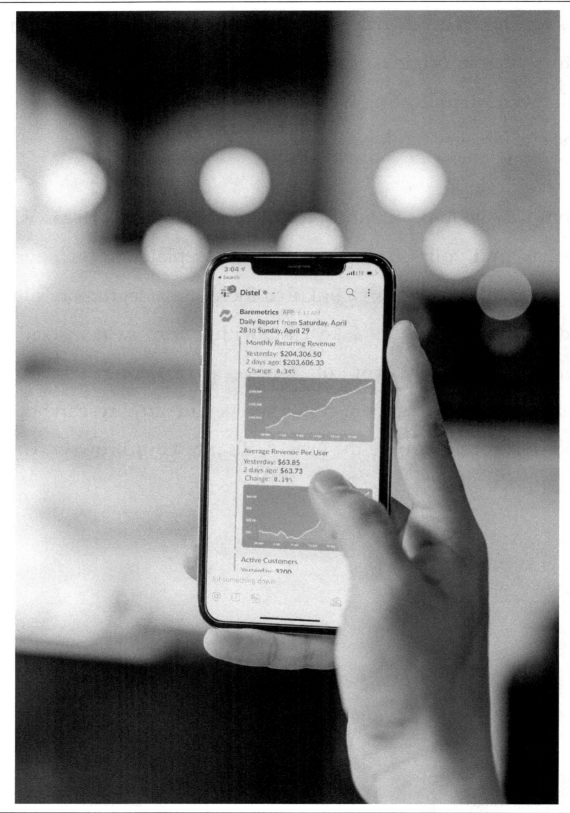

Fake Mobile Apps

Another common way scammers trick cryptocurrency investors is through <u>fake apps</u> available for download through Google Play and the Apple App Store. Although stakeholders can often quickly find these fake apps and get them removed, that doesn't mean the apps aren't impacting many bottom lines. Thousands of people have already downloaded fake cryptocurrency apps, <u>reports Bitcoin News</u>.

While this is a greater risk for Android users, every investor should be aware of the possibility. Are there obvious misspellings in the copy or even the name of the app? Does the branding look inauthentic with strange coloring or an incorrect logo? Take note and reconsider downloading.

Bad Tweets and Other Social Media Updates

If you're following celebrities and executives on social media, you can't be sure that you're not following impostor accounts. The same applies to cryptocurrencies, where malicious, impersonating bots are rampant. Don't trust offers that come from Twitter or Facebook, especially if there seems to be an impossible result. Fake accounts are everywhere.

If someone on these platforms asks for even a small amount of your cryptocurrency, it's likely you can never get it back. Just because others are replying to the offer, don't assume they aren't bots, either. You have to be extra careful.

Scamming Emails

Even if it looks exactly like an email you received from a legitimate cryptocurrency company, take care before investing your digital currency. Is the email the exact same, and are the logo and branding identical? Can you verify that the email address is legitimately connected to the company? The ability to check on this is one reason why it's important to choose a company that has real people working for it. If you have doubts about an email, ask someone who works there. And never click on a link in a message to get to a site.

Scammers often announce fake ICOs, or initial coin offerings, as a way to steal substantial funds. Don't fall for these fake email and website offers. Take your time to look over all the details.

Unfortunately, there are many ways that some Internet users exploit unsecure computing systems to mine or steal cryptocurrency.

How to Buy Bitcoin using PayPal

It is likewise feasible to shop for Bitcoin through charge processor PayPal. There are two ways to buy Bitcoin the usage of PayPal. The first, and maximum handy technique, is to purchase cryptocurrencies through the use of your PayPal account. The second choice is to apply the stability of your PayPal account to buy cryptocurrencies from a third-celebration issuer. This choice isn't always as handy as the first one due to the fact very few third party sites allow users to purchase Bitcoin with the use of the PayPal button.

Four cryptocurrencies – Bitcoin, Ethereum, Litecoin, and Bitcoin Cash – can be purchased without delay thru PayPal. With the exception of Hawaii, citizens of all states can both use their existing PayPal accounts or set up new ones.

To set up a crypto account with PayPal, the subsequent pieces of information are required: Name, Physical cope with, Date of Birth, and Tax Identification Number. There are some of the methods by which you may purchase Bitcoin via PayPal.

Some of them are:

- Existing balance in PayPal account.

-

- Debit card linked to PayPal account

-

- Bank account linked to PayPal account

-

It is not feasible to apply for a credit card to buy Bitcoin using PayPal. During the purchase system, PayPal will show a price. However, the inherent volatility of cryptocurrency charges method that those prices can exchange fast. You have to make sure which you have enough finances in your account to make the purchase.

When you buy Bitcoin without delay from PayPal, it makes cash off the crypto spread or the distinction between Bitcoin's marketplace charge and change fee among USD and the cryptocurrency. The enterprise additionally expenses a transaction fee for each purchase. These charges rely upon the dollar quantity of buy. For instance, a flat rate of $zero.50 is charged for purchases between $a hundred to $2 hundred. Thereafter, the fee is a percentage of the general dollar amount. For instance, a fee of two% of the whole quantity is charged for crypto purchases among $100 to $two hundred.

One downside of buying cryptocurrencies via PayPal is that you can't switch crypto outside the price processor's platform. Therefore, it isn't always feasible to switch cryptocurrencies from PayPal's pockets to an outside crypto wallet or your private wallet.

The other downside of using PayPal is that very few exchanges and online investors allow the charge processor to purchase payment. EToro is many of the few online investors who use PayPal to buy Bitcoin on its platform.

How to Buy Bitcoin with Credit Card

The technique to purchase Bitcoin with credit playing cards is just like getting the cryptocurrency with debit cards or thru computerized clearing house (ACH) transfers. You will want to go into your credit card details with the trade or online buying and selling firm and authorize the transaction. In trendy, however, it isn't always a terrific concept to purchase Bitcoin with credit cards. There are multiple motives for this.

First, not all exchanges permit Bitcoin purchases using credit cards because of associated processing expenses and the chance of fraud. Their selection to accomplish that may fit out inside the quality hobbies of customers. This is because credit card processing can tack extra fees onto such transactions. Thus, similarly to paying transaction charges, you will emerge as processing expenses that the alternate may also bypass onto you.

The 2nd motive is that credit card purchases can be high priced. Credit card issuers treat Bitcoin purchases as coins advances and charge hefty charges and interest quotes on such advances. For example, American Express and Chase both count purchases of cryptocurrencies as coins boost transactions. Thus, if you purchase $100 well worth of Bitcoin using an American Express card, you will pay $10 (current cash boost fee for such transactions) plus an annual percentage charge of 25%.

An oblique technique of buying Bitcoin using a credit card is to get a Bitcoin Rewards creditcard. Such playing cards characteristic like your normal rewards creditcard; besides, they offer rewards in the shape of Bitcoin. So, they make investments cash again earned from purchases into Bitcoin. An instance of a Bitcoin Rewards card is the BlockFi Bitcoin Rewards Credit Card.

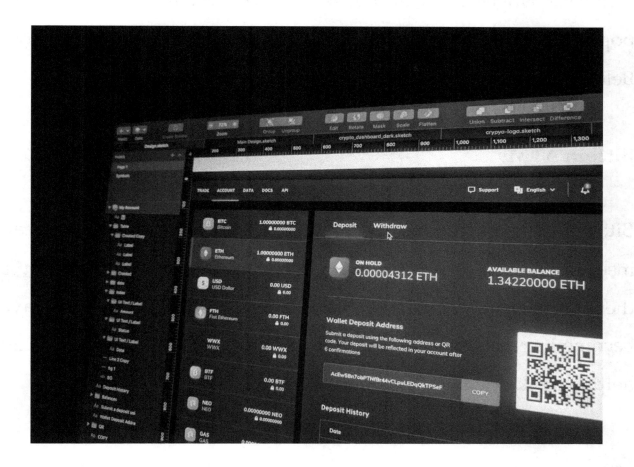

Beware, however, that the annual price on these playing cards may be steep, and there can be extra expenses associated with the conversion of fiat currencies into crypto.

Alternate Ways of Buying Bitcoin

While exchanges like Coinbase or Binance remain some of the most popular ways of purchasing Bitcoin, it is not the only method. Below are some additional processes Bitcoin owners utilize.

Bitcoin ATMs

Bitcoin ATMs act like in-person Bitcoin exchanges. Individuals can insert cash into the machine and use it to purchase Bitcoin that is then transferred to a secure digital wallet. Bitcoin ATMs have become increasingly popular in recent years; <u>Coin ATM Radar</u> can help to track down the closest machines.

P2P Exchanges

Unlike decentralized exchanges, which match up buyers and sellers anonymously and facilitate all aspects of the transaction, there are some peer-to-peer (P2P) exchange services that provide a more direct connection between users. <u>Local Bitcoins</u> is an example of such an exchange. After creating an account, users can post requests to buy or sell Bitcoin, including information about payment methods and price. Users then browse through listings of buy and sell offers, choosing those trade partners with whom they wish to transact.

Local Bitcoins facilitates some of the aspects of the trade. While P2P exchanges do not offer the same anonymity as decentralized exchanges, they allow users the opportunity to shop around for the best deal. Many of these exchanges also provide rating systems so that users have a way to evaluate potential trade partners before transacting.

How to Sell Bitcoin

You can sell Bitcoin at the same venues that you purchased the cryptocurrency, such as cryptocurrency exchanges and peer-to-peer platforms. Typically, the process to sell Bitcoin on these platforms is similar to the process used to purchase the cryptocurrency.

For example, you may only be required to click a button and specify an order type (i.e., whether the cryptocurrency should be sold instantly at available prices or whether it should be sold to limit losses) to conduct the sale. Depending on the market composition and demand at the venue, the offering price for Bitcoin may vary. For example, exchanges in South Korea traded Bitcoin at a Kimchi premium during the run up in its prices back in 2018.

Cryptocurrency exchanges charge a percentage of the crypto sale amount as fees. For example, Coinbase charges 1.49% of the overall transaction amount as fees.

Exchanges generally have daily and monthly withdrawal limits. Therefore, cash from a large sale may not be immediately available to the trader. There are no limits on the amount of cryptocurrency you can sell, however.

Chapter 3. Before You Begin

There are numerous matters that every aspiring Bitcoin investor desires. A cryptocurrency change account, private identity documents in case you are using a Know Your Customer (KYC) platform, a comfy connection to the Internet, and a method of charge. Likewise, it is recommended that you have your own private wallet outside of the trading account. Valid strategies of payment using this path consist of financial institution accounts, debit playing cards, and credit playing cards. It is likewise viable to get Bitcoin at specialized ATMs and via P2P exchanges. However, be aware that Bitcoin ATMs have been increasingly requiring authorities-issued IDs as of early 2020.

Privacy and protection are vital issues for Bitcoin traders. Even though there are no physical Bitcoins, it is also a bad idea to gloat approximately huge holdings. Anyone who profits the personal key to a public address at the Bitcoin blockchain can authorize transactions. Private keys must be kept in mystery; criminals might also attempt to steal them if they analyze large holdings. Be conscious that anybody can see the balance of a public deal you use. That makes it a good idea to maintain vast investments at public addresses that aren't immediately linked to ones that are used for transactions.

Anyone can view a history of transactions made at the blockchain, even you. While transactions are publicly recorded at the blockchain, figuring out user information isn't always. Most effective, a person's public key appears next to a transaction — making transactions exclusive however not nameless on the Bitcoin blockchain. In an experience, Bitcoin transactions are greater transparent and traceable than coins, but the cryptocurrency can also be used anonymously.

Following are some steps you need to follow if you want to invest in cryptocurrency:

Step One: Choose an Exchange

Signing up for a cryptocurrency trade will permit you to shop for, sell, and maintain cryptocurrency. It is generally an exceptional exercise to apply a change that lets its customers additionally withdrawal their crypto to their very own non-public online wallet for more secure preservation. This feature might not depend on the ones trying to change Bitcoin or other cryptocurrencies.

There are many styles of cryptocurrency exchanges. Because the Bitcoin ethos is about decentralization and man or woman sovereignty, some exchanges permit customers to remain anonymous and do not require users to go into private information. Such exchanges perform autonomously and, generally, decentralized, which means that they no longer have a primary factor of manipulation.

While such structures may be used for nefarious sports, they're extensively utilized to offer offerings for the arena's unbanked population. For certain classes of human beings – refugees or those dwelling in international locations with little to no infrastructure for authorities' credit or banking – anonymous exchanges can help convey them into the mainstream economy.

Right now, but, the maximum popular exchanges now not decentralized and do require KYC. In the United States, these exchanges include Coinbase, Kraken, Gemini, and Binance U.S., to name some. Each of those exchanges has grown appreciably inside the variety of capabilities they offer.

Coinbase, Kraken, and Gemini offer Bitcoin and a growing wide variety of altcoins. These 3 are probably the perfect on-ramp to crypto in the entire enterprise. Binance caters to a more superior dealer, imparting greater critical trading functionality and a better style of altcoins to choose from.

A vital thing to note whilst creating a cryptocurrency change account is to apply secure net practices. This consists of the usage of -aspect authentication and using a precise and lengthy password, together with a variety of lowercase letters, capitalized letters, special characters, and numbers.

Step Two: Connect Your Exchange to a Payment Option

Once you have chosen an exchange, you now want to collect your non-public documents. Depending on the exchange, these may consist of snapshots of a driving force's license, social security variety, in addition to statistics approximately your business enterprise and supply of funds. The records you could need can depend upon your location and the laws inside it. The system is largely the same as putting in place a standard brokerage account.

After the trade has ensured your identity and legitimacy, you can now join a payment choice. At most exchanges, you may connect your financial institution account without delay, or you could join a debit or credit card. While you may use a credit card to buy cryptocurrency, it's miles usually something that should be avoided because of the volatility that cryptocurrencies can revel in.

While Bitcoin is legal inside the United States, some banks no longer take too kindly to the idea and might query or even forestall deposits to crypto-associated web sites or exchanges. It is a great idea to test to make sure that your financial institution deposits at your chosen alternate.

There are various costs for deposits thru a financial institution account, debit, or credit card. Coinbase is a stable exchange for beginners and has a 1.49% charge for financial institution money owed, with a 3.99% rate for debit and credit playing cards. It is essential to analyze the charges associated with every fee choice to assist in pick out and trade or pick out which price choice works great for you.

Exchanges additionally rate fees in step with the transaction. This rate can both be a flat fee (if the trading quantity is low) or a per cent of buying and selling quantity. Credit cards incur a processing rate similarly to the transaction costs.

Step Three: Place an Order

Once you have selected trade and connected a charged alternative, you may now buy Bitcoin and other cryptocurrencies. In latest years, cryptocurrency exchanges have slowly turn out to be more mainstream. They have grown notably in terms of liquidity and their breadth of capabilities. The operational modifications at cryptocurrency exchanges parallel the exchange notion for cryptocurrencies. An industry that became as soon as the notion of as a rip-off or one with questionable practices is slowly morphing right into a valid one that has drawn interest from all huge players in the economic offerings industry.

Now, cryptocurrency exchanges have gotten to some extent where they have almost identical functions as their stock brokerage counterparts. Once you have located an exchange and linked a charging method, you are geared up to move.

Crypto exchanges these days provide some order types and methods to invest. Almost all crypto exchanges offer each marketplace and limit orders, and some also provide stop-loss orders. Of the exchanges stated above, Kraken gives the most order kinds. Kraken lets in for market, restriction, prevent-loss, prevent-restrict, take-earnings, and take-profit limit orders1

.

Aside from diffusion of order types, exchanges also provide approaches to set up habitual investments allowing clients to dollar fee average into their investments of desire. Coinbase, for instance, we could users set habitual purchases for every day, week, or month.

Step Four: Safe Storage

Bitcoin and cryptocurrency wallets are a place to shop virtual property extra securely. Having your crypto out of the trade doors and your personal wallet guarantees that only you have manipulated the personal key to your funds. It additionally gives you the ability to shop funds far away from an exchange and avoid the threat of your change getting hacked and losing your funds.

Some wallets have extra capabilities than others. Some are Bitcoin best, and some provide the potential to shop numerous types of altcoins. Some wallets also offer the capability to change one token for any other.

When it involves deciding on a Bitcoin wallet, you have some options. The first element you will need to understand about crypto wallets is hot wallets (online wallets) and cold wallets (paper or hardware wallets).

Hot Wallets

Online wallets also are called "hot" wallets. Hot wallets are wallets that run on internet-related devices like computer systems, phones, or capsules. This can create vulnerability due to the fact these wallets generate the private keys on your coins on those net-related devices. While a hot pockets may be very convenient in the way you're capable of access and make transactions along with your belongings quickly, storing your non-public key on a web-linked tool makes it greater vulnerable to a hack.

This can also sound far-fetched, but individuals who are not the usage of sufficient protection whilst using those hot wallets may have their price range stolen. This isn't always an rare prevalence and it can take place in some of approaches. As an instance, boasting on a public discussion board like Reddit about how a good deal Bitcoin you keep while you are the usage of little to no safety and storing it in a hot pockets would not be smart. That said, these wallets may be made to be relaxed so long as precautions are taken. Strong passwords, two-component authentication, and safe internet surfing have to be considered minimum requirements.

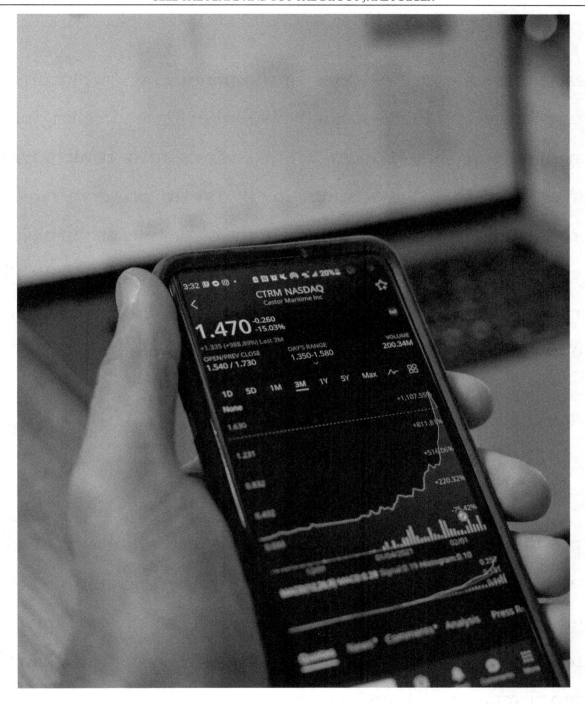

These wallets are nice used for small quantities of cryptocurrency or cryptocurrency that you are actively buying and selling on an exchange. You should liken a hot pockets to a bank account. Conventional financial wisdom might say to preserve handiest spending money in a bank account at the same time as the majority of your cash is in savings debts or different funding bills. The identical could be said for hot wallets. Hot wallets embody cell, computer, net, and exchange account custody wallets.

As stated previously, change wallets are custodial accounts provided by way of the alternate. The consumer of this pockets kind isn't always the holder of the personal key to the cryptocurrency that is held in this wallet. If an event were to arise where the change is hacked or your account becomes compromised, your budget could be lost. The phrase "now not your key, no longer your coin" is closely-repeated within cryptocurrency boards and groups.

Cold Wallets

The most effective description of a cold wallet is a pockets that is not related to the internet and consequently stands at a much lesser risk of being compromised. These wallets can also be referred to as offline wallets or hardware wallets.

These wallets keep a person's private key on some thing that is not linked to the internet and may come with software program that works in parallel in order that the user can view their portfolio with out putting their personal key at chance.

Perhaps the most secure manner to keep cryptocurrency offline is through a paper pockets. A paper wallet is a wallet that you can generate off of certain websites. It then produces each public and personal keys that you print out on a bit of paper. The capacity to get admission to cryptocurrency in these addresses is simplest viable if you have that piece of paper with the private key. Many people laminate those paper wallets and shop them in protection deposit packing containers at their financial institution or even in a safe of their home. These wallets are meant for excessive safety and long-time period investments because you can not quick sell or alternate Bitcoin saved this manner.

A more usually used type of cold wallet is a hardware pockets. A hardware pockets is commonly a USB power device that stores a person's non-public keys securely offline. Such wallets have serious benefits over hot wallets as they're unaffected by viruses that might be on one's pc. With hardware wallets, personal keys in no way are available contact together with your network-related computer or doubtlessly prone software. These gadgets are also commonly open supply, allowing the network to decide its protection thru code audits rather than a organisation declaring that it is safe to apply.

Cold wallets are the most cozy way to shop your Bitcoin or other cryptocurrencies. For the maximum component, but, they require a piece greater understanding to installation.

A proper way to installation your wallets is to have three matters: an alternate account to shop for and sell, a hot wallet to keep small to medium quantities of crypto you desire to change or promote, and a cold hardware pockets to keep large holdings for long-term periods.

Best cryptocurrencies on the market to invest in

Cryptocurrencies are almost always designed to be free from government manipulation and control, although as they have grown more popular this foundational aspect of the industry has come under fire. The currencies modeled after Bitcoin are collectively called altcoins, and in some cases "shitcoins," and have often tried to present themselves as modified or improved versions of Bitcoin. While some of these currencies may have some impressive features that Bitcoin does not, matching the level of security that Bitcoin's networks achieves has largely yet to be seen by an altcoin.

Below, we'll examine some of the most important digital currencies other than Bitcoin. First, though, a caveat: it is impossible for a list like this to be entirely comprehensive. One reason for this is the fact that there are more than 4,000 cryptocurrencies in existence as of January 2021. While many of these cryptos have little to no following or trading volume, some enjoy immense popularity among dedicated communities of backers and investors.

Beyond that, the field of cryptocurrencies is always expanding, and the next great digital token may be released tomorrow. While Bitcoin is widely seen as a pioneer in the world of cryptocurrencies, analysts adopt many approaches for evaluating tokens other than BTC. It's common, for instance, for analysts to attribute a great deal of importance to the ranking of coins relative to one another in terms of market cap. We've factored this into our consideration, but there are other reasons why a digital token may be included in the list, as well.

1. Bitcoin (BTC)
2.

The closest thing you'll get to a blue-chip cryptocurrency, <u>Bitcoin</u> has dominated the market since the first bitcoins were mined in January 2009 – but that doesn't mean it has always been smooth sailing. Bitcoin prices hit a high of around $20,000 in December 2017 before collapsing in 2018, reaching a bottom at $3,234 by the end of that year. Since then, however, Bitcoin has enjoyed a comeback as prices surged to more than $40,000 in January 2021 for a market cap of more than $1 trillion – meaning bitcoins accounted for more than 69% of the cryptocurrency market. Bitcoin has its fair share of volatility, as prices have pulled back since hitting this high, but being the biggest name in crypto gives it a worldwide acceptance that lesser-known rivals don't have, arguably making it the best cryptocurrency to buy for investors new to the asset class.

1. Bitcoin Cash (BCH)
2.

Bitcoin Cash (BCH) holds an important place in the history of altcoins because it is one of the earliest and most successful hard forks of the original Bitcoin. In the cryptocurrency world, a fork takes place as the result of debates and arguments between developers and miners. Due to the decentralized nature of digital currencies, wholesale changes to the code underlying the token or coin at hand must be made due to general consensus; the mechanism for this process varies according to the particular cryptocurrency.

When different factions can't come to an agreement, sometimes the digital currency is split, with the original chain remaining true to its original code and the new chain beginning life as a new version of the prior coin, complete with changes to its code.

BCH began its life in August of 2017 as a result of one of these splits. The debate that led to the creation of BCH had to do with the issue of scalability; the Bitcoin network has a limit on the size of blocks: one megabyte (MB). BCH increases the block size from one MB to eight MB, with the idea being that larger blocks can hold more transactions within them, and therefore the transaction speed would be increased. It also makes other changes, including the removal of the Segregated Witness protocol which impacts block space. As of January 2021, BCH had a market cap of $8.9 billion and a value per token of $513.45.

1. Litecoin (LTC)

2.

Litecoin, launched in 2011, was among the first cryptocurrencies to follow in the footsteps of Bitcoin and has often been referred to as "silver to Bitcoin's gold." It was created by Charlie Lee, an MIT graduate and former Google engineer. Litecoin is based on an open-source global payment network that is not controlled by any central authority and uses "scrypt" as a proof of work, which can be decoded with the help of CPUs of consumer-grade. Although Litecoin is like Bitcoin in many ways, it has a faster block generation rate and hence offers a faster transaction confirmation time. Other than developers, there are a growing number of merchants who accept Litecoin. As of January 2021, Litecoin had a market cap of \$10.1 billion and a per token value of \$153.88, making it the sixth-largest cryptocurrency in the world.

1. Ethereum (ETH)
2.

The first Bitcoin alternative on our list, <u>Ethereum</u>, is a decentralized software platform that enables <u>Smart Contracts</u> and Decentralized Applications (DApps) to be built and run without any downtime, fraud, control, or interference from a third party. The goal behind Ethereum is to create a decentralized suite of financial products that anyone in the world can have free access to, regardless of nationality, ethnicity, or faith. This aspect makes the implications for those in some countries more compelling, as those without state infrastructure and state identifications can get access to bank accounts, loans, insurance, or a variety of other financial products.

The applications on Ethereum are run on its platform-specific cryptographic token, ether. Ether is like a vehicle for moving around on the Ethereum platform and is sought by mostly developers looking to develop and run applications inside Ethereum, or now, by investors looking to make purchases of other digital currencies using ether. Ether, launched in 2015, is currently the second-largest digital currency by market cap after Bitcoin, although it lags behind the dominant cryptocurrency by a significant margin. As of January 2021, ether's market cap is roughly 19% of Bitcoin's size.

In 2014, Ethereum launched a pre-sale for ether which received an overwhelming response; this helped to usher in the age of the initial coin offering (ICO). According to Ethereum, it can be used to "codify, decentralize, secure and trade just about anything." Following the attack on the DAO in 2016, Ethereum was split into Ethereum (ETH) and Ethereum Classic (ETC). As of January 2021, Ethereum (ETH) had a market cap of $138.3 billion and a per token value of $1,218.59.

In 2021 Ethereum plans to change its consensus algorithm from proof-of-work to proof-of-stake. This move will allow Ethereum's network to run itself with far less energy as well as improved transaction speed. Proof-of-stake allows network participants to "stake" their ether to the network. This process helps to secure the network and process the transactions that occur. Those who do this are rewarded ether similar to an interest account. This is an alternative to Bitcoin's proof-of-work mechanism where miners are rewarded more Bitcoin for processing transactions.

1. Binance Coin (BNB)
2.

Like Ethereum, Binance Coin is much more than a cryptocurrency – as a matter of fact, Binance Coin was originally hosted on Ethereum until the Binance decentralized exchange, or DEX, went online in 2017. The Binance DEX is a platform much like Ethereum, albeit with a different mission. The Binance DEX is a decentralized platform where users can not only buy and sell binance coins but also use BNB to convert other cryptocurrencies from one to another. This has made the Binance DEX the biggest cryptocurrency exchange on the planet by volume and has helped fuel the popularity of the digital asset. Most importantly, the Binance DEX offers a discount to users who pay transaction fees on the exchange with BNB – a smart strategy that keeps users on the platform and helps sustain Binance Coin's growth.

1. Tron (TRX)
2.

The past year brought extreme upheaval within the entertainment industry, leaving it ripe for disruption. This is exactly the sort of opportunity the founders of Tron must have been hoping for when they built a decentralized, blockchain-based platform for sharing content. Whereas many of the biggest entertainment companies in the world profit from gathering and selling data about their users, using Tron leaves no such footprints behind. While it protects users, Tron also allows creators to monetize their content directly via Tronix, Tron's form of cryptocurrency. The platform has gained fame and notoriety in equal measure over the last few years due to the antics of Tron Foundation founder Justin Sun, but no matter how you feel about him, it's undeniable that Tron is an ambitious idea – and while it isn't going to overthrow <u>Netflix</u> (ticker: <u>NFLX</u>) tomorrow, it is an excellent speculative investment.

1. Chainlink (LINK)
2.

Chainlink is a decentralized oracle network that bridges the gap between smart contracts, like the ones on Ethereum, and data outside of it. Blockchains themselves do not have the ability to connect to outside applications in a trusted manner. Chainlink's decentralized oracles allow smart contracts to communicate with outside data so that the contracts can be executed based on data that Ethereum itself cannot connect to.

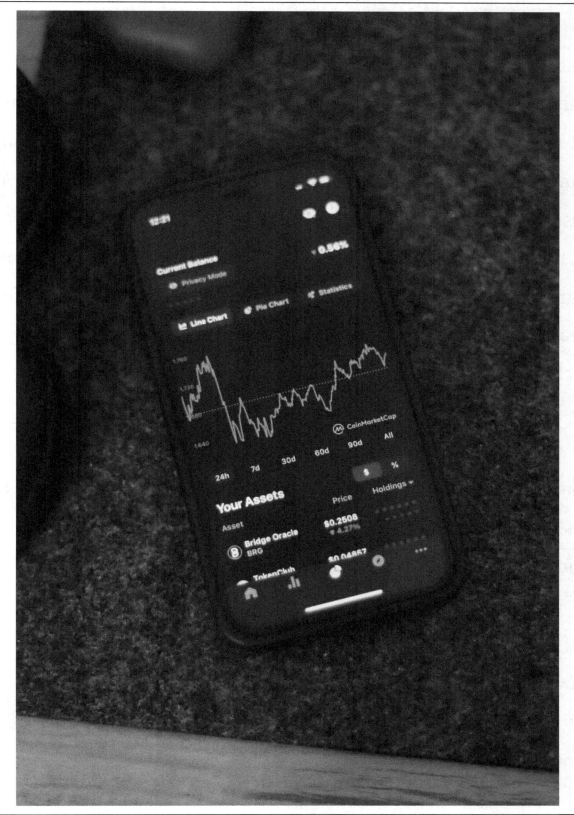

Chainlink's blog details a number of use cases for its system. One of the many use cases that are explained would be to monitor water supplies for pollution or illegal syphoning going on in certain cities. Sensors could be set up to monitor corporate consumption, water tables, and the levels of local bodies of water. A Chainlink oracle could track this data and feed it directly into a smart contract. The smart contract could be set up to execute fines, release flood warnings to cities, or invoice companies using too much of a city's water with the incoming data from the oracle.

Chainlink was developed by Sergey Nazarov along with Steve Ellis. As of January 2021, Chainlink's market capitalization is $8.6 billion, and one LINK is valued at $21.53.

1. USD Coin
2.

The stablecoin, which hit the markets in September 2018, is managed by a consortium called CENTRE, launched by peer-to-peer company Circle and crypto exchange Coinbase. Their aim, according to their website, is to "bring stability to crypto". It was trading at $1 with a market cap of $9.12bn as of 9:38am GMT on 9 March.

1. Cardano
2.

Cardano is an "Ouroboros proof-of-stake" cryptocurrency that was created with a research-based approach by engineers, mathematicians, and cryptography experts. The project was co-founded by Charles Hoskinson, one of the five initial founding members of Ethereum. After having some disagreements with the direction Ethereum was taking, he left and later helped to create Cardano.

The team behind Cardano created its blockchain through extensive experimentation and peer-reviewed research. The researchers behind the project have written over 90 papers on blockchain technology across a range of topics. This research is the backbone of Cardano.

Due to this rigorous process, Cardano seems to stand out among its proof-of-stake peers as well as other large cryptocurrencies. Cardano has also been dubbed the "Ethereum killer" as its blockchain is said to be capable of more. That said, Cardano is still in its early stages. While it has beaten Ethereum to the proof-of-stake consensus model it still has a long way to go in terms of decentralized financial applications.

Cardano aims to be the financial operating system of the world by establishing decentralized financial products similarly to Ethereum as well as providing solutions for chain interoperability, voter fraud, and legal contract tracing, among other things. As of January 2021, Cardano has a market capitalization of $9.8 billion and one ADA trades for $0.31.

1. Tether (USDT)
2.

Tether was one of the first and most popular of a group of so-called <u>stablecoins</u>, cryptocurrencies that aim to peg their market value to a currency or other external reference point in order to reduce volatility. Because most digital currencies, even major ones like Bitcoin, have experienced frequent periods of dramatic volatility, Tether and other stablecoins attempt to smooth out price fluctuations in order to attract users who may otherwise be cautious. Tether's price is tied directly to the price of the US dollar. The system allows users to more easily make transfers from other cryptocurrencies back to US dollars in a more timely manner than actually converting to normal currency.

Launched in 2014, Tether describes itself as "a blockchain-enabled platform designed to facilitate the use of fiat currencies in a digital manner." Effectively, this cryptocurrency allows individuals to utilize a blockchain network and related technologies to transact in traditional currencies while minimizing the volatility and complexity often associated with digital currencies. In January of 2021, Tether was the third-largest cryptocurrency by market cap, with a total market cap of $24.4 billion and a per-token value of $1.00.

1. Monero (XMR)

2.

<u>Monero</u> is a secure, private, and untraceable currency. This open-source cryptocurrency was launched in April 2014 and soon garnered great interest among the cryptography community and enthusiasts. The development of this cryptocurrency is completely donation based and community driven. Monero has been launched with a strong focus on decentralization and scalability, and it enables complete privacy by using a special technique called "ring signatures."

With this technique, there appears a group of cryptographic signatures including at least one real participant, but since they all appear valid; the real one cannot be isolated. Because of exceptional security mechanisms like this, Monero has developed something of an unsavory reputation—it has been linked to criminal operations around the world. While this is a prime candidate for making criminal transactions anonymously, the privacy inherent in Monero is also helpful to dissidents of oppressive regimes around the world. As of January 2021, Monero had a market cap of $2.8 billion and a per-token value of $158.37.

1. Stellar
2.

Stellar is an open blockchain network designed to provide enterprise solutions by connecting financial institutions for the purpose of large transactions. Huge transactions between banks and investment firms that typically would take several days, a number of intermediaries, and cost a good deal of money, can now be done nearly instantaneously with no intermediaries and cost little to nothing for those making the transaction.

While Stellar has positioned itself as an enterprise blockchain for institutional transactions, it is still an open blockchain that can be used by anyone. The system allows for cross-border transactions between any currencies. Stellar's native currency is Lumens (XLM). The network requires users to hold Lumens to be able to transact on the network.

Stellar was founded by Jed McCaleb, a founding member of Ripple Labs and developer of the Ripple protocol. He eventually left his role with Ripple and went on to co-found the Stellar Development Foundation. Stellar Lumens have a market capitalization of $6.1 billion and are valued at $0.27 as of January 2021.

1. Ripple (XRP)
2.

XRP is a digital asset built for payments. It is the native digital asset on the XRP Ledger—an open-source, permissionless and decentralized blockchain technology that can settle transactions in 3-5 seconds.XRP can be sent directly without needing a central intermediary, making it a convenient instrument in bridging two different currencies quickly and efficiently.

Ripple diverges from much of its cryptocurrency competitors in a number of ways. Ripple is an invention of Ripple Labs, and the Ripple token is being used in high-speed and low-cost money transfers worldwide.

Ripple Labs has announced a number of partnerships with leading money transfer services, with more financial market partnerships expected in the future.

Unlike many cryptocurrencies that trade on hopes and dreams, Ripple is being used in the real world today, showing signs of future adoption within the financial market community. Ripple rise in value over 36,000% in 2017, but similar gains may not be likely going forward

1. EOS (EOS)
2.

EOS is the native cryptocurrency for the EOS.IO blockchain platform with smart contract capabilities. The company Block.one created EOS.IO in September 2017 and it now has over 100 dapps with thousands of daily active users. It enables decentralized apps, or dapps, to be created by software developers. The platform is more scalable than many other blockchain networks, with the ability to process one million transactions per second without any fees. Its dapp development capability makes

EOS similar to _Ethereum_ with the notable distinction that transaction confirmations are done through a different type of consensus system. Block producers are chosen by the EOS ecosystem through a voting mechanism known as delegated-proof-of-stake (DPoS). In order to vote, users must stake tokens for three days without selling them, putting them at risk of losing money should the price of the token drop during that time. There is no maximum supply limit of EOS tokens. The delegated proof-of-stake model uses inflation, capped at 5% annually, to fund transactions and pay block users. Many competitors, including Ethereum, have a transaction fee for transferring coins or tokens from one wallet address to another. EOS concluded its year-long ICO in May of this year, raising a total of $4 billion. The longer-duration ICO was done in an attempt to create an orderly market for EOS without the dramatic run-up and sudden crash common to cryptocurrencies when launched.

YTD performance for EOS is flat, with less volatility than has been seen with some competitors. Enthusiasm for the project remains high, and EOS is one of the most actively traded cryptocurrencies on exchanges.

1. Polkadot (DOT)
2.

Polkadot is a unique proof-of-stake cryptocurrency that is aimed at delivering interoperability between other blockchains. Its protocol is designed to connect permissioned and permissionless blockchains as well as oracles to allow systems to work together under one roof.

Polkadot's core component is its relay chain that allows the interoperability of varying networks. It also allows for "parachains," or parallel blockchains with their own native tokens for specific use cases.

Where this system differs from Ethereum is that rather than creating just decentralized applications on Polkadot, developers can create their own blockchain while also using the security that Polkadot's chain already has. With Ethereum, developers can create new blockchains but they need to create their own security measures which can leave new and smaller projects open to attack, as the larger a blockchain the more security it has. This concept in Polkadot is known as shared security.

Polkadot was created by Gavin Wood, another member of the core founders of the Ethereum project who had differing opinions on the project's future. As of January 2021, Polkadot has a market capitalization of $11.2 billion and one DOT trades for $12.54.

Chapter 4. Are cryptocurrencies a good investment?

Cryptocurrencies may go up in value, but many investors see them as mere speculations, not real investments. The reason? Just like real currencies, cryptocurrencies generate no cash flow, so for you to profit, someone has to pay more for the currency than you did.

That's what's called "the greater fool" theory of investment. Contrast that to a well-managed business, which increases its value over time by growing the profitability and cash flow of the operation.

As NerdWallet writers have noted, cryptocurrencies such as Bitcoin may not be that safe, and some notable voices in the investment community have advised would-be investors to steer clear of them. Of particular note, legendary investor Warren Buffett compared Bitcoin to paper checks: "It's a very effective way of transmitting money and you can do it anonymously and all that.

A check is a way of transmitting money too. Are checks worth a whole lot of money? Just because they can transmit money?"

For those who see cryptocurrencies such as Bitcoin as the currency of the future, it should be noted that a currency needs stability so that merchants and consumers can determine what a fair price is for goods. Bitcoin and other cryptocurrencies have been anything but stable through much of their history. For example, while Bitcoin traded at close to $20,000 in December 2017, its value then dropped to as low as about $3,200 a year later. By December 2020, it was trading at record levels again.

This price volatility creates a conundrum. If bitcoins might be worth a lot more in the future, people are less likely to spend and circulate them today, making them less viable as a currency. Why spend a bitcoin when it could be worth three times the value next year?

Legal Risks for Cryptocurrency Investors

Along with the explosion of interest in digital currency and all of its implications for both new and traditional businesses, there is a growing need for clarity regarding the legal implications of these new technologies and currencies. As governments around the world, regulatory agencies, central banks, and other financial institutions are working to understand the nature and meaning of digital currencies, individual investors can make a great deal of money investing in this new space. On the other hand, <u>investors assume certain legal risks when they buy and sell cryptocurrencies</u>.

While digital currency might be easy to confuse for conventional electronic money, it is not the same; similarly, it is unlike conventional cash currencies because it cannot be physically owned and transferred between parties. Much of the murkiness of the legal standing of digital currency is due to the fact that the space has only recently become popular as compared with more traditional currency and payment systems. Below, we'll explore some of the emerging legal implications associated with investing in cryptocurrencies.

Cryptocurrencies as Property

One of the most critical legal considerations for any cryptocurrency investor has to do with the way that central authorities view cryptocurrency holdings. In the U.S., the IRS has defined cryptocurrencies as property, rather than as currencies proper. This means that individual investors are beholden to capital gains tax laws when it comes to reporting their cryptocurrency expenses and profits on their annual tax returns, regardless of where they purchased digital coins.

This aspect of the cryptocurrency space adds layers of confusion and complexity for U.S. taxpayers, but the difficulty does not end there. Indeed, it remains unclear whether digital currency investors who have purchased their holdings on foreign exchanges must face additional reporting measures come tax time. According to a report by CNBC, "anyone with more than $10,000 abroad usually needs to fill out the Report of Foreign Bank and Financial Accounts (FBAR)...with the Treasury Department each year. Another law--the <u>Foreign Account Tax Compliance Act</u>, or FATCA--requires certain U.S. taxpayers to describe their overseas accounts on Form 8938, when they file their taxes with the IRS."

Former federal tax prosecutor Kevin F. Sweeney offered a hint as to how foreign cryptocurrency exchanges could complicate tax matters for U.S. digital currency investors: "there probably is an FBAR requirement, but I wouldn't go as far as to say there always is one," he explained, adding that the lack of guidance from the IRS has created a "black hole" of uncertainty for investors and tax professionals alike. "It would seem awfully unfair if they would expect taxpayers to know that--and to then issue penalties for taxpayers who didn't do that--when practitioners can't even 100% figure out if there's an FBAR requirement," Sweeney added.

All of this suggests that digital currency investors should take special precautions to follow the advice of tax professionals when it comes to reporting cryptocurrency profits and losses. <u>Because the rules are constantly changing</u>, what may have been legally permissible last year or even months ago may now be cause for legal concern.

Decentralized Status

One of the great draws of many digital currencies is also a potential risk factor for the individual investor. Bitcoin (BTC) has paved the way for other cryptocurrencies in that it is <u>decentralized</u>, meaning that it has no physical presence and is not backed by a central authority. While governments around the world have stepped in to assert their regulatory power in various ways, BTC and other digital currencies like it remain unattached to any jurisdiction or institution. On one hand, this frees investors from being beholden to those institutions. On the other hand, however, this status could result in legal complications. The value of digital currencies is dependent entirely upon the value that other owners and investors ascribe to them; this is true across all currencies, digital or fiat. Without a central authority backing the value of a digital currency, investors may be left in the lurch should complications with transactions or ownership arise.

Another potential risk associated with cryptocurrencies as a result of their decentralized status has to do with the particulars of transactions. In most other transactions, currency with a physical presence changes hands. In the case of <u>electronic money,</u> a trusted financial institution is involved in creating and settling deposits and debt claims. Neither of these concepts applies to cryptocurrency transactions. Because of this fundamental difference, legal confusion between parties in various types of digital currency transactions is a real possibility. Once again, because of the decentralized state of these currencies, the path of legal recourse in these situations can be difficult to assess.

Business Registrations and Licensing

A growing number of businesses are taking advantage of digital currencies as a form of payment. As in other financial areas, businesses may be required to register and obtain licensure for particular jurisdictions and activities. Owing to the complex and evolving legal status of digital currencies, this area is significantly less clear for businesses operating in the crypto market. Companies which only accept cryptocurrencies, for example, may not need to register or obtain licenses at all. On the other hand, they may be required to submit to special considerations depending upon their jurisdiction. The onus of responsibility falls on business owners and managers to insure that they are following proper legal procedure for their operations at both the local and state levels. At the federal level, for example, financial institutions must maintain certain activities related to protections against <u>money laundering</u> and fraud, transmission of funds, and more. Considerations like these also apply to businesses dealing with digital currencies.

Fraud and Money Laundering

There is a widespread belief that cryptocurrencies provide criminal organizations with a new means of committing fraud, money laundering, and a host of other financial crimes. This may not directly impact most cryptocurrency investors who do not intend to use this new technology to commit such crimes. However, investors who find themselves in the unfortunate position of being a victim of financial crime do not likely have the same legal options as traditional victims of fraud.

This issue also relates to the decentralized status of digital currencies. When a cryptocurrency exchange is hacked and customers' holdings are stolen, for instance, there is frequently no standard practice for recovering the missing funds. <u>Digital currency investors thus take on a certain amount of risk by purchasing and holding cryptocurrency assets</u>. It is for this reason that developers and startups related to digital currency have focused such a great deal of attention on creating secure means of holding digital coins and tokens. Still, while new types of wallets are being released all the time, and while cryptocurrency exchanges are always improving their security measures, investors have so far not been able to fully eliminate the legal risks associated with owning cryptocurrencies, and it's likely that they never will.

Dropshipping Business Model on a Budget

The Risk-Low E-Com Guide to Create Your Online Store and Generate Profits with less than 47$

By

Jake Folger

Table of Contents

Introduction 248

Chapter 1. What is Dropshipping? 250

1.1 Benefits of dropshipping 251

Chapter 2. How Dropshipping Works 258

2.1 Awareness about the Supply Chain 259

2.2 The Supply Chain Process...259

2.3 What is Fulfillment? 261

2.4 The Steps to make Order Fulfillment 262

Chapter 3. Why dropshipping is one of the best way to make money in 2021...264

3.1 Dropshipping Is The E-Commerce Future 265

Chapter 4. Niche And Product Selection 268

4.1 Steps how to search your right niche 269

4.2 Creating a good niche 273

Chapter 5. How to start dropshipping business in 2021 277

1. Commit yourself for starting a dropshipping business 278

2. Dropshipping business idea to chose....................................282

3. Do competitor research...283

4. Choose a dropshipping supplier...283

5. Build your ecommerce store 284

6. Market your dropshipping store..284

7. Analyze your offering 286

Chapter 6. How To identify Best Suppliers For Your New Dropshipping Business 288

6.1 The Importance of Selecting The Right Suppliers 289

6.2 Finding Your Dropshipping Suppliers 289

Chapter 7. Setting Up Your Dropshipping business On A Budget 297

1. Research Your Options 298

2. Create a Plan to Stick 298

3. Find Your Niche 299

4. Set Up Your eCommerce website 299

5. Make Meetings With Your Suppliers 300

6. Start Selling 301

7. Optimize Your Site 301

Chapter 8. Mistakes To Avoid When Developing Your Dropshipping Business 303

1. Worrying About Shipping Costs. 305

2. Relying Much on Vendors. 305

3. Expecting Easy Money. 305

4. Making Order Difficult to Access. 306

5. Not Enough Brand Display. 306

6. Return Complications. 306

7. Selling Trademarked Products 307

8. Picking the Wrong Field 308

9. Poor Relationship With Suppliers 308

10. Lowering Price To Extreme Levels 309

11. Poor Website Structure 309

Chapter 9. Smooth Running tips for Your Dropshipping Business 311

1. Add Value 312

2. Focus on SEO and marketing 313

3. Marketing Your Dropshipping Business 313

4. Social Media Source 314

5. Customer Ratings & Reviews 314

6. Email Marketing 315

7. Growth Hacking 315

Chapter 10. How To Maximize Your Chances Of Success? 316

1. Things To Remember 317

Conclusion 320

Introduction

With very little startup expenses, dropshipping is an innovative business model.

A dropshipping business is where an owner finds a collection of distributors to deliver and offer goods for their website. However, as in an e-commerce business, instead of owning the merchandise, a third party does much of the distribution and logistics for them. That third party is usually a wholesaler, who on behalf of the business "dropships" the consumer's goods.

When you start a retail shop, there are several factors to consider, but among the most significant aspects, you have to decide whether you'd like to store inventory or have a wholesale distributor. You must purchase goods in bulk, stock, unpack and send them to customers of your products if you want to store inventory. You may, therefore, contract the phase of storing, packaging and exporting to a drop-ship supplier by picking a wholesale distributor. As direct fulfillment, a drop-ship supplier is often described, but both definitions may be used to define the same service.

The wholesaler, who usually manufactures the product, delivers the product at the most basic, any time anyone buys a product, and you get a part of the sale for the product marketing.

Unless the client puts an order for it, you don't pay for the thing.

Dropshipping is an internet-based business model that draws novices and experts alike to choose a niche, create a brand, market and earn money, with probably the minimum entry barriers.

Chapter 1. What is Dropshipping?

Dropshipping is a retail model of e-commerce that enables retailers to offer goods without maintaining any physical inventory. The company sells the product to the buyer through dropshipping and sends the purchase order to a third-party seller, who then delivers the order directly on behalf of the retailer to the customer. Dropshipping sellers may not need to spend in any commodity stock, inventory or storage room and do not manage the phase of fulfillment.

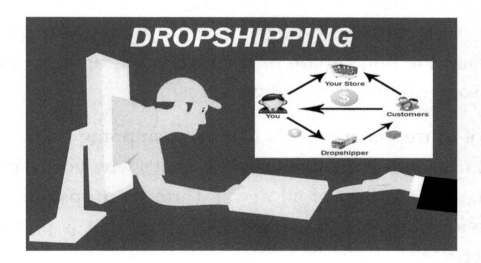

Dropshipping is a form of retail fulfillment, where the goods are ordered from a third-party retailer instead of a store stocks products. The goods are then delivered directly to the customer. This way, the vendor doesn't have to personally manage the product. A familiar sound? Maybe not, but dropshipping is a fulfillment model utilized by 35 percent of online stores.

This is mostly a hands-off process for the store. The retailer doesn't have to buy stock or, in any manner, meet the orders. The third-party retailer, instead, takes control of the product itself.

For startups, dropshipping is great since it does not take as much as the conventional sales model. You don't have to prepare, pay overhead, & stock merchandise in a brick-and-mortar store. Instead, you start an online shop to purchase bulk goods and warehouse space from vendors that already have products.

In dropshipping, the merchant is solely responsible for attracting clients and handling orders, ensuring you'll be a middleman effectively. Despite this, through pricing up the goods you offer, you can gain the lion's share of the profits. It's an easy model of business, so one that can be really successful.

Millions of entrepreneurs switch to dropshipping to get started because it takes less hassle and capital. That's why you're probably interested. And the best of all news? Through dropshipping, you can create a company right from your laptop that is profitable in the long term.

There are several pitfalls and benefits, of course, and it is essential that we check at them before you launch your own e-commerce dropshipping firm. However, once you realize the positives and negatives of dropshipping, it'll be a breeze to learn how to do so effectively.

1.1 Benefits of dropshipping

For aspiring entrepreneurs, dropshipping is a smart business move to start with, which is accessible. You can easily evaluate multiple business concepts with a small downside with dropshipping, which helps you to think a lot about how to pick and sell in-demand goods. Here are a couple more explanations why dropshipping is a popular business.

1. Little capital is required

Perhaps the greatest benefit to dropshipping is that an e-commerce website can be opened without needing to spend thousands of dollars in stock upfront. Typically, retailers have had to bundle up large quantities of inventory with capital investments.

For the dropshipping model, unless you have already made the transaction and have been charged by the consumer, you may not have to buy a product. It is possible to start sourcing goods without substantial up-front inventory investments and launch a profitable dropshipping company with very little capital. And since you are not committed to sales, as in a typical retail sector, there is less chance of launching a dropshipping shop through any inventory bought up front.

2. Easy to get started

It's also simpler to operate an e-commerce company because you don't have to interact with physical products. You don't have to take stress with dropshipping about:

- Paying for a warehouse or managing it
- Tracking inventory for any accounting reasons
- Packing & shipping your orders
- Continually ordering products & managing stock level
- Inbound shipments and handling returns

3. Low overhead

Your overhead expenses are very minimal, and you don't have to deal with buying inventory or maintaining a warehouse. In reality, several popular dropshipping stores are managed as home-based enterprises, needing nothing more to run than a laptop & a few operational expenses. These costs are likely to rise as you expand but are still low relative to standard brick-and-mortar stores.

4. Flexible location

From almost anywhere via an internet connection, a dropshipping company can be managed. You can operate and manage the business as long as you can effectively connect with vendors and consumers.

5. Wide selection of goods to sell

Because you don't really have to pre-purchase any items you market, you can offer your potential clients a variety of trending products. If an item is stored by vendors, you will mark it for sale at no added cost at your online store.

6. Easier for testing

Dropshipping is a valuable form of fulfillment for both the opening of a new store and also for company owners seeking to measure consumers' demand for additional types of items, such as shoes or whole new product ranges. Again, the primary advantage of dropshipping is the opportunity to list and likely sell goods before committing to purchasing a significant quantity of stock.

7. Easier to scale

For a traditional retail firm, you would typically need to perform three times as much work if you get three times the amount of orders. By using dropshipping vendors, suppliers would be liable for more of the work to handle extra orders, helping you to improve with fewer growth pains & little incremental work.

Sales growth can often bring extra work, especially customer service, however companies which use dropshipping scale especially well comparison to standard e-commerce businesses.

8. Dropshipping starts easily.

In order to get started, you need not be a business guru. You don't really require some past company knowledge, honestly. You will get started easily and learn the rest while you move along if you spend some time to learn its basics.

It is too easy to drop shipping, and it takes so little from you. To help you out, you don't need a warehouse to store goods or a staff. You don't need to think about packaging or storage either. You do not even have to devote a certain period of time in your shop every day. Surprisingly, it's hands-off, especially once you get underway.

All of this means that today you can begin your company. Within a matter of hours, you will begin getting it up and running.

You're going to need some practical skills and the right equipment and tools. You will be equipped with the skills you have to jumpstart your own dropshipping company by the time you've done it.

9. Dropshipping grow easily.

Your business model doesn't even have to alter that much at all when you scale up. As you expand, you'll have to bring more effort into sales and marketing, but your daily life will remain almost the same.

One of the advantages of dropshipping is that when you scale, the costs do not spike. It's convenient to keep rising at a fairly high pace because of this. If you choose to build a little team at any stage, you can manage about anything by yourself, too.

10. Dropshipping doesn't need a big capital.

Since you need very little to start a dropshipping business, you can get underway with minimal funds. Right from your desktop, you can create a whole corporation, and you do not need to make any heavy investment. Your costs would be reasonably low even as your company grows, particularly compared to normal business expenses.

11. Dropshipping is flexible.

This is one of the greatest advantages. You get to be a boss of your own and set your own regulations. It's one of the most versatile occupations anyone can try.

With just a laptop, you can operate from anywhere, and you can operate at the hours that are most comfortable for you. For founders that want a company that fits for them, this is perfect. To get stuff done, you won't have to lean over backward. You choose your own pace instead.

Dropshipping is indeed flexible in that it allows you plenty of space to create choices that fit for you. Whenever you choose, you can quickly list new items, and you can change your plans on the move. You should automate it to work when you're gone, whether you're going on holiday. You get the concept prospects are limitless.

12. Dropshipping manages easily.

Because it doesn't need you to make several commitments, with no hassle, you can manage everything. When you have found and set up suppliers, you are often exclusively liable for your e-commerce store.

Chapter 2. How Dropshipping Works

Dropshipping functions by third-party suppliers, which deliver goods for each order on a just-in-time basis. When a sales order is received by the retailer, they transfer the requirements to the supplier—who manufactures the product.

While dropshipping is used by many e-commerce retailers as the base of their business processes, dropshipping can be used successfully to complement traditional retail inventory-stocking models. Because dropshipping does not create any unused surplus inventory, it may be used for analysis purposes before committing to sale on a marketplace, such as testing the waters.

Dropshipping works because, with the aid of a third party such as a wholesaler or an e-commerce shop, a dropshipper fulfills orders to deliver the goods for an even cheaper price. The majority of dropshippers offer goods directly from Chinese suppliers because the prices of most products in China are very poor. If the wholesaler's price is 5 dollars for a product. A dropshipper sells it for $8 and retains $3 for himself. The bulk of dropshippers target nations with higher purchasing power.

2.1 Awareness about the Supply Chain

You'll see the word "supply chain" a lot in here. It seems like a fancy lingo for the business, but it actually applies to how a product transfers from seller to consumer. We'll use this to explain the method of dropshipping.

2.2 The Supply Chain Process

You, the merchant, are only one puzzle piece. An effective dropshipping mechanism depends on several parties all acting in sync together. The supply chain is just that: producer, supplier, and retailer coordination.

You should split down the supply chain into three simple steps:

- The producer manufactures the goods and supplies them to wholesalers & retailers.

Let's say maker A is manufacturing bottles of water. They are marketed in bulk to manufacturers and wholesalers after the bottles come off the assembly line, who switch around & resell the bottles to dealers.

- Suppliers and wholesalers market the products to dealers.

For a particular type of product, a retailer like yourself is searching for a supplier. An arrangement to operate together is then reached between the retailer and the supplier.

A little point here: Although you may order directly from product producers, purchasing from retailers is always much cheaper instead. There are minimum purchasing criteria for most suppliers that can be very high, and you will still have to purchase stock & ship the goods.

So, purchasing directly from the producer might seem quicker, but you would profit more from buying from distributors (dealing with the little profit).

Suppliers are often convenient since all of them are skilled in a specific niche, so the type of items you need can be quickly identified. This also implies that you'll get started to sell super quick.

- Retailers sell goods to buyers.

Suppliers & wholesalers should not market to the public directly; that's the task of the retailer. The last move between the product & the consumer is the supplier.

Online stores from which customers buy goods are provided by retailers. The merchant marks it up again to reach at the final price after the wholesaler rates up the items. By "markup," we apply to fixing a premium that covers the product's cost price and gives you a benefit.

It's that! From start to end, it is the whole supply chain. In business, it's a simple but crucial concept.

You may have noted that no other group has been alluded to as a dropshipper. That is because there is no particular function for "dropshipper." Dropshipping is actually the activity of somebody else delivering goods. Technically, producers, retailers, and merchants will all be dropshippers.

Later on, we'll discuss how to start a retail dropshipping company in this guide. In other terms, you can learn how to become a trader who buys commodities from wholesalers to market to the public. This may indicate that through an online storefront, you sell through eBay or even your own website.

Remember what it's like for the consumer now that you realize what the supply chain is like.

2.3 What is Fulfillment?

Order fulfillment that's all the steps a corporation requires in having a fresh order and bringing the order into the hands of the customer. The procedure includes storing, picking & packaging the products, distributing them and sending the consumer an automatic email to let them know that the product is in transit.

2.4 The Steps to make Order Fulfillment

There are some steps involved in order fulfillment, which are as under:-

1. Receiving inventory.

Essentially, there are two approaches for an eCommerce company to manage inventory. It can decide to receive & stock the in-house inventory, or it can employ an outsourcer for eCommerce order fulfillment to take control of the inventory and other associated activities. The organization would be liable for taking stock, inspecting the product, marking, and maintaining the inventory method if it opts for the first alternative. If the business wishes to outsource or dropships, the order fulfillment agent or supplier can perform certain duties.

2. Storing inventory.

 If you plan to stock the inventory yourself, after the receiving portion is finished, there'll be another list of assignments waiting for you. Shelving the inventory and holding a careful watch on what goods come in and what goods are going out would be the key activities on the list so that you can deliver the orders without any complications.

3. Processing the order.

Businesses who outsource order fulfillment do not have to get through the nitty-gritty of order delivery since they actually move on to their partner's order request and let them manage the rest. This is the phase where the order is taken off the shelves, shipped to a packaging station, examined for any damage, packed and transferred to the shipping station for businesses who handle their own product.

4. Shipping the order.

The best delivery strategy is calculated based on the scale, weight and precise specifications of the order. A third-party contractor is typically contracted to complete this phase.

Returns Handling. For online shoppers, the opportunity to refund unwanted goods quickly is a big factor in the purchase phase. You ought to design a crystal straightforward return policy that is readily available to all the customers and workers to ensure the receipt, repair and redemption of the returned goods are as successful as practicable. It will help you prevent needless confusion and errors by making this step automated.

Chapter 3. Why dropshipping is one of the best way to make money in 2021.

According to Forrester (analyst) Reports, the magnitude of online retail revenues would be $370 billion by the end of 2017. In comparison, 23 percent, which amounts to $85.1 billion, would come from dropshipping firms. To many businesses, like startups, this sheer scale alone is attractive.

An online retailer following this concept appears similar to its traditional e-commerce competitors by appearance. Dropshipping may be a well-kept mystery in the e-commerce world as consumers just think about the goods, price and credibility of the shop rather than how the goods are sourced and who delivers the shipments.

In summary,' dropshipping' is a business strategy in which the supplier does not directly hold the inventory or process the orders in his or her control. Both orders are delivered directly from a wholesaler and delivered. This encourages the supplier to concentrate on the business's selling aspect.

Many major e-commerce names, such as Zappos, began with dropshipping. For those that seek motivation, billion-dollar dropshipping internet store Wayfair or the milliondollarBlinds.com are top examples today.

Five explanations of how the dropshipping business strategy appeals to both startups and experienced entrepreneurs are offered below. These issues in traditional e-commerce have been nagging challenges, which can be addressed with the dropshipping model immediately.

3.1 Dropshipping Is The E-Commerce Future

It seem that dropshipping will be the future of e-commerce. Here are some main reasons which explain this concept.

Sourcing of Product:

Conventional e-commerce stores must directly import supplies from wholesalers, frequently based in various countries. They often need goods to be bought in bulk and are then shipped prior to being promoted and distributed to the local warehouse. A lot of time, money & resources are required for the whole phase. The presence of expensive intermediaries, such as banks, freight shipments and export-import brokers, also involves it.

The dropshipping model, however, enables manufacturers to market goods for large quantities of each product without needing to think about sourcing. The entire method is substantially simplified with just a turn-key e-commerce storefront such as Shopify and a dropshipping software like Oberlo. The retailer may choose to notify the distributors via e-mail to tell them that their supplies are now being shipped to the store. The most of the procedure can be quickly handled from the dashboard, such as uploading product images, updating pricing and order monitoring.

Storage

A traditional e-commerce store, particularly as it carries multiple or large products, requires large storage spaces. It might be imaginable to store ten to 100 items, but storing 1,000 or 1,000,000 items will cost a real fortune that is not within the reach of a start-up. This high warehouse rent issue is addressed by the dropshipping model since the goods remain with the distributor or wholesale retailer until they are bought.

Order fulfillment

Many pioneers of e-commerce do not foresee investing most of their time picking, packaging and delivering orders. They should, of course, outsource the order fulfillment for ease to a boutique e-commerce fulfillment, such as ShipMonk. The dropshipping model, however, facilitates hands-free shipment, since the whole packaging and shipping process is in the possession of the wholesaler or distributor.

Cataloging & photography

A conventional e-commerce shop owner has to take professional-quality images of items that may be very pricey, like a decent digital camera, a light panel, lighting and some more. For a dropshipping control software, this issue is fixed, as the "product importing" function allows for instant picture import.

Scalability

Wayfair.com is a major online dropshipping store that holds 10,000 vendors of more than eight million items. Yes, $8 million. By this business model, such huge scalability is made possible.

Because the retailer just has to work on the publicity and customer care aspect, they don't have to think about the warehouse's rent and other operating expenses skyrocketing.

In conclusion, the dropshipping paradigm offers the ability for tiny startups with minimal capital to contend with large and medium online stores comfortably, rendering the field of e-commerce an equal environment for everyone. That being said, plan in the future to see more e-commerce shops adopting this model.

Chapter 4. Niche And Product Selection

You want a business to start, but the thing that holds you down is the market niche that you feel you need to pick. And, honestly, it can be tricky: you might mention all your interests & passions and yet feel like you haven't hit the singular thing that you were expected to do.

Yet, it can trigger paralysis to place some sort of burden on yourself to choose the very right niche.

Certainly, in choosing a suitable niche business, you like to do your careful research, but it's easier to get up and run than to wait around. You will try ideas that way, enter the market earlier, and benefit from the victories and losses. That way, too, you can still take what you have gained from previous attempts, so step on with fresh concepts if the first company does not take off.

4.1 Steps how to search your right niche

Using the following five methods to find your niche, whether you're unable to determine or you need more information to work with.

1. Identify your interests & passions.

This could be something that you have achieved before. But, if you haven't, quickly make a compilation of 10 topical passions and areas of passion.

Business isn't easy, and it can challenge you at any stage. If you work in an area you don't care for, the likelihood of leaving will increase significantly — especially like a first sole proprietor.

This doesn't mean that a better match has to be found. You can stay with it if you are excited about any part of running the business. If you don't care about the issue, you might not be able to easily find the drive to persevere within.

2. Identify problems that you can solve.

You're able to get to narrow down your choices with your list of ten topics in hand. You first need to identify challenges that your target clients are facing to build a viable enterprise, then decide if you can potentially fix them. Here are a few items you should do to find issues in different niches.

3. Research your competition.

There is not always a bad thing in the presence of competition. It can actually show you that you've discovered a market that's lucrative. Although you do have to do an in-depth analysis of competing pages. Build a fresh spreadsheet and start tracking all the competing websites that you can find.

And find out whether there's already an opening in the crowd to stick out. Are you still willing to rate the keywords? Is there really a way to distinguish and build a unique offer for yourself? Here are some indications that you will enter a niche and flourish, even though it is already covered by other sites:

- Content of poor quality. In a niche where several company owners are not delivering high-quality, informative content that suits the viewer, it's easy to outrank the competitors.

- Lack of transparency. By establishing an authentic and accessible identity in a niche where most platforms are faceless and unnecessarily corporate, many internet marketers have disrupted whole industries.

- The lack of paid competitiveness. If you have noticed a keyword with a relatively high search rate but little competition with paying ads, there is undoubtedly a potential for you to upset the business.

4. Determine the profitability of the niche.

You need to have a fairly decent understanding now about what niche you're about to get into. You might not have limited your selection down to a particular region of the topic, but you've certainly noticed a few suggestions that you feel pretty good about. It's important to have an idea at this stage about how much money you have the opportunity to make in your niche. A fine way to go to continue your search is ClickBank.

So, browse the category's best brands. That is not a positive indication if you can't locate any offers. It could mean that the niche could not be monetized by someone.

You're in luck if the quest throws up a good amount of products — just not an excessive amount of products. Take notice of pricing points such that your own goods can be marketed in a fair way.

Bear in mind, though, that you may not have to launch your organization with your own product offering. You should collaborate in your niche with product makers, marketers and site owners to start earning commissions when working on your innovative solution.

5. Test your idea.

You are now prepared with all the knowledge you need to pick a niche, and checking your proposal is the only thing needed to do. Setting up a landing page for pre-sales of a product you're producing is one easy way to do this. Through paying ads, you will then push traffic to this page.

That doesn't actually mean that you are not in a viable niche, even though you don't get pre-sales. Your message may not be quite correct, or you haven't found the right deal yet. You will maximize conversions by using A/B split testing to figure out whether there is something preventing the target group from taking action or not.

You will sell to two fundamental markets: customer and corporation. Such divisions are reasonably clear. "For example, if you sell women's clothes from a department shop, shoppers are your target market; if you sell office supplies, companies are your target market (this is referred to as "B2B" sales). In certain instances, for example, you could be selling to both corporations and people if you operate a printing company.

No company, especially a small one, can be everything to all individuals. The more you can describe your target group broadly, the stronger. For even the larger corporations, this method is recognized as building a market and is crucial to growth. Walmart and Tiffany are also stores, but they have somewhat different niches: Walmart caters to bargain-minded customers, while Tiffany tends to luxury jewelry buyers.

"Some entrepreneurs make the error of slipping into the "all over the map" pit instead of building a niche, believing they can do many things and be successful at all of them. Falkenstein warns that these individuals soon learn a difficult lesson: "Smaller is larger in market, and smaller is not across the map; it is extremely focused."

4.2 Creating a good niche

Keep in mind these important to create a good niche:

1. Make a wish list.

Who do you like to do business with? Be as descriptive as you are capable of. Identify the regional spectrum and the kinds of firms or clients that you want your organization to target. You can't make contact if you do not really know whom you are going to do business with. Falkenstein cautions, "You must recognize that you can't do business with everyone." Otherwise, you risk leaving yourself exhausted and confusing your buyers.

The trend is toward small niches these days. It's not precise enough to target teens; targeting adult, African American teenagers with the family incomes of $40,000 or more is. It is too large to target corporations that market apps; it is a better aim to target Northern California-based firms that offer internet software distribution and training that have sales of $15 million or more.

2. Focus.

Clarify what you intend to sell, knowing that a) to all customers, you can't be all items and b) smaller is better. Your specialty isn't the same as that of sector you are employed in. A retail apparel corporation, for example, is not a niche but a sector. Maternity clothes for corporate mothers" may be a more specific niche."

Using these strategies to assist you in starting this focus process:

- Create a compilation of the greatest activities you do and the talents that are inherent in many of them.

- List your accomplishments.

- Identify the important things of life that you've experienced.

- Look for trends that reflect your personality or approach to addressing issues.

Your niche should emerge from your desires and expertise in a normal way. For instance, if you spent 10 years of working in such a consulting firm and also ten years working for such a small, family-owned company, you may actually have to start a consulting company that specializes in limited, family-owned businesses.

3. Describe the customer's worldview.

A good corporation utilizes what Falkenstein called the Platinum Rule: "Do to the others as they're doing to themselves." You will define their desires or desires as you look at the situation from the viewpoint of your prospective clients. Talking to new clients and recognizing their biggest issues is the perfect approach to achieve this.

4. Synthesize.

Your niche can begin to take shape at this point when the opinions and the desires of the consumer and desire to coalesce to create something different. There are five attributes of a Strong Niche:

- In other terms, it relates to your long-term view and carries you where you like to go.
- Somebody else needs it, consumers in particular.
- It is closely arranged.
- It's one-of-a-kind, "the only city game."
- It evolves, enabling you to build multiple profit centers and yet maintain the core market, thus guaranteeing long-term success.

5. Evaluate.

It is now time to test the product or service proposed against the five requirements in Phase 4. Perhaps you'll notice that more business travel than that you're ready for is needed for niche you had in mind. That indicates that one of the above conditions is not met-it will not carry you where you like to go. Scrap it, and pass on to the next proposal.

6. Test.

Test-market it until you have a balance between the niche and the product. "Give individuals an opportunity to purchase your product or service, not just theoretically, but actually put it out there." By giving samples, such as a complimentary mini-seminar or a preview copy of the newsletter, this can be accomplished. "If you spend enormous sums of cash on the initial trial run, you're possibly doing it wrong," she says. The research shouldn't cost you a bunch of money:

7. Go for it!

It is time for your idea to be implemented. This is the most challenging step for many entrepreneurs. But worry not: if you have done your research, it would be a measured risk to reach the business, not simply a chance.

Chapter 5. How to start dropshipping business in 2021

It's not easy to learn the way to start a dropshipping company, as with any type of business. Nevertheless, it's a perfect first move in the world of business. Without keeping any inventory, you may sell to customers. You do not have to pay upfront for goods. And if you are passionate about your new venture, in the long term, you will create a sustainable source of revenue.

In this complete dropshipping guide, suggest taking the following market and financial moves if you are considering dropshipping.

Others are mandatory from the start, and others are only a smart idea, so it will save you time and stress down the line by coping with them up front.

Dropshipping is a method of order fulfillment that helps shop owners to deliver without stocking any stock directly to buyers. If a consumer orders a commodity from a dropshipping shop, it is delivered directly to them by a third-party retailer. The client pays the selling price that you set, you pay the market price of the vendors, and the rest is benefit. You never need to maintain goods or spend in inventory.

You are responsible for designing a website and your own label, as well as selecting and promoting the items you choose to offer in the dropshipping business strategy. Your corporation is therefore liable for the expense of shipping and for setting rates that result in a reasonable profit margin.

Steps For Starting A Dropshipping Profitable Business

Learn to find high-margin products, introduce them to your business, and easily begin selling them.

1. Commit yourself for starting a dropshipping business

Dropshipping, as in any other business, needs considerable effort and a long-term focus. You're going to be deeply surprised if you're looking for a six-figure benefit from 6 weeks of part-time employment. You would be far less likely to get frustrated and leave by entering the organization with reasonable assumptions regarding the commitment needed and the prospects for benefit.

You'll need to spend heavily when beginning a dropshipping venture, utilizing one of the two following currencies: time or funds.

Investing time in dropshipping business

Our recommended strategy, particularly for the first dropshipping developers, is bootstrapping & investing sweat equity to develop your company. For various factors, we prefer this method over spending a huge amount of money:

- You will understand how the organization works inside out, which, as the enterprise expands and scales, will be crucial for handling others.

- You would know your clients and business personally, helping you to make smarter choices.

- You would be less inclined to waste huge amounts on vanity ventures that are not vital to success.

- You will build some new talents that will enable you a stronger entrepreneur.

Realistically, most persons are not ready to leave their work in order to ramp up their own online shop for six months. It might be a little more complicated, but even though you're already doing a 9-to-5 job, it's surely feasible to get underway with dropshipping, assuming you set reasonable standards for your customers about customer support and delivery times. When you continue to expand, as much as working capital and profitability allow, you will move into working long hours on your company.

Both companies and entrepreneurs are specific, but it is feasible to produce a monthly income stream of $1,000-$2,000 within 12 months of working around 10 to 15 hours per week to develop the firm.

Excited regarding starting a new business but not knowing where to begin? This informative guide will show you how to identify great products with strong sales potential that are newly trendy.

If you have the choice of working long hours on your company, that's the best option to increase your profit prospects and the possibility of good dropshipping. It is particularly beneficial in the early days to concentrate all the energies on publicity when creating traction is essential. It would normally take approximately 12 months of full-time jobs based on our knowledge, with a heavy focus on publicity for a dropshipping firm to replace an annual full-time salary of $50,000.

For a very small payout, it might sound like a lot of work, but bear these two points in mind:

When the dropshipping company is up and going, it would actually require considerably less time than from a 40-hour-per-week work to maintain it. In terms of the reliability and scalability that the dropshipping paradigm offers, much of your expenditure pays off.

You establish more than just a revenue stream when you develop a company. You also build an asset that you will market in the future. Be sure that when looking at the true return, you remember the equity valuation you are accruing, and also the cash flow produced.

Investing money in dropshipping business

By spending a lot of capital, it is feasible to develop and grow a dropshipping company, but we suggest against it. We attempted all methods to growing an enterprise (bootstrapping it ourselves vs. outsourcing the procedure), and while we were in the trenches doing much of the work, we had the most progress.

In the early stages, it is vital to have someone who is profoundly involved in the company's future to construct it from the ground up. You would be at the hands of pricey engineers, developers, and advertisers who will easily eat away whatever money you produce without knowing how your organization operates at any stage. You don't have to do everything it yourself, but at the start of your company, we highly advocate becoming the primary motivating power.

To have your company started and operating, you would, though, require a modest cash reserve in the $1,000 range. For limited administrative costs (like web hosting and dropshipping providers), you may need this and to pay some incorporation fees, which we will cover below.

2. Dropshipping business idea to chose

The second phase in studying how to launch a dropshipping company is to do the market research required. You want to find a niche you are interested in and make choices based on how effective it can be, almost like though you were starting a grocery shop and checking at the numerous sites, rivals, and developments. But the fact is, it's tricky to come up with product concepts to offer.

Niche goods also have a more passionate client base, which, through increasing awareness about the items, will make marketing to unique audiences simpler. A good entry point to begin dropshipping without cash could be health, clothes, makeup goods, appliances, phone accessories, or yoga-related pieces.

Any instances of dropshipping stores in a niche may be:

- Dog bow and ties for dog lovers

- Exercise equipment for fitness

- iPhone cases and cables for iPhone owners

- Camping gear for campers

To try the dropshipping business ideas, you may also use the appropriate techniques:

Google Trends could really help you identify whether, as well as the seasons in which they tend to trend, a product is trending up or down. Notice the search volume is not indicated by Google Patterns. But if you're using it, be sure to use a keyword tool such as Keywords Everywhere to cross-check your data to determine the popularity of the product in search.

3. Do competitor research

You want to check about your competitors so that you know what you're trying to sell in your shop and appreciate the way they operate. Your competitors may have great success hints which can help you develop a better marketing strategy for your dropshipping firm.

Limit your study to only five other dropshipping firms, like one or two major players such as Walmart or Ebay, if your business has a number of competitors (that is a positive thing in dropshipping). It will help you remain centered and prepare your next phase.

4. Choose a dropshipping supplier

Choosing a supplier for dropshipping is a crucial move towards creating a profitable dropshipping business. A dropshipping company does not have any goods to ship to consumers without vendors and would thus cease to operate.

At this stage, you analyzed what goods you want to offer and realize that they can be profitable, and you want to know where to find a provider of dropshipping that provides you with the high-quality service that you need to grow. By linking Oberlo to the online store, eCommerce platforms such as Shopify provide a plug-and-play style alternative to find possible suppliers.

5. Build your ecommerce store

An eCommerce platform such as Shopify is the next what you need to launch a dropshipping business. This is the home where you deliver traffic, offer goods, and payments are processed.

These type of platforms makes the e-commerce website simple to create and launch. It is a complete commerce service that connects you to sell and receive payments in several ways, like online, sell in different currencies, and conveniently manage products.

To use e-commerce websites, you don't need to become a programmer or developer either. They have resources to assist with anything from domain name ideas to logo design, and with the store creator and Payment processing themes, you are quickly able to modify the feel and look of your store.

6. Market your dropshipping store

It's time to talk about promoting your new shop, now that you know to start a dropshipping firm. You may want to bring more work into your marketing and promotional activities while developing the dropshipping business strategy to stick out in your market.

You will invest time working on selling and supporting the company in the following ways, with too many stuff about dropshipping being processed:

- Paid ads (Facebook & Google).

For a Facebook ad, the average cost is about 0.97 cents per click, that's not too bad if you're new to social media advertising. Facebook ads are extensible, goods can perform ok on them, and they click into the desire of people to purchase momentum. You can run Google Shopping Ads and target lengthy keywords that are more likely to be purchased by shoppers. Typically, with Google ads, there is more price competition, but it might be worthy of your time to check it out.

- Influencer marketing.

You may have a low funds for marketing your business as a new dropshipper. Influencer marketing is also an affordable way to target audience because individuals are more likely than traditional advertising to trust influencers. When you go this route, start negotiating an affiliate fee versus a flat rate with the influencer. It's a win-win situation, as every sale they're going to make money off, and the cost is going to be less for you.

- Mobile marketing.

Smartphone marketing is a broad term referring to a company that connects with clients on their mobile phones. You can start with a VIP text club, for example, and encourage website users to sign up for the exclusive promotions & deals. Or provide client support through Messenger in a live chat session with shoppers. You can create automated qualified leads, customer loyalty, and cart abandonment campaigns with a mobile marketing tool such as ManyChat to drive sales and profits for your dropshipping business.

Stay updated on what channels are operating and which are not, as with any profitable online business, especially if you invest money in them like paid ads. You can always adjust your marketing plan to lower costs as well as maximize revenue as you keep growing and improve your business.

7. Analyze your offering

You should start looking at the consequences of your diligent work after you've been promoting and operating your dropshipping company for some time. Any analytics will help you address some critical online shop queries, like:

- Sales

What are my channels with the highest performance? Where am I expected to put more ad dollars? What else are my favorite items for sale? What are my greatest clients?

- Behavior of shoppers

Do citizens buy more on their laptops or cell phones? For each unit, what's the conversion rate?

- Margins of profit

Why are the most profitable pieces and variant SKUs? What do my month-over-month revenue and gross income look like?

To track web traffic over time and optimize your search engine optimization activities, you can even use resources like Google Analytics & Search Console. Plus, you review the results monthly to guarantee that your overall plan succeeds with your business, whether you are utilizing third-party software for your social network or messenger marketing.

You want to build a data-informed analytics framework while building a dropshipping e-commerce store. Remain compatible with what you evaluate over time and calculate the consistency of your store against simple KPIs. This will encourage you to make better choices for your store, so move your small business over time to the next level.

Chapter 6. How To identify Best Suppliers For Your New Dropshipping Business

Dropshipping is a model for eCommerce that is increasingly attractive. That is because launching a dropshipping company is simpler (not to say less expensive) than managing inventory for a traditional digital storefront.

The whole model of drop shipment is focused on the retailer doing its job well and delivering orders timely and effectively. It goes without saying, therefore, that identifying the appropriate supplier is one, if not the most important, and a step towards creating a successful brand. If an order is messed up by your supplier/seller, you and your organization are liable, so the trick is to find someone who adheres to the schedule and is open to discuss any problems

The advantages and disadvantages of dropshipping are well known, but it has become far less obvious that the most significant part of beginning a dropshipping business is choosing the right vendors for your WooCommerce shop. Until now.

6.1 The Importance of Selecting The Right Suppliers

A special model for eCommerce is Dropshipping. To retain their own inventories, conventional online retailers compensate. Those expenses are all but offset by dropshipping, so dropshipping would not need substantial start-up investment.

In the other side, dropshipping suggests that you place the destiny of your eCommerce store in the possession of others.

With the dropshipping system, retailers focus on wholesalers, manufacturers, and dealers who meet the orders of the retailers.

The dropshipping puzzle has several parts, and for the greater image, each component is critical. Among those pieces, one of the most significant is dropshipping suppliers. In reality, the finest dropshippers know that a dropshipping eCommerce store can make or break the efficiency and overall reliability of dropshipping suppliers.

6.2 Finding Your Dropshipping Suppliers

It needs you to partner with manufacturers, wholesalers, & distributors to start a dropshipping business. You want to identify vendors who improve the dropshipping business rather than compromise it.

Research Your Products

You have to figure out what types of things you can sell before you can start finding and working with vendors.

You want to address queries in specific, such as:

- Where does the item come from?
- How long would manufacturing take?
- How is it done?

Are there factors of height or weight which might make fulfillment more complicated or more costly?

The purpose is not expertise; however, you want to get to know the goods so that you can help determine which ones are suitable for dropshipping.

Understand the supply chain and recognize the considerations

You need to get familiar with dropship supply chain after nailing down your goods. In other terms, you should to know how it works for dropshipping.

For dropshipping, the items never really go into the hands of the dealer. Instead, an order is issued by the retailer, and a supplier who manages packing and delivery initiates fulfillment. In this way, the dealer is like the director of a dropshipping company.

You can't sell goods if you don't have reputable vendors, which suggests that you don't have a dropshipping business.

You need to get familiar with dropship supply chain since nailing down your products. In other terms, you need to understand how it functions for dropshipping.

For dropshipping, the items never really go into the hands of the dealer. Instead, an order is issued by the retailer and a supplier who manages packing and delivery initiates fulfilment. In this manner, the retailer is just like the director of a dropshipping company.

You can't sell goods if you don't have reputable suppliers, which suggests that you don't have a dropshipping business.

Search for Dropshipping Wholesalers on Google

You will identify the major vendors for your preferred commodities or product types with a Google search.

When you build a preliminary list, by studying the next few queries, take notice of the various characteristics of dropshipping suppliers.

- What is supplier location?

- Will the retailer link with your WooCommerce shop so that fresh orders are immediately submitted for fulfillment?

- What (if any) is the sum of minimum order (MOQ)?

- What support (e.g., mobile, email, chat, etc.) does the provider offer?

- What kind of range of items does the retailer offer?

Subscribe to Dropshipping Suppliers Directories

And if lots of choices pop up in the Google searches, directories will bring even more options. For a broad selection of items, these repositories comprise of web lists of dropshipping vendors and wholesalers.

You should recognize that some of the finest are premium directories, such as Salehoo and Worldwide Labels, implying they need paying subscriptions. There are a lot of free directories accessible that you can access at no fee, like Wholesale Central. Free directories, though, are occasionally obsolete. Newer vendors do not exist, and suppliers are also listed who are no longer in operation.

Usually, premium directories vary in cost from $20 a month for lifetime access to a few hundred bucks. You can find the expense of a premium directory to be beneficial, with free directories often hit-

or-miss. There are also premium directories, like Doba, explicitly customized for dropshipping.

Figure Out Your Competitor's Suppliers

It follows that you must see what your competitors do if you want to be successful in the dropshipping field. Do any acknowledgment, in fact, to see which manufacturers are meeting their requirements.

There are a lot of methods to do this, but testing the markets that the competitors sell is the best.

If the supplier is not listed on the page, by making your own order, you will always show the supplier. Since the retailer is pleased, an invoice or packaging slip from them would possibly be included with the shipment. To ask about a partnership with your own dropshipping company, you can then contact the supplier directly.

Attend Trade Seminars

Trade shows have been considered to be an efficient place for manufacturers to set up and grow their companies. So, if you haven't been to a trade seminar yet, add it to the end of the list of to-do events.

You network with other participants within dropship supply chain, like distributors and dropshipping wholesalers, at trade shows. You get an insider's view on current and future products that you should introduce to your online store. For dropshipping businesses, you even get to "talk shop" face-to-face, which is also the most successful way to do business.

Join Industry Groups and Networks

Trade shows facilitate with locating vendors for dropshipping firms, yet another effective resource is business networks and groups.

The majority of retailers, like the identities of their dropshipping vendors, are not willing to share the secrets of their performance. The individuals who enter business groups, however, want to share, learn, & develop. Through being part of the dropshipping network, you will get valuable insight from industry professionals. Your colleagues, for instance, might recommend better suppliers or alert you about suppliers in order to avoid.

Connect with the Manufacturers

Not all manufacturers supply to consumers directly, although there are those who do. Until picking vendors for your eCommerce dropshipping shop, suggest reaching out to the producers of the goods that you will market.

You have far higher margins when a producer chooses to be the distributor than with a traditional retailer or wholesaler. Manufacturers, on the other hand, frequently impose minimum order amounts that could need bigger orders. You might find yourself with considerable inventory to deal in this situation, which is intended to circumvent dropshipping.

Ask the vendor to recommend vendors for you if a manufacturer won't work with you. A recommendation, after all, indicates that the agreements and commitments between a manufacturer and a supplier is successful. For that cause, it is definitely worth putting suggested vendors on your list of possibilities.

Order Samples

There's no substitution for firsthand knowledge, no matter how many feedback or testimonials you find. This is why ordering samples is the next phase in finding the correct dropshipping suppliers for the business.

Ordering samples teaches you a few key things about a supplier. First one is that you get to know the product's consistency yourself.

The second is that you will see how delivery is done by the retailer, and what shipment packaging seems to if a different vendor is involved, and how long it takes to ship and distribute. Suppliers will execute the requests, so buying samples provides you with an idea of what your clients will feel.

Confirm Contract Terms & Fees

You compiled several options, removed any but the most suitable possibilities, ordered tests to assess certain vendors, and decided on your dropshipping company with the right supplier (or suppliers). Negotiating deal conditions and payments is the last option left to do.

New businesses with unproven consumer bases have fewer bargaining leverage relative to mature companies with established customer bases. When it comes to communicating the margins, this is especially true.

Since dropshipping means that you don't have to hold your inventory, there would be low margins. The bulk of inventory costs and expenditures involved with meeting your orders is borne by your supplier(s). With dropshipping, because prices are smaller, gross margins are often lower than if you stored and delivered orders personally.

With margins generally poor, the fees concerned may be the biggest distinction between vendors. Such suppliers, for instance, charge flat per-order rates that are applied to the overall cost of the goods. Per-order payments typically vary from $2 and $5 to cover delivery and shipping costs (although big or unwieldy goods can require higher fees).

In the end, you want to select the supplier(s) that satisfies your specifications and give contracts of appropriate terms.

Chapter 7. Setting Up Your Dropshipping business On A Budget

The establishment of a dropshipping company as an eCommerce business is a perfect way to earn money. Managing a business without the hassle of product and shipping logistics is the most convincing aspect of a dropshipping store

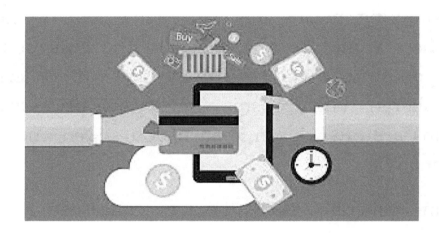

You have already heard stories from businessmen about how costly it is to start a business. This involve accounts of hopelessly pursuing buyers or firms failing because of bleak financials to remain afloat. Do not let this scare you from launching a dropshipping store, as this model enables you to offer low-risk products.

What you need to do is get the orders and call the supplier-the rest is up to them.

There are very few financial barriers associated with the establishment of a dropshipping store when it comes to financing the company. In fact, with around zero initial investment, you can get underway with an online store.

Here's a 7-step feasible plan for launching a dropshipping shop on a budget shoestring.

1. Research Your Options

You'll need to do some research before beginning some form of business.

It requires getting online and finding out the competitors that offer related goods. To see just what each has to suggest, you'll also want to spend a little time investigating the future vendors and distributors.

Each shipping group will have a specific way of doing stuff and pricing models, therefore pay careful attention to those specifics so that you can ensure that you team up with your dropshipping store with the right party.

2. Create a Plan to Stick

You'll need to get a solid plan in progress before you can launch your business activities. A budget is used with this. It's important to decide what your budget is, whether you have $100 or $500 to get underway and ensure that you adhere to it. The easiest way to achieve so is to maintain good track of all your spending to guarantee that as you start up your store, you do not go over the budget.

3. Find Your Niche

In reality, many believe that it is an impossible task. It may be really challenging to appeal to all. Instead, rather than attempting to market could product under the sun, choose the goods focused on a particular niche.

Select a particular area of the business, such as organic pet food or dog clothes, if you decide that you want to market animal-related items.

When you can refine your attention down, you can have a much higher sales rate, and you are more likely to be noticed when customers are looking for a particular form of a product. Your small shop can get lost in the noise of competitors if your focus is too big.

4. Set Up Your eCommerce website

This is the phase through which you finally launch and set up your site with a dropshipping store.

Three of the most successful eCommerce sites accessible to sellers today are Shopify and Wix. It's quick to get started, as well as its user-friendly interface, also for sellers who are not especially tech-savvy, makes configuration and maintenance easy.

With monthly prices of less than $40, Shopify and Wix are both inexpensive alternatives, making it a perfect way to get off on a budget in the digital marketplace. You may also open a Modalyst store to boost the delivery and streamline the distribution process.

You're able to move on to the next stage after you have set up a simple online storefront that has your products selected.

5. Make Meetings With Your Suppliers

When it comes to choosing which provider to use it for your dropshipping shop, there are lots of decisions out there. Because you've done your homework in phase one already, now is the moment where your decision is formalized. Through entering into a contract with the commodity distributor(s) of your choosing, you will do so. Any of the most successful shipping partners makes it simple to get started, and in no time, unlike having to pay such upfront costs, you will be on your way.

The most relevant issues you are asking your prospective suppliers are:

- Do you keep all products in stock?

- How do you care the returns?

- What is your normal or average processing time?

- In which areas do you ship to? Do international shipping available?

- What kind of support did you offer?

- Is there any limit for orders?

You would have a solid understanding about how your suppliers conduct their company until you meet a supplier who addresses certain questions to your satisfaction. In addition, as a seller dealing for them, you'll realize what you need to do. You're on the path to a successful working partnership at this point.

6. Start Selling

Oh, congratulations. In launching your online store, this is one of most exciting steps. It's time to add your product details to your website and start selling until you have all your arrangements and agreements in order.

If customers are not aware of the products, you will not have enough sales, to begin with. You'll want to waste more time and money on ads if this is the case. By beginning with low-cost advertisements on Instagram and Facebook, or advertising on blogs as well as other websites which have a common audience, you will keep advertising costs reasonably small.

7. Optimize Your Site

You should take some time to customize the website until you have some revenue and knowledge under your belt. You can do all this earlier in the process, but waiting to see what is really working before you start to make changes is often a good idea.

There are a broad variety of customization choices for sites such as Shopify and Modalyst, including templates that change the way your website looks and plugins to can customize how your website works. The primary aim here is to tweak the site in ways that make it smoother for your clients and more organized.

As you've seen, all it takes to set up an online store is a few steps, and most of them don't need any money. You're not lonely if you're excited about being an owner of an eCommerce company just don't have a ton of money to launch with. This is why so many platforms are accessible that make it easier to get started without investing a million in the process.

Making sure that it works and prepare a strategy that you will use to guide you when keeping under your budget by setting up your dropshipping business, no matter how small it might be.

Chapter 8. Mistakes To Avoid When Developing Your Dropshipping Business

In an environment that jumps at the chance to make a business deal quick and convenient, Dropshipping tends to have a no for retailers. It might seem like, now, acquiring the goods and marketing with a bit of savvy are your only worries. Yet, if you wish to hold the company afloat, you should not forget about the client's perspective. True, the boring duties of inventory, order filling, and then ensuring shipping can be passed on.

The dropshipping company, however, does not waste any time thinking about the feelings of your client. How do you assume if your client is going to be satisfied? The buyers are the ones who put the money back. Anything falls out the window if they're not satisfied. You would need to consider the duties and what failures typically trigger it all to backfire in order to completely enjoy the advantages of utilizing dropshipping.

Here are a common mistake that leads to the failure end of your dropshipping business, so you should hold these mistakes in mind all the time.

1. Worrying About Shipping Costs.

While shipping costs might be a doozy, it's never productive to stress. In this area, you will need to decide under which your priorities lie. Shipping prices can vary all over the board, depending on where orders come from. This stress can be relieved by setting a flat rate and generally evens out with time. Not only does this make things easier for you, but it's also simple and easy for customers.

2. Relying Much on Vendors.

By putting much trust in such a vendor, a good number of crises can arise. For example, they may go out of business or increase their rates on you if you only use one vendor. They might run out of the items that you expect them to supply. Where would you be then? This is why there should always be a backup for you. It is smart to write up the contract with your vendors for your own insurance to remain aware of your requirements. This will ensure that everyone involved has agreed to uphold what you demand.

3. Expecting Easy Money.

Dropshipping, as we've already established, offers a degree of ease that can seem to make your work easier. Yet, you can't ignore how critical your product is in marketing and all the competition you're going to face. This involves analysis and the creation of a unique approach that will allow the product more attractive than that of anyone else.

4. Making Order Difficult to Access.

When you assure your consumers a simple and quick procedure, they'll want to see the proofs. Set approximate location-based ship dates and require suppliers to keep you posted on the status of the order so that you can keep the consumer aware. This way, you can track shipments whenever you anticipate them to come longer than expected and easily fix issues.

5. Not Enough Brand Display.

Through dropshipping, it may be hard to guarantee the brand remains to be seen in the customer's overall experience. You may not want people to forget regarding you, so it's important to insert as many locations as possible into your brand. You should have customized packing slips, stickers and custom exterior packaging to hold the name included after delivery. Sending a follow-up thank you message or a survey to remind about of you and prove them you think for their feedback at the same time is also not a bad idea.

6. Return Complications.

If you do not have a system for returns set up, things can get messy very quickly. You and your vendor will have to establish a refund policy to avoid this. Customers are going to wait for their refund expectantly, and being disorganized on that front and will not make them feel good. They may also need guidelines explaining how or where to return the product. Organizing a structure for this will save a good amount of confusion and irritation for both you and the client.

7. Selling Trademarked Products

When most people learn about dropshipping and realize that it is not that complicated to do the process, they picture all the things they might sell and make a quick buck.

Many of these goods are items which have been trademarked by a manufacturer. Selling these goods without the manufacturer's specific consent to be a retail agent will lead you to legal issues. This can not only lead to the end of your online shop, but you can also be held personally responsible.

You should, consequently, look at generic items which you can add to your variety of products for sale. Best still, you should swap in goods with white marks. They are plain goods that are available to those who rebrand them through the manufacturer. You will order and get these items customized to suit the brand and display them.

8. Picking the Wrong Field

Once you have abandoned thoughts of selling any product you come across, by concentrating on one field, you can develop your dropshipping business.

You might, however, select the wrong niche in which to operate. Maybe you should pick a niche that isn't lucrative. This may be that it's out of vogue or it's simply not meant for shopping online.

Therefore, to see what will earn you money, you have to do proper market analysis. "Market research" might sound like a complex process in which only major brands participate.

Simple Google searches will, therefore, show you what individuals are interested in and where they purchase them.

9. Poor Relationship With Suppliers

Your vendors are part of your business; they promise that you have the best goods and that they supply your consumers with them. You can be inclined, though, to consider them as workers and handle them as though they are in the hierarchy on a lower rung.

They're not. They are your friends, without whom it would be effectively dead for your dropshipping business. Therefore, you can establish a better relationship with them.

This will have its benefits. When negotiating costs for commodity stock, a strong partnership will work in your favor.

10. Lowering Price To Extreme Levels

Reducing your prices to knock out your competition is also one of the dropshipping failures to avoid.

This is a logical way for you to rise your dropshipping business, you might think. You could have been no farther from the facts. Very low prices indicate to potential customers that your product may be of poor quality.

11. Poor Website Structure

The progress of your dropshipping company depends on the shopping experience your clients have when they browse your online store.

Thus, you have to make sure everything is convenient for them. However, you could rush through the process of establishing your website due to low barrier for entrance into dropshipping. Many beginners do not have the coding skills required to construct an online store.

In conclusion, the primary interest is the customer's experience. Although inventory management and shipping are not your responsibility, you can also ensure that all is well handled. All of these dropshipping failures can be prevented with adequate preparation and careful management, and the business can better manage.

Chapter 9. Smooth Running tips for Your Dropshipping Business

Well, you've done your research, decided to agree on the right dropship goods and roped in the right possible supplier. All of you are planned to begin dropshipping goods and make the mullah! Setting up the company, though, is typically one thing, but a totally different ball game is to manage it on a day-to-day basis. Even if it's a dropshipping company, there are various facets of running a business that you have to remember as a retailer: marketing, refunds, refunds, repairs, inventory, distribution, customer service, and far more. So dive into all these different aspects of managing a dropshipping business.

So far, when covered a lot of details, it involves everything from the fundamentals of dropshipping to the nuances of finding a niche and managing the business. You should have much of a base by now to begin investigating and establishing your own dropshipping company comfortably.

It's possible to get confused and lose track about what's really necessary, with too much to consider. That's why we've built this list of key elements for success. This are the main "must-do" acts that can make the new company or ruin it. If you can perform these effectively, you would be able to get a bunch of other stuff wrong and yet have a decent probability of success.

1. Add Value

The most important performance element is making a good roadmap on how you will bring value to your clients. In the field of dropshipping, where you can contend with legions of other "me too" stores carrying related items, this is critical for both corporations, but even more so.

With dropshipping, it's reasonable to think you're marketing a product to consumers. Yet good small merchants realize that they are offering insights, ideas and solutions, not just the commodity they deliver. You assume you're an e-commerce seller, but you're in the information industry as well.

If you can't create value by quality data and advice, price is the only thing you're left to contend on. While this has been an effective technique for Walmart, it will not help you grow a successful company for dropshipping.

2. Focus on SEO and marketing

The opportunity to push traffic to the new platform is a near second to providing value as a main key factor. A shortage of traffic to their sites is the #1 concern and annoyance faced by modern e-commerce retailers. So many retailers have been slaving away on the ideal platform for months just to unleash it into a community that has no clue it exists.

For the success of your company, advertising and driving traffic is completely necessary and challenging to outsource well, particularly if you have a limited budget and bootstrap your business. In order to build your own SEO, publicity, outreach and guest posting abilities, you have to consider taking the personal initiative.

Within the first 6 - 12 months, where no one know who you are, this is particularly crucial. You need to devote at least 75 percent of your time on publicity, SEO and traffic development for at least 4 to 6 months after your website launch, which is right, 4 to 6 months. You can start reducing and coast a little on the job you put in until you've built a strong marketing base. But it's difficult, early on, to bring so much emphasis on advertising.

3. Marketing Your Dropshipping Business

Marketing is indeed a subjective field, and that there are a billion strategies which can be used to position your brand successfully whilst driving awareness and sales of your brand. It will even help you root out the remainder of the market if the approach is well planned.

4. Social Media Source

Social networking is one of the most efficient ways to promote, advertise, attract clients and share content, so when social networks are now used for digital marketing, it comes as no surprise. For example, Facebook has more than 1.7 billion active members from diverse walks of life, and it is this diversity that makes it so appealing to online marketers.

One thing to note is that it's important to content. No matter how perfect a platform is or how good the product you are offering is, without high quality content backing it up, it means nothing.

5. Customer Ratings & Reviews

A few bad customer ratings will actually ruin a business in dropshipping business model. Think about it: As you order online from websites like ebay and aliexpress, the quality ranking and what other consumers had to tell about it will be one of the determining purchase variables, too, with decrease delivery. A few positive feedback will also give you an advantage over the competition because that is what will help you convert traffic to your website successfully.

6. Email Marketing

In a digital marketer's pack, this one of the most neglected tools. To keep your clients in the loop for any major changes within company, email marketing may be used: Price increases, promotions, coupons, content related to the commodity, and content unique to the industry are only some of the forms email marketing may be utilized.

7. Growth Hacking

Growth hacking is a cheap but highly productive way to get online creative marketing campaigns. A few definitions of growth hacking involve retargeting old campaigns and featuring in your own niche as a guest writer for a popular website. Any of this commonly involves content marketing.

Chapter 10. How To Maximize Your Chances Of Success?

There are only a couple more tips you should adopt to maximize the chances of long-term growth if you are willing to take the plunge and attempt dropshipping. Second, that doesn't mean you can approach a dropshipping business because it's risk-free simply because there are no setup costs involved with purchasing and managing goods. You're also spending a lot of time choosing the right dropshippers while designing your website, so consider it as an investment and do careful preliminary research.

1. Things To Remember

What do you want to sell? How profitable is the surroundings? How can you gain clients and distinguish yourself? Inside the same room, is there a smaller niche that is less competitive? When they find a particular market and curate their goods like a pro, most individuals who operate a purely dropshipping model have seen the most growth, ensuring that any last item they offer is a successful match for their niche audience with their brand.

After you develop your list of possible dropshippers, carry out test orders and then watch for the items to arrive, thinking like a consumer. How long can any order take? What is the feeling of unboxing like? What is the commodity standard itself? This will help you distinguish between possible dropshippers or confirm that positive consumer service is offered by the one you want.

Note that the goods themselves may not be the differentiator for your business.

After you have chosen your dropshippers and products, note that the products themselves may not be the differentiator for your business. So ask what else you should count on to make the deal. This is another explanation why test orders are a wonderful idea since they encourage you to obtain the item and explain its functionality and advantages as a client might. In a way which really shows it off, you can even take high-quality, professional pictures of the product. Armed with exclusive explanations of the goods and images that are separate from all the other product photos, you would be able to start standing out.

Your bread and butter is definitely going to be a well-executed campaign strategy, so devote time and money on each section of it, from finding your potential audience to interacting with influencers on social media in your niche. Targeted commercials can be a perfect way to kick start your site to bring your name on the mind of your client base.

When it relates to your return policies, delivery contact and customer support, ensure your ducks are in a line. You'll need to do what you could to serve as the buffer between a dropshipper and your client if something goes wrong somewhere in the process. Understand the typical cost of return for each item so that you will notice whether it is large enough to denote a quality issue. If you suspect a consistency problem, talk to your dropshipper or try a different supplier to your issues.

Eventually, note that dropshipping is not a model of "all or nothing." Many of the more profitable corporations follow a hybrid model, making or shipping in-house some goods and employing dropshippers to fill the gaps. The dropshippers are not the key profit-drivers for these firms but are instead a simple, inexpensive way to provide clients with the "extras" they can enjoy. Before you put it in-house, you can even use dropshipped products for upsells, impulse sales, or to try a new model.

As long as you consider the above tips to ensuring that the one you chose is suitable for your business needs, there is definitely a lot to learn from the streamlining and flexibility of using a dropshipper. You will make your dropshipping store run for you in no time with a little of research, negotiation, and setup!

Conclusion

So that concludes our definitive dropshipping guide. You now learn how to set up to kick start your new dropshipping business if you've made it here. Starting up your own business often involves a certain degree of dedication, effort, and ambition to make things work, much as in every other undertaking in life. It's not only about building the business but also about pushing through and knowing how to manage it on a daily basis.

The greatest feature of dropshipping is that you will practice in real-time by checking your goods and concepts, and all you have to do is drop it from your shop if anything doesn't work. This business concept is indeed a perfect opportunity for conventional business models to try out product concepts. Dropshipping creates a secure place to innovate to see what happens without incurring any substantial damages that will surely give business owners the courage to state that they have a working idea of how the market works. The dropshipping business model is an interesting business model to move into with little initial expense and relatively little risk.

A perfect choice to drop shipping if you are only starting to sell online and would like to test the waters first. It's a great way to start your business, even if the margins are low.

As dropshipping can still get started with little investment, before they build their market image, businessmen can start with that too.

Ecommerce sites such as Ebay, Shopify, Alibaba and social networking, such as Instagram, Twitter, Reddit, provide vast expertise in user base and content marketing. It also helps newbies to know about establishing an online store, optimizing conversions, generating traffic and other basics of e-commerce.

That's what you need to learn about beginning a dropshipping. Just note, it's not the hard part to launch your dropshipping store, the real challenge is when you get trapped, and your stuff is not being sold. Do not panic, and keep checking as it happens. You're going to get a product soon that sells well.

Short Stays Real Estate with No (or Low) Money Down

The 7+1 Creative Strategies to Create Passive Income from Home Using the AirBnb Business Model in 2021

By

Jake Folger

Table of Contents

Introduction 326

CHAPTER 1: Understand Income and Importance of Passive Income 330

  1.1 Active Income 330

  1.2 Portfolio Income 333

  1.3 Passive Income 335

  1.4 Taxing of passive income 339

  1.5 Why Passive Income Beats Earned Income 340

  1.6 Reasons Why Passive Income Is So Important 342

CHAPTER 2: Passive income ideas to help you make money in 2021 349

  2.1 How many streams of income should you have? 350

  2.2 Passive income ideas for building wealth 351

  2.3 Selling information products 351

  2.4 Rental income 352

  2.5 Affiliate marketing 354

  2.6 Flip retail products 356

  2.7 Peer-to-peer lending 357

  2.8 Dividend stocks 359

  2.9 Create an app 360

  2.10 REITs 361

2.11 A bond ladder 363

2.12 Invest in a high-yield CD or savings account 365

2.13 Buy Property..366

2.14 Rent out your home short-term through Airbnb 367

2.15 Air BnB Business as a Passive income Strategy 368

2.16 Advertise on your car 373

2.17 Invest in Stocks...374

2.18 Make Your Car Work for You.......................................375

2.19 Sell your Videos 376

2.20 Create YouTube Videos 377

2.21 Write an eBook 377

2.22 Sell Digital Products...378

2.23 CPC Ads (Cost Per Click) 379

2.24 Minimize your taxes on passive income 380

CHAPTER 3: Airbnb Offers The Best Passive Income Generation Strategy...382

3.1 Understand the Vacation Rental Industry 383

3.2 Create a Maintenance Management System 384

3.3 Put Together a Vacation Rental Marketing Strategy 385

3.4 Invest in Property Management Tools 386

3.5 Outline Your Guest Management Strategy 388

3.6 Set a Reasonable (But Competitive) Price..............................389

3.7 How an Airbnb Business Works 390

3.8 The Bottom Line 402

Conclusion 404

Introduction

If you are a forward-focused person, you can dream of leaving the profession to enjoy a retirement life that is simpler, or you might even consider early retirement. But a dream is only a wish without a plan. You need to contemplate passive income to put a few wheels on the dream. There are also plenty of different options for passive income and rationales of how to build it. Passive income is the money you collect that doesn't cause you to do a lot of "active" work in order to continue to earn it. In essence, you may do much of the work in advance and do some extra effort to earn an income. For instance, to keep the money flowing, if you develop an online course, you only need to update the content. Likewise, passive income strategies like renting out property and/or building a blog can take some effort to get up and running, but while you sleep, they would eventually earn you cash. You've already heard the word, "make money when you're sleeping." This is the main attraction that allows individuals to generate passive income. Even when you're not working, you can develop something (a course, a blog, e-book, videos, and/or an online store) which generates income. Or you can own something that helps you to earn passive income (property or stocks).

So why do you need to build passive income?

In the presence of a full-time job, your salary is your biggest income tool, a tool that usually requires your active involvement. Even if you enjoy your career, you wouldn't mind making some additional money without the tears, blood, sweat, and time commitment of another job. If you lose your job or want to generate an extra source of income when you are no longer productive or if you outlive your retirement fund, developing a passive income will improve your wealth-building strategy, create the opportunity to retire early, and save you from a total loss of income.

And how much money can passive income generate?

Generally, passive income won't make you wealthy overnight, so ignore those get-rich-quick schemes you've read about. But, over the long term, consistent, profitable passive income strategies will produce some serious money. Depending on the income stream, we're talking about anything from two to three thousand dollars to thousands of dollars.

Some people like to think of investing when we mention "passive income" because, with the least amount of effort, it can yield the greatest returns. But you should think about your retirement plan & passive income as two distinct subjects. The entire premise behind the long-term investment is to produce retirement income. If your fund options are good and they offer a match, you want to make sure you invest in your company retirement plan, like that of a 401(k). These are great choices for establishing a powerful pension plan, but before a certain age, you will face taxes as well as penalties for every withdrawal. You need to let your money grow only for the long term with retirement planning and not touch it. However, a form of low-effort income which can be accessed at any time should be passive income. After you are debt-free and have some cash left, one way to build passive income is by buying real estate and leasing it out to tenants. Rental property may be a fantastic source of additional income, but it is not the most passive option because, unless you employ a property management company, you will have to put a lot of effort and time into maintaining the property. You need to be in charge of your property if you go on the rental property route. Pay off your own home first before you buy a rental property, and buy your investment property with cash. You must not go into debt in order to purchase property for rent. You could develop something like an informative blog and/or a YouTube tutorial series to be able to generate online traffic if you have a bright idea that appeals to a particular audience. You might sell commercial space on your blog or ad spots on your channel if your content is engaging and it sees ample regular traffic. You can sit back, relax, and reap sources of passive income after you put in the heavy lifting. The list of ideas for passive income could go on indefinitely. Never go for any passive income strategies that promise a fast return or require large sums of money upfront. Your other financial targets would be sabotaged by them. In this book, we will present ideas that are steady, profitable, and trustworthy.

CHAPTER 1: Understand Income and Importance of Passive Income

There are three main categories of income:

Active income

Portfolio income

Passive income

1.1 Active Income

Active income alludes to money made as a result of the provision of service. Examples of active income are wages, tips, salaries, fees, and income from companies in which there is material involvement. The owner must meet the criteria for "material participation," which is based on hours worked or other factors, in order for income from a company to be considered active rather than passive. The most popular example of active income is income earned in the form of a paycheck from an employer. "Money from business activities is deemed "active" for the self-employed or someone else with an ownership interest in a corporation if it meets the criteria of material participation by the Internal Revenue Service (IRS). That implies one of the following is valid, at least:

- The taxpayer works during the year in the corporation for 500 or more hours.
- The taxpayer performs the majority of the company's work.
- Over the year, the taxpayer works for more than 100 hours in the company and no other employee works more hours than the taxpayer.

However, income earned is treated as passive income if someone earns income from a company in which they do not actively participate. Meanwhile, portfolio income is income from investments, like dividends and capital gains. Depending on the legislation at the time, these various forms of income can be taxed differently. At present, for instance, portfolio income is taxed at lower rates than active income.

Example of active income from a business

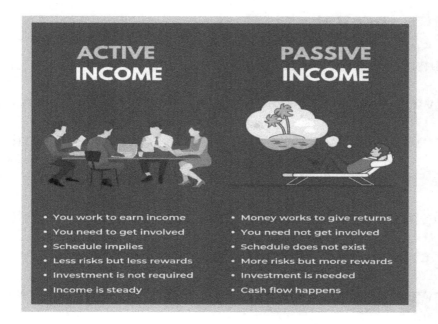

John and Laura are not married to each other. They have a 50% interest in an online business. John performs the majority of the day-to-day work in the business. Therefore, his income is considered active by the IRS. On the other, Laura helps with the marketing activities. She, however, works less than 100 hours a year in the business. It is for this very reason that her income from the business is considered passive income by the IRS. The material participation rule was established to prevent individuals that do not actively participate in a business from using it to generate tax losses which they, otherwise, could have written off against their active income.

1.2 Portfolio Income

Income from the portfolio is money received from investments, interest, dividends, and capital gains. Portfolio income streams are often known to be dividends received from investment properties. It is one of three main income groups. Active income and passive income are the others. Most income from the portfolio enjoys favorable tax treatment. Dividends and capital gains are charged at a much lower rate as compared to active income. Furthermore, portfolio income is not subject to Medicare or Social Security taxes. Income from the portfolio contains dividends, interest, and capital gains. Compared to active or passive income, portfolio income typically enjoys favorable tax treatment. Money from the portfolio is not subject to withholding from Social Security or Medicaid. One way to maximize portfolio income is to invest in an ETF that purchases dividend-paying stocks. Income from the portfolio does not come from passive investments. Moreover, portfolio income is not received from daily business activity. It is earned because of dividends, taxes, and capital gains or interest paid on loans. For tax purposes, the categories of income are important. Passive income losses can not necessarily be offset against portfolio or active income.

Ways to Increase Portfolio Income

Following ways can be employed for increasing portfolio income:

Purchase High-Paying Dividend Stocks

Investors can enhance their portfolio income by purchasing stocks that pay above-average dividends. Dividends can be paid directly to the shareholder. Moreover, dividends can also be used to buy additional shares in the company.

Purchase Dividend Exchange-Traded Funds

A cost-effective way to maximize portfolio income is to buy ETFs that explicitly track high-paying dividend stocks. For example, the FTSE High Dividend Yield Index is tracked by the Vanguard High Dividend Yield ETF. There are 396 stocks that have high dividend yields and are included in the index. For other dividend ETF options, the selection criteria concentrate on how many consecutive years the company has paid a dividend and/or on companies that have a history of raising their annual dividend payments.

Write Options

An investor can write call options against their stock holdings to enhance his portfolio income.

1.3 Passive Income

Passive income are earnings that come from a limited partnership, rental property, or another enterprise in which an entity is not actively engaged, such as a silent investor. Proponents of passive income tend to be boosters of the working lifestyle of a work-from-home and/or be-your-own-boss. Colloquially, it has been used on the part of the person receiving it to describe money being earned periodically with little or no effort. When used as a technical term, passive income is defined by the IRS as either "net rental income" or "income from an enterprise in which the taxpayer does not participate materially" and may include self-charged interest in some cases. Passive income is a source of income that may require some initial effort or investment but continues to generate payments in the future. Examples are music and book royalties and house rent payments. Passive income is the return on savings accounts. Passive income is created by a limited partnership in which a person owns a share of a company but does not engage in its functioning. Passive income consists of earnings generated from rental property, a limited partnership, or some other enterprise in which a person does not engage actively. Usually, taxes are charged on passive income. Portfolio income is perceived by a few analysts as passive income, and interest and dividends will also be considered as passive income. In order to earn and maintain, passive income needs little to no effort. When an earner puts in one of those little efforts to produce income, it is called progressive passive income. In many ways, a passive income investment can make an investor's life easier. This is true when a hands-off strategy is followed. Examples of passive income investment strategies include - Peer-to-Peer Lending, Real Estate, Dividend Stocks, and Index Funds. These four choices suggest different risk and diversification levels. As with any kind of financial investment, calculating the anticipated returns in relation to a passive income opportunity versus the loss potential is important. The main types of passive activities are explained below:

Cash flows from property income, including cash flows from a property or from any piece of real estate, capital gains, rent through resource ownership such as rental income, and in the form of interest from financial asset ownership.

Trade or business-related activities in which an individual does not engage in a company's operations other than investing during the year.

Royalties, that is, payments initiated by one corporation (the licensee) to another firm/person (the licensor) for the right to use the intellectual property of the latter (music, video, book).

Standards for Material Participation

The standards for material participation include:

- Five hundred plus more hours toward an activity or a business from which you are earning
- If the participation for that tax year has been "substantially all."
- Up to 100 hours of commitment and at least as much as every other person involved in the operation
- Material involvement in at least five of the past 10 tax years
- For personal services initiatives, material engagement at any point in three previous tax years

According to the IRS, there are two passive activity categories. Rentals, including equipment and real estate, are the first type; and businesses are the second type, where the individual does not engage materially on a daily, continuous and significant basis.

Examples of passive activities

The following are considered passive activities:

- Equipment leasing
- Limited partnerships

- Partnerships, S-Corporations, and LLCs where the individuals do not materially participate
- Rental real estate (some exceptions apply)
- Sole proprietorship or farm where the individual does not materially participate

1.4 Taxing of passive income

There are various forms of passive income, ranging from capital gains and dividends. Then the question arises whether the passive income is taxable or not. The brief response is, yes. Tax rates can differ depending on how long the assets are kept, the amount of benefit gained, and/or net income on each form of passive income.

Short-Term Passive Income Tax Rates

For assets retained for a year or less, short-term gains apply and are taxed as ordinary income. In other words, at the same rate as your income tax, short-term capital gains are taxed. The prevailing tax rates for short-term gains are as follows: 10 percent, 12 percent, 22 percent, 24 percent, 32 percent, 35, and 37 percent.

Long-Term Passive Income Tax Rates

Long-term capital gains (assets that are held for more than one year) are taxed at three rates: zero percent, fifteen percent, and twenty percent, based on your income bracket.

Taxing of real estate income

With lower tax rates, investing in real estate and high yield rental assets is now even more advantageous for individuals. The authorized business income deduction is now a twenty percent deduction on the taxable income while buying and holding real estate. This deduction of 20 percent now requires investors to subtract a portion of the real estate investment holdings, which may lead to a higher ROI.

1.5 Why Passive Income Beats Earned Income

income Earned is the income that you earn when you work the job full-time or run a business. Notice that, in most instances, "running business" doesn't require rent real estate corporate. Money gained from royalties, rents, & stakes in the limited partnerships is passive income. Income from the portfolio is the income from interest, dividends, and stock sales capital gains. Earned income would be subject to heavy taxation at all levels. Earned money should be utilized to rapidly create wealth, but your wealth must be transferred into the portfolio and passive income pools in order to reduce your tax position. Earned incomes are subject to FICA taxation and the full marginal income tax rate. There are undoubtedly ways of minimizing tax liability, such as operating an S-earned Corporation's revenue, investing in the firm and currently earning deductible expenditures, etc., but high marginal tax rates would also be subject to net income. The issue with earned money is that you still have to spend more cash in order to minimize tax liability. Passive incomes from the rental property aren't subject to the high operational tax rates. Rental property income is privileged by amortization and depreciation and contributes to a much lesser effective rate of tax.

Let's assume, for instance, you now own a rental property, which nets 10,000 dollars before the depreciation & amortization. Let's just say that $8,000 is the total amount of depreciation and amortization. It leaves with a taxable revenue of $2,000. You can pay a tax equivalent to 740 dollars if you fall in the 37 percent tax bracket. Yet you see an effective rate tax of just 7.4 percent as we equate the $740 with the amount raised ($10,000). If you made the same 10,000 dollars in the earned income, in order to minimize the amount available to tax, you would need to expend more. Otherwise, with $10,000 into taxable income, you'd pay $3,700, meaning you're in 37 percent tax brackets. With the rental real-estate, every year, you don't have to be paying for depreciation. It's a ghostly cost which you have to claim. That's why, from a tax standpoint, passive income knocks out earned income.

1.6 Reasons Why Passive Income Is So Important

It's no wonder passive income's, and for a good cause, one of the most thought about, sought after aspects of personal finance. Passive income will have an incredibly positive effect on only about any financial situation, from creating vast wealth to avoiding a paycheck-to-paycheck lifestyle. But that poses the question: why does passive income matter so much? In short, passive income's essential because in financial life, it provides flexibility, prosperity, and independence. In addition, because your time & resources do not limit passive income, it may have a beneficial and important impact on the ability to build wealth. Passive income, in different words, is 1 of the easiest ways to upgrade the financial condition. But if that's not compelling enough, we've listed the top reasons why passive income's important.

Improved financial stability

One of the most significant milestones you will hit on the road to prosperity is monitory stability. In different words, even if you really can see your financial position and realize, with certainty, that you're capable of coping with a powerful financial storm, so then you're on a very stable path. If you may count on the money rolling inside without having to fight for every cent of it, even more than that, so financial security is just a nearby corner. More money which comes in more you can be secure and comfortable in the finances. It helps you in relaxing, look at the bigger picture, & make smarter financial decisions because you don't have to grind for every dollar you earn, which, in turn, increases your financial health. This is a magnificent little cycle & one of key reasons why passive income is playing such a major role in personal finance.

Less reliance on a paycheck

The discomfort that comes with living paycheck to paycheck is not comparable by any means. And if it is your case, then one of the best moves you can take is to add a bit of the passive income in your life. There is no secret in that sometimes it may get a bit stressful as you trade time for dollars. And the more you will distance yourself from a focus on the next paycheck, the lighter it can be in your life. One of the greatest advantages of passive income is avoiding the paycheck-to-paycheck lifestyle.

It's easier to achieve your goals

Did you ever say to yourself, " only If I made extra money, then I could accomplish my monetary goals much more quickly..."? Well, that's just another explanation why the passive income's so awesome. It doesn't what financial targets you're trying to attain; you can accomplish your goals much quicker if you build certain passive income sources that enable you to make money all the time of day.

More freedom to pursue your passions

You will unexpectedly find yourself with the opportunity to pursue your passions or, for that matter, your ideal job, along the same line as avoiding the paycheck to the paycheck lifestyle, while you get some of the passive income flowing through the bank account. Remember that it's easy to end up trapped in a position you can't bear when you focus on the active income to make ends meet. It is tough enough to leave a career. But it is particularly tough to leave a job if you don't have sufficient money to pay the rent that is due in two weeks. On the other hand, you have the opportunity to do the things you really want to do when you have a stable stream of passive income running into the finances of yours. Passive income, to put plainly, offers you choices. & with those choices, independence comes.

Location independence

Likewise, in many ways, passive income encourages you to live and working from anywhere you like. Since you don't have to work constantly to earn a passive income, so you don't have to be working from a particular position either. You could tour the world if you like, as far as you earn passive income sufficient to support your lifestyle. And plenty of people do.

Early retirement

Retirement is, to some degree, for many people, that may only be done later in life. Although, if you're building any passive income sources, retirement may not be far away as you thought. Really, if you love the thought of retirement at a young age, so then your primary financial priority should be passive income. If it means creating a company that operates even without you needing to be present there, participating in real estate, or a mix of few different sources of income, if you desire to stop working at a young age, passive income is necessary.

More financial margin

 more financial margins you will build in life, better off you will be in personal finance. In different words, the more distance you've between the expenditures & your income, the better it will get for financial life. And when you produce a constant stream of the passive income per month, it becomes much simpler to build the financial margin. Let's say, for instance, that your monthly gross expenditures increase up to 3,000 dollars. Now, if you're earning $4,000 inactive household revenue, then the monthly margin is $1,000. Yeah, that's not bad. However, if you add an additional $2,000 in passive monthly income in to the mix, life just got a lot better.

Reduced stress

There's one unity between all, after everything we've spoken about so far. It's plain; passive revenue has a distinctive way to reduce the financial burden. A passive income life is considerably less difficult than a life deprived of it. Because your financial security, margin, independence, and too much more are improved by passive income, it's only logical that it will help alleviate your financial burden. So, if financial condition makes you feel a little tightened around the collar, you may just want to give passive income a little more priority.

It's exciting

Passive income is not constrained by the effort and time that you can put into it. In different words, at all the hours of night and day, passive income can be earned, including while you are sleeping.

Yet, at the same time, making money is incredibly thrilling. There's nothing like waking up in the morning thinking that you've won a few hundred bucks while you're sleeping. And the more you are enthusiastic about the financial condition, the more probable you are to continue to improve it.

CHAPTER 2: Passive income ideas to help you make money in 2021

Passive income may be a wonderful way of helping you produce more cash flow, & global upheaval created primarily by the pandemic is evidence of the importance of having many income sources. Passive income lets you cross the gap whether you unexpectedly become jobless or even whether you willingly take the time from work away with the pandemic tossing the working condition of most people into disarray. You might get the cash rolling in from passive income even while you follow your primary career, or if maybe you can build up a good passive income pool, you may need a little to kickback. Anyway, you are granted additional protection from passive income. And if you are concerned about being capable of saving enough money to reach your retirement objectives, accumulating capital through passive income also is a tactic that could be appealing to you. Regular earnings from a party other than the employer or the contractor are counted as passive income. IRS (Internal Revenues Service) notes that passive revenue will come from 2 sources: a company or a rental property in which one is not directly participating, such as paying book royalty or dividends on securities. Most individuals agree that passive income's about getting more for nothing. It's got get-wealthy-quick charm, but it also includes work in the end. What you offer is work upfront. You may do any or all the job upfront in practice, but the passive income also requires some extra labor along the way too. To keep the passive dollars flowing, you might have to save your merchandise updated or well-maintained rental property. But if you're dedicated to the approach, it could be a perfect way to make income, and by the way, you'll build some more financial stability for yourself.

2.1 How many streams of income should you have?

"When it comes to generating revenue sources, there is no "one size fits all" advice. How many revenue streams you have can depend on where you are financially and what your potential financial targets are? But it is a decent beginning to get at least a handful. "With multiple lines in the sea, you'll attract more fish. Rental assets, revenue-producing shares, and company ventures are a perfect way to diversify your income stream, in addition to the earned income produced by your human capital. You'll want to make sure, of course, that bringing work into a new passive income stream would not cause you to lose sight of the other sources. So, you want your efforts to be aligned and make sure you pick the right options for your time.

2.2 Passive income ideas for building wealth

So, if you're considering building a passive income source, look at these techniques and absorb what this takes to succeed with them, whereas still recognizing the dangers involved with each strategy.

2.3 Selling information products

One common passive income approach is to produce information products, such as e-books, or video or audio lessons, and then kick back while cash rolls inside from product sale. Via platforms such as Skillshare, Udemy, and Coursera, courses could be distributed & sold. Otherwise, you may think of a "freemium model"-making a free content follow-up and only charging for the more comprehensive details or for the ones who wish to learn more. Language teachers or / & stock-picking guidance, for instance, can use the model. Free material serves as a demonstration of talents and can draw those who want to be going to the next stage. You may use advertising (or sponsor) to make your revenue as the third alternative for this concept while offering information or material on a free forum like YouTube to a growing audience. Take the love of music or video games, for instance, and transform it into the content.

Opportunity

The Information products will have an outstanding revenue stream, so after the initial time outlay, you quickly make money.

Risk

development of this product typically requires a huge amount of effort. And it needs to be good in order to make great money off it. There isn't space out there for trash. If you wish to be competitive, you must create a strong base, advertise your products & prepare for other products. Unless you get very lucky, one product isn't business. Generating more outstanding products is the easiest way to market an established good. You could create a strong income stream once you understand the business model.

2.4 Rental income

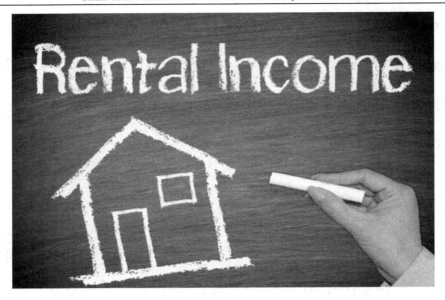

A successful way of earning passive income is to invest in rental properties. But more work is always needed than people expect. You could risk your money if you do not take the time to know how to create a profitable venture.

Opportunity

If you want to earn the passive incomes from the rental properties, then you must determine three things:

- Financial risk of owning property.
- Property's total expenses and costs.
- How much profit you need on investment.

For example, suppose your objective is to make $10,000 in a year in the rental income. At the same time, your property has monthly mortgages of 2,000 dollars and charges another 300 dollars in one month for the taxes & other expenses. In this scenario, you will have to cost 3,133 dollars in the monthly rent for accomplishing your objective.

Risk

few questions should be considered: Is there a marketplace for a property? How if you have a homeowner who pays off the property late or harms it? Suppose you cannot rent the property out? The passive income could be significantly impacted by any of the variables. And pandemic also has raised new threats. You could suddenly have occupants who could no longer afford their rent because of the economic crisis, although you may already have a mortgage of your own to be paying. Or, if earnings fall, you couldn't be capable of renting out homes for as far as you did before. So, to secure yourself, you'll want to consider these threats and have a contingency plan in place.

2.5 Affiliate marketing

However, with affiliate advertising, website owners, "influencers" on social media or blogs support the goods of third parties by including a link to the product on the forum or the social media network. The best-known associate partner maybe Amazon, but Awin, ShareASale and eBay, are all among the bigger brands. And for those watching to develop a following and sell goods, TikTok and Instagram have become major websites. To attract attention to the blog or else steer people to goods and services which they may like, you might also start growing an email list.

Opportunity

The site owner receives a fee if visitors click on the link and make a transaction from a third-party associate. The commission may vary from 3-7 %, so it would obviously need substantial traffic to the site to produce serious revenue. But you could be able to make some serious coin if you may expand the following or even have a more profitable niche (like tech, fitness, or financial services). Affiliate advertising is deemed passive, and, in principle, only by adding a link to your social media platform or website, you will gain money. In fact, if you cannot draw readers to the site to tap on the link and purchase anything, you won't earn anything.

Risk

You'll have to be taking time to develop content and generate traffic if you're just starting out. Building a following will take important time, and you'll need to discover the best formula to reach the crowd, a task that could take a while on its own. Worse, the audience might be likely to fly to the next famous influencer, topic, or social media site after you've expended all that energy.

2.6 Flip retail products

Make use of online sales sites like Amazon or eBay, and offer goods you find nowhere at prices of cut-rate. You will arbitrage the difference between the prices between your purchase & selling, and you will be able to create a following of the people who monitor your transactions.

Opportunity

The price disparities between what you'll find & what average customer will be capable of finding would encourage you to take advantage of them. If you've contact that may help you obtain affordable goods that some other individuals can locate, this might work extremely well. Or you might be capable of uncovering useful products which others have completely missed.

Risk

Although deals can happen online at any moment, you'll probably have to rush to find a reputable source of goods to help keep this strategy passive. And you're just going to have to know the competition so that you don't buy at a price that's too much. Otherwise, in order to market, you can finish up with goods that nobody needs. Moreover, you may be forced to slash the price drastically in order to make the product worthwhile for the buyers.

2.7 Peer-to-peer lending

Peer-to- peer (or P2P) loan's personal loan supports by the intermediary of third-party like LendingClub or Prosper between you & borrower. Funding Circle that targets firms & has greater borrowing caps, and Payout, which targets better collateral losses, are other players.

Opportunity

You generate income as a lender from interest payments made on loans. Yet, you face the possibility of default because the loan is insecure, implying you might end up with nothing. You must do two things to cut the risk:

By paying smaller sums on different loans, diversify the lending portfolio. Minimum investment for each credit is $25 at Prosper.com and LendingClub.

To make educated choices, evaluate old data on the prospective borrowers.

Risk

It takes time to learn the lending metrics of P2P because it's not completely passive, and you'll want to vet your prospective borrowers closely because you ought to pay particular attention to payments earned when you're engaging in several loans. If you intend to create profits, whatever you make for interest can be reinvested. Economic recessions may also make the high-yielding personal loans more likely to default candidates because if the COVID-19 manages to harm the economy at higher than historical rates, these loans will go bad.

2.8 Dividend stocks

The Shareholders in companies with dividend-yielding securities receive a payout from the company at regular intervals. The Companies pay the cash dividend out of the earnings on a quarterly basis, and what you need to be doing is to own stock. Per-share of stock, dividends are funded, meaning the more shares that you hold, the larger your compensation.

Opportunity

Since stock income is not linked to any operation other than the actual financial investment, it may be one of the most passive ways of money-making to own dividend-yielding securities. In your bank account, the money will simply be deposited.

Risk

Choosing the correct stocks is a tricky aspect. Without carefully researching company issuing stock, too many novices leap into the market. You have to study the website of each organization and be acquainted with their financial statements. 2 to 3 weeks you can spend researching each venture. That said, without wasting a massive amount of time analyzing firms, there are some ways to participate in the stocks dividend-yielding. ETFs, or Exchange-traded fund, are strongly recommended for income generation. ETFs are hedge vehicles containing collateral such as equity, commodities & bonds but trading like stocks. The ETFs are an excellent alternative for novices because, due to much lower prices than mutual funds, they are easier to understand, affordable, highly liquid, and offer much higher potential returns. Another key risk's that the stocks or the ETFs will decrease dramatically over short periods of time, particularly in times of volatility, such as when the financial markets were shocked by the Coronavirus crisis in 2020. Economic uncertainty may also cause certain firms to fully cut the dividends, while the diversified funds can experience less of a pinch.

2.9 Create an app

Creating an app may be a method to invest time in advance and then enjoy rewards over time. Your software may be a game or one that allows smartphone users to execute any feature that is difficult to do. Users download it once the application is public, & you can generate revenue.

Opportunity

There's a big upside to an app if you can create something that captures your audience's fancy. You'll think about how it's best to generate revenue. You could run in-application advertisements, for example, or else make users pay a small fee to use the app. You'll definitely add incremental improvements to keep the product current and popular as the app gains attention or you get feedback.

Risk

Perhaps the greatest risk here's that you spend your time unprofitably. You have no financial drawback here if you contribute little to no money to the project (and/or money which you'd have spent otherwise, for instance, on hardware). It's a competitive market, though, and genuinely popular applications must give consumers a persuasive benefit of experience. If your app gathers some data, you would also want to ensure that it is in accordance with privacy rules, which vary across the globe.

2.10 REITs

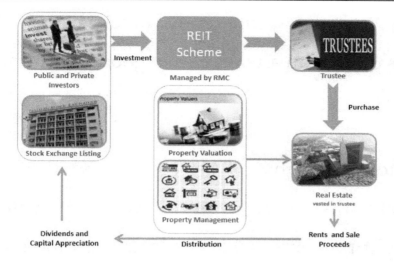

For a corporation that owns and manages real assets, REIT is a real estate investment trust, which is a fancy word. REITs have a special legal arrangement such that although they pass over any of their income to owners, they pay no or little corporate income tax.

Opportunity

In the stock exchange, you can purchase REITs much as every other business or dividend stock. You're going to earn whatever the REITs payout as a payout, and the strongest REITs have an annual record of growing their dividend, meaning over time, you might have an increasing supply of dividends. Specific REITs could be more expensive, like dividend stocks, than buying an ETF composed of hundreds of REIT stocks. Fund offers instant diversification, which is inherently much better than owning specific stocks & you can always earn a good return.

Risk

You'll have to be capable of selecting good REITs, much like dividend stocks, that means you'll have to evaluate any of the firms you might purchase, which indeed is a time-taking process. Also, while it is a passive activity, if you do not know what you're doing, you might lose a lot of money. And neither are REIT dividends safe from difficult economic times. If REIT does not produce enough income, this would possibly have to slash or totally remove its dividend. So just when you want it, most of the passive income could get hit.

2.11 A bond ladder

bond ladder's sequence of bonds maturing over a number of years at various periods. The phased maturities help you to reduce the risk of reinvestment, which is a risk of locking up your cash as bonds offer interest rates that are too low.

Opportunity

bond ladder's a traditional passive investment that for decades has attracted near-retirees and retirees. You will sit back to collect the interest payments, and you "extend the ladder," transferring the principle into different package of bonds as the bond matures. For starters, you could start off with one year, three years, five years, and seven years of bonds. In the year that 1st bond matures, you have two years, four years, and six years of bonds left. You may use proceeds from the newly aged bond to purchase another one year or roll out an eight-year bond with a longer-term, for example.

Risk

Bond ladder reduces one of the big dangers of purchasing bonds, the possibility that you may have to purchase a new bond as the bond develops when the interest rates will not be attractive. Bonds, too, come with the other risks. Although the federal government backs Treasury bonds, corporate bonds aren't, meaning you could risk your principal. And to diversify the exposure & eliminate the risk of someone bond harming your total portfolio, you'll want to buy multiple bonds. Many investors move to bond the ETFs because of these issues, which include a diversified fund of bonds that you may put up on a ladder, removing the possibility that a single bond will harm your returns.

2.12 Invest in a high-yield CD or savings account

Investing in an online bank's high-yield deposit certificate (CD) or savings account will help you to produce passive income and get one of the country best interest rates as well. In order to make money, you won't even have to leave home.

Opportunity

You'll want to do a fast check of the nation's great CD rates or the top savings accounts to make the most of your CD. Going to the online bank instead of the local bank is typically far more advantageous since you will be able to pick the highest rate available in the region. And if the financial firm is backed by the FDIC, you will also receive a fixed return of principal of up to 250,000 dollars.

Risk

Your principal is secure as far as the bank is backed by FDIC and under limits. So, it is just as secure a return as you'll find to invest in a CD or savings account. Nevertheless, though the accounts are secure, these days, they return even less than before. And with Federal Reserve aiming at 2% inflation, the least in the short run, you're going to miss out on inflation. A savings account or CD can, though, yield less than keeping your cash in cash or in a non-interest paying checking account where you will earn about zero.

2.13 Buy Property

Real estate can be a decent way to make a passive income, depending on where you invest and when. There has been a rapid growth in the value of property in common cities such as Toronto- 44 percent in Canada alone in the last five years. You will find some lower-cost properties by purchasing pre-construction condos, which will rise in value by the time it is eventually completed, enabling you to sell the property once it is complete for a profit. Like for all investments, it can be dangerous, so if you're new to the market, it's better to talk to a real estate agent to help you purchase the correct investment property.

2.14 Rent out your home short-term through Airbnb

This simple approach takes advantage of space that you don't need anyway, and converts it into an opportunity to make some money. Whether you're leaving for summer and/or have to be outside of the town for some time, or maybe even you want to fly, try renting your present space out while you're gone.

Opportunity

On a variety of websites, including Airbnb, you may list space and set rental conditions yourself. With limited additional work, you'll receive a check for efforts, particularly if you rent to a tenant who might be in place for a couple of months.

Risk

You do not have a lot of financial downsides here, but it's a gamble that's atypical of the most passive investors to let strangers stay in your house. Tenants can, for instance, even deface or ruin your property or steal valuables even.

2.15 Air BnB Business as a Passive income Strategy

Airbnb is an online website for selling and renting urban homes. It ties hosts and travellers and promotes the rental process without owning any rooms on its own. Moreover, it cultivates a cooperative economy by allowing private flats to be leased by property owners. Airbnb is an internet platform which links individuals that wish to rent the homes to an individual in that area who are searching for a room. It currently surrounds more than 100 thousand cities in the world and 220 countries. The name of the business derives from the "air mattress B and B." Engaging in Airbnb is a way for hosts to gain some money from their home, but with the possibility that it may be damaged by the visitor. The benefit could be comparatively cheap lodging for visitors, but with the possibility that property wouldn't be as advisable as the listing has made it look. For less than the cost of a hotel bed, travellers may also book an Airbnb. The traveler's biggest concern is that the property could not live up to its listing. The primary concern for hosts is that their property may be badly damaged by guests.

Airbnb

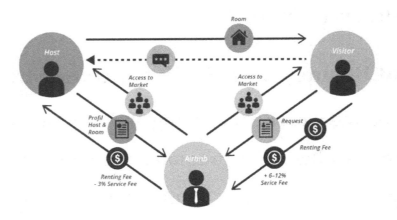

The Advantages of Airbnb

It offers the following advantages:

Wide Selection

Airbnb hosts list several different categories of properties on the Airbnb website, like single rooms, a suite of rooms, moored yachts, , whole homes, studios, houseboats, even castles.

Free Listings

In order to list the assets, hosts don't have to be paying. Listings may contain written descriptions, captioned photographs, and user profiles so prospective visitors can have the knowledge about hosts a little better.

Hosts Can Set Their Own Price

It is the host's prerogative to decide how much to charge per night, per week, or /and per month.

Customizable Searches

The Guests can filter the Airbnb database and not only through date & location, however also by price, property type, amenities, and the host's language. To further limit their search, they may also add keywords (such asclose to the Louvre').

Additional Services

Airbnb has increased its services to include events and restaurants in recent years. In addition to a list of available hotels for the dates they expect to visit, individuals searching by the venue can see a list of opportunities provided by nearby Airbnb hosts, like classes and sightseeing. Restaurant listings also contain Airbnb hosts' reviews.

Protections for Guests and Hosts

As a protection for customers, before transferring the funds to the host, Airbnb keeps the guest's payment for 24 hours following check-in. For guests, Airbnb's Host Guarantee program "provides security for up to $1,000,000 in damage to covered property in eligible countries in the rare incident of guest damage."

The disadvantages of Airbnb

It has the following demerits:

What You See May Not Be What You Get

Booking Airbnb accommodation is not like booking a space with a big hotel chain, where you have a fair promise that the property will be as described. Individual hosts, though some may be more truthful than others, create their own listings. Previous visitors, however, often post updates about their experiences, which may offer a more critical perspective. To make sure the listing is correct, review the reports of other guests who have stayed at the Airbnb house.

Potential Damage

The greater concern for hosts is potential that their property will be damaged. Although most stays go without incident, when the Airbnb hosts assumed they were renting to a peaceful household, there are reports of entire houses being trashed by thousands of partygoers. Some insurance is offered by Airbnb's Host Guarantee program, mentioned above, but it does not cover anything, like cash, rare artwork, jewellery, and pets. Also, hosts whose homes are destroyed can experience significant inconvenience.

Added Fees

A number of extra charges are imposed by Airbnb (just like, of course, hotels and other lodging providers). To cover Airbnb's customer care and other programs, travelers pay a guest management fee of 0 percent to 20 percent on top of the reservation fee. Prices are shown in the currency that the customer chooses, provided it is sponsored by Airbnb. Banks or issuers of credit cards can, where applicable, add fees. And though listings are free, to cover the cost of handling the transaction, Airbnb charges a service fee of at least 3 percent for each reservation.

It Isn't Legal Everywhere

Would-be hosts need to review their municipal zoning codes before listing their properties on Airbnb to make sure it is legal to rent their properties. To receive special permits or licenses, hosts may also be required.

2.16 Advertise on your car

By merely driving your car across town, you can be able to raise some additional income. Contact a specialized advertisement firm to determine your commuting patterns, like when and how many miles you drive. The firm will "wrap" your car with the ads at no cost to you if you're a match with one of their advertisers. Newer vehicles are being searched by agencies, and drivers should have a clear driving record.

Opportunity

If you're still putting in the miles anyway, though you may have to get out and drive, then this is a perfect way to earn hundreds every month at little to no added expense. It is reasonable to pay drivers by the mile.

Risk

Be extra cautious about locating a reputable operation to work with if this idea seems good. In this space, many fraudsters set up schemes to try to bilk you out of thousands.

2.17 Invest in Stocks

When you look at the wealthiest people in the world, it's pretty fair to conclude that their deep, endless savings accounts are a result of their major investment in stocks. Warren Buffett reads 500 pages a day, but he doesn't read your usual mystery novel. He reviews the annual corporate reports. He better knows whether or not a company is doing well by reviewing annual reports each day, which helps him improve his decision to invest in stocks. While the act of investing in stocks is very passive, the analysis that goes into it is active. Nevertheless, investing in shares will help you gain passive income that goes well beyond what your value is worth at your 9 to 5 work. So, if you enjoy reading about the success of different firms, consider this passive income approach.

2.18 Make Your Car Work for You

Driving is another everyday practice that you can translate into passive income. When you're just walking around, why not pick up a commuter or two to run errands? Uber can help you make money by taking people to their designated destination by driving your vehicle. You may also put ads on your vehicle to collect cash as you drive around. When your car is not used while you're on holiday, driving, or just during a normal workday, it will still make money. You will make thousands of dollars with an app like Getaround by renting out your car if you're not using it. Plus, drivers of Getaround vehicles get the best parking spaces in town, a $50 monthly rental credit on any vehicle they want, and one million U.S. dollars in primary insurance coverage.

2.19 Sell your Videos

We live in a day and age where video content fascinates hundreds and thousands of humans. You would want to take out your phone and hit the record if you still find yourself in the middle of drama and excitement. To allow you to make some passive income, you can sell stored content. Why? It is because the video can be sold to a news site. And you can make some recurring income for weeks, months, and maybe even years if the video takes off. Of course, being at cultural gatherings such as marches, rallies, and festivals is the best way to get in on the action. You'll find ways for your material to be sold anywhere there's controversy. And corporations will pay you to make viral videos along with providing a share of total earnings if you are successful at creating engaging content.

2.20 Create YouTube Videos

The passive income source that just keeps on giving is YouTube. You'll find that you can make a regular income from your YouTube channel, from funded videos to ad sales. Creating videos on a regular basis for a long time is the key to creating a profitable YouTube channel. If you stick with it in the long run, you will finally start reaping the benefits of passive income.

2.21 Write an eBook

In 2009 and 2010, e-books came onto the scene and are now a hugely successful content medium. While they first became popular a few years ago, to this day, there is still a very decent chunk of individuals who make passive income from writing e-books. It's an insanely dynamic business, of course. Yet, you might find yourself with a nice slice of the profits if your writing chops are stellar. You could build a fanbase of loyal readers by designing how-to e-books on famous niches and marketing them.

2.22 Sell Digital Products

You can make digital goods if you're trying to create your own products rather than selling someone else's. You can sell your digital goods online using Shopify. From e-books, educational classes, PDFs, custom graphic templates, stock images, or some other digital goods, digital products will contain anything. Selling these items is the epitome of passive income, and with immediate updates, the whole operation can be streamlined on Shopify.

Car Wash

Car wash is a perfect way to earn a semi-passive income. Although a car wash will need daily cleaning, it is something you can either contract out or do once a week. We are talking about the very simple car wash that is cinderblocks, a pressure washer, and the powered coin, as a side note. It's certainly a corporation vs. a passive income stream if you're trying to run a drive-through car wash.

2.23 CPC Ads (Cost Per Click)

You get really paid whenever anyone clicks on your link and signs up for something or orders something through affiliate ads. On the other hand, show advertisements charges depend on the volume of traffic and eyeballs that you receive on their ads. On the other hand, for CPC advertisements, also known as "cost per click" ads, anytime someone clicks on an ad, you get paid no matter what they do after that. You don't have to hope or pray that they're buying anything or signed up for something. Any single click takes money into your account with the bank. Does that mean that all day long you can go to your own website and click on ads? It is not realistic since the corporation will inevitably find out what you are doing and cut you off. With all that in mind, it should not be a part of your plan here to click on your own ads. Instead, aim to build up traffic so that more and more viewers every day see the ads.

2.24 Minimize your taxes on passive income

A passive income may be a wonderful side-income generation strategy, but you can still create a tax burden for your effort. But by setting yourself up as a business and building a savings portfolio, you can reduce the tax bite and plan for your future, too. However, this solution will not work with all these passive strategies because to qualify. You will have to be a legal organization.

Register with the IRS to make your company receive a tax identification number.

Then call a broker, such as Charles Schwab or Fidelity, who will open a self-employed retirement account.

Determine the type of savings account that will fit well for your needs.

CHAPTER 3: Airbnb Offers The Best Passive Income Generation Strategy

rental vacation industry is rising quickly. It is real quick indeed as a matter of fact. The sector is currently generating 57,669 million dollars in sales, according to recent analysis reports from Statista.com. The revenue is awaited to grow to a market value of 74,005 million dollars by 2023 and is projected to see an average growth rate of 6.4 percent. This data illustrates just how broad & robust the holiday rental management industry is. And you should expect demand for Airbnb property management to pursue to grow over the coming years with the growth of Airbnb rental properties in recent years. Therefore, if one day you are aiming to become a manager of Airbnb property, now is a great time to be entering the business. But how are you able to get started? We will supply you with what you have to know regarding how to be an Airbnb vacation rental property manager. We're going to teach you what this takes to handle rental Airbnb properties, particular instruments you're going to be needing before you start, and stop points for the beginners for achieving successful property management. So, without further ado, over here are all six steps to beginning an Airbnb property management career in real estate.

3.1 Understand the Vacation Rental Industry

Just like some other business, without learning at least the fundamentals of this area, you can't succeed. However, no formal qualification is necessary to become an Airbnb property manager, and many find success with the only diploma of high school in this profession. Thorough knowledge of how the holiday rental industry & Airbnb run is what you need to have. So, if you don't already have it, having this information now is the 1st step to being the manager of the Airbnb properties. Ideally, as Airbnb hosts yourself, you should have some experience. If you've already hosted your rental property on Airbnb, run it yourself, you can show to potential buyers which you know exactly what you are doing. Furthermore, this will allow you to be prepared better to predict challenges, recognize potentially troublesome travelers, and cope with common issues. But if you don't have the experience, through online guides and classes, you can empower yourself about the rental vacation industry & how Airbnb works.

There are plenty of those out there that can help you create a good base on which you have to learn. For instance, you may take marketing coursework to know how to extend your scope and get bookings more and business courses to know how to manage a company, keep records, & file tax. As an Airbnb property manager, it'll help you improve your creditability. Before you start, another significant point to learn is where the Airbnb hosts invest in rentals for the short-term. You'll know the place to find customers looking for management support with this detail.

3.2 Create a Maintenance Management System

Managing rental of short-term rentals ensures that you'll get visitors checking in & out repeatedly. One of many duties of the property managers, of course, is to review property before visitors visit & after they depart. Every now & then, operators of holiday rentals must also conduct repairs to ensure that the properties are in perfect shape. This is vital to ensure the happiness of both your customer and guests. For instance, imagine having visitors who had parties and had rental property trashed before leaving. Nobody with such a situation is going to be happy to step into a rental. As a consequence, before addressing the issue, the manager of Airbnb property can never leave the maintenance as an afterthought or even wait for the property owner to receive several inquiries. In addition, to offer high-quality care on their behalf, great short-term property rental operators often work alongside a dependable maintenance team. Your staff should include, among others, plumbers, house cleaners, and electricians. For any check-in, these entities will ensure that Airbnb assets you handle are tip to top.

3.3 Put Together a Vacation Rental Marketing Strategy

The most significant tasks of property managers are promoting and selling holiday rentals to attract prospective visitors. Today, there are millions of listings on Airbnb & more rental sites for the short-term, which is creating rivalry among the Airbnb hosts. It is why one of the first things potential users would like to know is how you're going to get reservations and increase their occupancy rates for Airbnb. As a consequence, you must have a basic comprehension of tactics and methods for property marketing. Therefore, having a marketing campaign that will draw Airbnb visitors to the holiday rentals you run is the next step towards being Airbnb properties manager. Start by writing an enticing listing that will maximize the probability of retaining a high rate of occupancy & a positive flow of cash. To make rental properties under your management stand out, think about investing in advanced photography & videography facilities, also branding services. Moreover, selling holiday rentals suggests that you have to go outside the listing platform. It is why active rental managers of Airbnb use social media and also SEO to meet the target tenant audience. If you don't know how it works, before you begin handling rentals in the short term, we strongly suggest that you begin to read about real estate marketing.

3.4 Invest in Property Management Tools

You can handle them with hard work and a few spreadsheets as you become manager of Airbnb property for the first time when you have only some rental properties underneath your belt. This becomes difficult, though, as you continue to add more assets to manage. How are thirty check-ins & cleanings going to be done in 1 day? At an early point, it is best to begin thinking about it so that you're planning yourself & your company for success and expansion. Using real estate management of property software that allows to automate & remain structured is the best approach for this.

In order to operate their businesses more effectively, modern holiday rental property supervisors rely a lot on technology. There are several high-tech solutions that make it easy to handle Airbnb rental, from the smart lock to invoicing, pricing, and the guest screening software systems. You will even find holiday rental apps which will synchronize schedules and handle multiple Airbnb profiles for free from different platforms. Not only does the use of such instruments make your life more effective as a manager of real estate properties, but they can also give you the strategic edge to keep rising. Mashboard, for instance, is a software that lets managers of Airbnb property connect with their customers and find the right properties for those to expand their business.

3.5 Outline Your Guest Management Strategy

Amazing client care is one of the abilities that any manager of real estate property wants to provide when handling both conventional and holiday rentals. It is how effective operators of Airbnb assets set themselves away from the audience. A good selling point, particularly for Airbnb travelers, is customer service that goes beyond and beyond. Getting a guest engagement plan ensures that during their visit, the services can be open to visitors and their demands at whatever time. Expect the short-term visitors to have to inquire or inquire over something. You must be capable of responding in a timely way to such unannounced requests. How can you treat a case, for instance, where the visitor has misplaced keys to a holiday rental and can't get in? There will be a contingency in it and other cases for a successful Airbnb property manager. In addition, to manage communication with visitors, managers of top-performing properties also have automation tech systems in place. Airbnb guests really enjoy great customer service & show this by posting favorable feedback. This, in essence, helps to get more bookings & boost cash flow, that will surely make the customers happier. As you could see, one of the most critical skills for good management of Airbnb property is definitely customer service, so don't consider it as an afterthought.

3.6 Set a Reasonable (But Competitive) Price

To become a manager of Airbnb property, the only thing you need is a pricing plan. Usually, the holiday rental manager takes a percentage cut from the real host's secured rental fee. A selection of online outlets recommends anywhere from ten to twenty-five percent. At the same time, others believe that more consumers would be drawn by charging the lowest price; that isn't the case. Customers base their options on the quality o facilities rendered by property managers-not dependent on costs. Thus, providing the lowest price means that you don't have top-tier facilities for owners of Airbnb property. You need to take several factors into account in order to fix the correct price. First of all, as stated, is what kind of services you are providing. Naturally, for something that you don't sell, you do not charge. Look at experience instead, what distinctive points of selling you may give, and set rate accordingly. The local economy and what the other rental property (short-term) managers in the area charge, the seasonal demands, also current events, you will need to remember. Ultimately, you need to set a fair price which you are sure will be getting you back that your service is worth.

3.7 How an Airbnb Business Works

Nearly everyone has listened to Airbnb or has used it. It is the platform for online home rentals that helps hosts renting vacant private short-term accommodation from a single room to whole homes. Airbnb launched in 2007 & has expanded exponentially to have listings in further than 65 thousand cities in the world with more than three million available properties. Here is how to start a sustainable Airbnb company if you have sufficient rental space and are searching for additional revenue. Through uploading photographs and details of the room for rent, the first move is to be a host on Airbnb and register the home. When an Airbnb property's listed, travelers searching for a room in the host area will access it. Guests may use a number of requirements to check for Airbnb listings, like:

- Availability dates

- Destination

- No. Of rooms, such as bedrooms and washrooms

- Price

- Host language

- Amenities such as hot tub, breakfast, pets allowed, and etc.

- Facilities like air conditioning, parking,etc.

Prior to booking the chosen space through the Airbnb guest may establish a contact with hosts directly for gathering additional information through the Airbnb service of messaging.

Access

Along with browser access, Airbnb offers mobile applications for Android and Apple IOS devices.

Security

For security purposes, the hosts are expected to provide Airbnb with appropriate identification. Travelers should post the reviews of hotels to create a trustworthy group (and the hosts may review the guests). The Reviews aren't anonymous.

Guest Services

Airbnb offers a stable payment platform for the guest's calmness of mind, and fees to the hosts are deferred until 24 hr after the arrival of the guest. In the event that any difficulties are faced during the renting time, Airbnb has a 24-hour hotline for the guest.

Fees

Host sets the price for lodging. Moreover, Airbnb charges under-mentioned fees:

Host: Three % transaction payment fee

Guest: six to twelve % booking fee

The Hosts can also ask for a security deposit & could well charge a cleaning fee.

Taxes

Airbnb could apply provincial, state, or city taxes for guest bookings depending on the jurisdiction.

Travelers Prefer Airbnb Rentals

One of the best things about operating an Airbnb company is that, for several reasons, travelers choose Airbnb over motels, hotels, or hostels:

Cost: Usually, Airbnb rent is much inexpensive than a similar hotel room. In certain instances, an entire house may be rented through Airbnb for the cost of a single suite of the hotel, depending on the location.

Living locally: Living the life of a local person is the key advantage of the Airbnb service. Most guests of Airbnb choose to stay inside the community and explore the destination way the locals do, instead of renting a generic hotel room.

Privacy: customers of Airbnb are not continuously surrounded by visitors and workers at the hotel.

Peace & quiet: the Airbnb rents are usually more secure and do not suffer from loud hotel events, such as guest exits early in the morning, young children, maid service, and traffic.

Witness what you get already: Unlike a hotel where you can see a snapshot of similar rooms on their Airbnb page at best, you get full images and explanations of the real premises.

Diversity: From yachts and boathouses to castles and lighthouses, Airbnb has an immense variety of available accommodations.

Home comforts: Airbnb has a homey atmosphere of a real living space instead of generic hotel spaces (few have resident pets even). Kitchens allow the guests to cook their own food if they desire to save money on outside dining or have dietary issues.

Friends or Family: Through Airbnb, you may save a lot of money by renting a whole apartment/ house/condo rather than the multiple rooms of a hotel for family and friends.

Is Renting Your Space Permissible or Advisable?

Ensure you're legally permitted to be an Airbnb host into jurisdiction before you plan to start an Airbnb business, & you're prepared to respect local laws & regulations. Depending on the state/ city or regional rules, municipal laws governing the hosting of paid visitors will vary greatly; they are absolutely banned in some areas whilst they're subject to occupancy tax in others if space is condominium or apartment, check to view if it is allowed to sub-let the premises. There are also regulations in place for apartment landlords & condominium societies to prohibit an owner from renting the units out as Airbnb rooms. Renting your apartment out without the knowledge of your landlord will have you evicted. Neighborhood ties are also a significant concern. In the area, a few inconsiderate or loud Airbnb guests will easily turn you in a pariah. If none of the challenges are insurmountable, it could be an outstanding opportunity of home-found business to become an Airbnb host.

Are You Committed to Becoming a Host

There are a variety of additional concerns to remember prior to making a definitive decision to host Airbnb:

Would you like to start a business? Then Starting an Airbnb company is like establishing any business- that you need enthusiasm, entrepreneurial spirit, & the ability to make the required effort, starting off with doing relevant background analysis and developing business plans.

Do you've energy? It could take a great amount of time to be a landlord, particularly for the short-term rents. You'll have to:

- Manage reservations and reply to interactions with prospective tenants.
- Plan to meet the guests to give out or receive keys
- ensure the property, including fresh linen, breakfast supplies, is cleaned properly and ready for the arrival of the guest (if applicable)
- Fix some property maintenance problems such as plumbing and pest control, electrical & appliance repair
- Be accessible to the visitors on a 24 into 7 basis if the property has any problems.

Demand: The deciding factor in the popularity & price of rented accommodation is visitor demand. The highest places for rental returns are:

 sought-after tourist destinations with high hotel rates (famous neighborhood ranks higher on the Airbnb searches)

situated Centrally, close to visitor attractions, shops & public transport,

Featuring panoramic views and facilities like parking, balconies, etc.

Seasonality: Demand for the property in the northern hemisphere will definitely drop drastically in winters (unless you're renting a ski chalet). In comparison, rental accommodation demand in colder southern locations (like Arizona) decreases dramatically in summers.

What are the marketing aims? Are you trying to earn a little cash or create a stable income on the side? The financial portion of the business plan must show target market analysis and reasonable forecasts of your property's future rental income. The income from the Airbnb contract depends upon:

Before you start thinking about leaving your job & making a living through running an Airbnb company, make sure that by seeing rental prices & booking regularity for comparing Airbnb listings of your area, you carefully examine the revenue potential of your property.

Extra costs: In addition to booking fees paid by Airbnb, there are extra costs involved with Airbnb hosting, including:

Insurance: Standard insurance plans for homeowners do not include the use of the property for commercial uses, including renting on Airbnb. Airbnb has a free host compensation insurance policy in Canada, U.K., U.S., and many other nations, offering up to 1 million dollars in guarantees against personal harm or property loss. If your place is not protected by Airbnb policies, please contact your insurance provider to see if there is sufficient coverage.

Business Licenses: Airbnb hosts are being required by more & more cities to hold a business license.

Repair and Cleaning: You want to keep rental properties in top condition all the time in order to keep your Airbnb host ranking at a high standard, which includes extensive cleaning during guest stays and daily repairs. The charges will contribute to your expenses if you have to sub-contract cleaning and repair duties.

Listing and Pricing Your Property on Airbnb

Accurately describe the place and make this stand out. Note that Airbnb is an online marketplace & you have to be thinking like a realtor to make listing stick out from the competition in order to optimize guest interest in your house. Start by looking at the same Airbnb listings inside the region and consider the amenities/features and prices listed. If this works, make a spreadsheet. The definition of your listing must be precise, comprehensive, complete, and highlight, which makes it special. Comprehensively define the facilities and functionality of your room also as any regulations or preferences of visitors. Providing high-quality photographs of the room is incredibly necessary. Airbnb has specialist availability of photography service in certain places if you are unable to do this yourself.. You don't want visitors to be upset because the room isn't as advertised or you've exaggerated amenities. Note that the guest rankings would be partially dependent on the accuracy of your listing description.

Price Your Listing Competitively

You should also get an idea of how to market your listing from your analysis of similar listings. It needs to be competitively priced to keep the property consistently booked (and increase profits).

Improving Your Host Ranking

Higher the property pops up in rankings, the more probable it's to be chosen by visitors, so having good rankings of Airbnb is crucial to the success of Airbnb business. Airbnb rankings are like internet search rankings. And by building confidence and offering a fantastic experience to your visitors, you will boost your rankings.

Build Trust

Airbnb community's based on trust and guests would be searching for hosts with contact information, credentials, and favorable feedback.

Verification

For the new hosts, verification is highly essential: change your profile and include other details like the email address, phone number, Facebook profile, and etc. For giving prospective visitors some confidence that you're a reliable host.

References

You should post the references from colleagues, co-workers, relatives, business partners, etc., to build more trust. For the other Airbnb users, you may even write references.

Provide Great Customer Service

Like any entrepreneur would tell you, the cornerstone of any successful business is customer care, and becoming an Airbnb host has no difference. Positive ratings, better search scores, and more bookings reward hosts of Airbnb who have the best experience of the guest. The hosts with the most popular are:

Responsive

The Hosts that can not be bothered for responding in a timely manner (or at some) to inquiries are a big turnoff for visitors. In reality, Airbnb keeps track and rates your replies to guests accordingly. With higher search rankings and improved bookings, the host who has the highest ratings of response is awarded. At all times, Airbnb mobile application will help you to keep connected. All the time when visitors are present, be available through phone and check up with them on extended trips and see if there's something more you may do to maximize the services.

Update Their Calendars Regularly

Keeping your calendar current, also enhancing the guest experience, boosts the Airbnb rankings of search.

Fix All Problems quickly

When a guest mentions problems like leaky taps or a burned-out lightbulb, it should be repaired promptly and render an apology to the guest. Sure ways to boost the guest rankings is to provide five-star service.

Act on Their Reviews

Fix the issue and benefit from the failures if a visitor writes a critical review. React to complaints all the time in a respectful way.

3.8 The Bottom Line

In real estate, there are many ways of earning profits. The growing success in the U.S. housing sector of Airbnb and other short-term rentals has created opportunities not just for real estate developers but also for property managers. Today, there is a great demand for vacation rental managers, and industry analysts expect that over the coming years, there will be national growth. Therefore, imagine being an Airbnb property manager if you're looking for a profitable means of generating passive income.

Conclusion

In a nutshell, passive income is money that comes at regular intervals without having to invest a large amount of work into generating it. By blogging, one method of producing passive income may be achieved. If you've figured out how to produce content that attracts sufficient traffic to the host advertising, you can make a product that your customers would want to purchase. From a basic e-book to a sophisticated app that produces sales for several years after it is released, passive income could be anything. Similarly, people have a lot of things, and they still look for cheap places to store this. What might be simpler than asking people to pay you for storing their things? An investment on a large-scale in purchasing storage facilities (with the cash) or anything simple like offering the basement or the shed might entail creating passive income by offering storage. All you'll need is to make sure their goods are clean and stable. You will make money by selling them to others against such charges if you've any things that you don't use at all times, which others will love to borrow. As rental items, useful items such as a tractor, trailer, kayak, trampoline, or your own lawn even may give you passive income. With the support of platforms like Airbnb, this also involves renting spare rooms out in your home. Upload the pictures of items, fix a date, and tell the world they're ready for the rent on your favorite social networking site. The reason why it is necessary to have passive income is that it will help increase your financial consistency. The more passive income you make, the easier it becomes to be consistent with your financial life, from consistently saving to consistently spending to consistently donating. One of the strongest and most relevant aspects of a sound financial condition is passive income. It is beneficial for you in several ways, from enhancing your financial health to reducing your financial burden.

The Complete Startup Crash Course

How Digital Entrepreneurs Use Continuous Innovation to Create Radically Successful Businesses and How You Can Copy Them

By

Jake Folger

Table of Contents

Introduction 408

CHAPTER 1: Lean Start-up 412

  1.1 Learn to build a Lean Start-up 415

CHAPTER 2: Importance of Market Research 423

  2.1 Develop an understanding of the Market Research..........424

  2.2 Collection of information through Market Research 425

CHAPTER 3: Digital Entrepreneurship 432

CHAPTER 4: The Best Business 443

  4.1 Start your own online Dropshipper business 444

  4.2 How to Find and Work with Reliable Dropshipping Suppliers

 458

Conclusion 492

Introduction

An entrepreneur is a clever fellow who wants to create an enterprise in circumstances of intense complexity. More than often, a company's priorities don't always fit the ways people need or want a service or product. New products and new projects stall at some stage or don't live up to their full potential. It is where the Lean Startup model comes in. The core philosophy behind the Lean Startup model, which is an evolution of astute businessmen's management style, promotes an atmosphere that allows new concepts to thrive while finding ways to reduce waste. Sometimes as challenging as it may be, the only way ahead might be to ditch what you have and start again from scratch. In stagnation or unfavorable economic conditions, we all are advised to do something for less. All of you must be well aware of the idea of having to do a great many things with little money along with reinventing ourselves or our systems to cater to the ever-changing needs of our consumers. Astute entrepreneurs have insight plus know means and strategies of evaluating success.

Additionally, they can determine the next steps of action, find shortcomings, and make commensurate changes to change with the changing circumstances and atmosphere to develop and further innovate. It is generally accepted that hard work and determination, combined with historical predictors, are automatic performance measures. However, the future is uncertain, and the old methods of working are just not applicable. The management of the previous century does not work with the instability of today's economy. Frustrated with conventional strategies and approaches to entrepreneurship, the creative entrepreneurs begin looking for other ideas to bring to the test. They all have come up with the Lean Startup model that focuses on innovation and getting to know customers' needs and habits to create a better product or service. It focuses on the correct process, that is, to work better and not simply harder to solve difficult circumstances. Whether it is a start-up of tech, small businesses, or a project inside a big corporation, Launching a new organization has long been a hit-or-the-miss proposition. According to the decades-old formula, you always write a marketing strategy, pitch this to the investors, build a team, launch a product, & start to sell it as much as you possibly can. & somewhere in the chain of events, you will inevitably suffer fatal failure. Most of the time, the odds aren't in your favor. A recent study by Harvard Business School reveals that 75 percent of all start-ups crash. But lately, the important countervailing factor has arisen, one which can make the task of beginning a business less dangerous. It's a technique called the "leaned start-up," & it encourages experimentation over the elaborate organizing, customer input over intuition, & iterative designs over conventional "big designs upfront" expansion. While methodology's only a few years old, and its constructs like "minimum viable product" & "pivoting" — have rapidly taken hold in the start-up community, & business schools have already started modifying the curricula to explain them. The lean start-up movement is changing traditional thinking around entrepreneurship. Newest ventures of every sort try to boost the chances of survival by pursuing the ideals of struggling quickly and learning quickly. Despite methods name, some of the greatest payoffs can be earned by the major corporations that embrace it in the long run. This book shall explore in deep as to how digital entrepreneurs utilize continuous creativity to build fundamentally profitable companies and how you can imitate them.

CHAPTER 1: Lean Start-up

lean start-up is a strategy used on behalf of an established business to create new companies or launch a new product. Method of lean start-up advocates the development of products that customers have already shown they want so that as quick as product's launched, a market will already exist. It is in contrast to creating a brand and then hoping the demand would emerge. Developers of Product can measure consumers' interest in a product & determine how the product may need to be clarified by employing lean start-up principles. The process is referred to as validated learning & can be used to prevent unnecessary usage of the resources in the creation & development of products. If innovation is likely to be failed by lean start-ups, it'll fail cheaply and quickly instead of gradually & expensively, thence the word "fail-fast." Lean start-up's example of customers dictating the type of goods that the respective markets deliver, instead of deciding what products they would be provided.

LEAN STARTUP

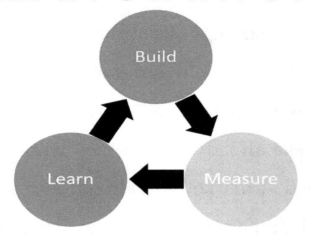

Lean Start-ups vs. the Traditional Businesses

When it comes to hiring, the lean entrepreneurship approach often differentiates itself from the conventional company model. Lean start-ups attract employees who can adapt, learn, and work efficiently, whereas conventional firms recruit employees based on knowledge and expertise. Lean start-ups employ multiple financial recording metrics also; they concentrate on the customer acquisition expenses, lifetime consumer value, client churn rate, & how viral the product maybe, instead of relying on revenue statements, balance sheets, and cash flow statements.

Requirements for the Lean Startup

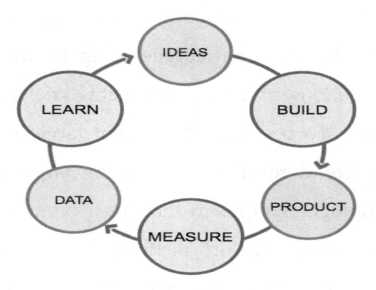

Experimentation is perceived by the lean start-up approach to be extra valuable than comprehensive planning. A waste of time is viewed as five years of business plans designed on unknowns, and consumer response is paramount. Instead of the business models, Lean start-ups use business concepts focused on assumptions that are easily checked. Before proceeding, data doesn't have to be completed; it only has to be more than enough. The start-up easily changes to limit the losses & return to the production of goods consumers want when customers do not respond. Failure is generally regarded as the rule. Following this strategy, entrepreneurs validate their theories by engaging with prospective consumers, investors, & partners to evaluate their responses to product specifications, packaging, delivery, and customer retention. With the data, entrepreneurs make tiny changes to goods called iterations, and big adjustments known as pivots fix any major issues. To best suit the current target consumer, this testing process could result in exchanging target customers or altering the product. A problem that must be addressed is first defined by the lean start-up method. It then produces the minimum workable product or smallest product type that enables entrepreneurs to offer prospective buyers. This strategy is simpler and less risky than checking final product production, and decreasing the risk that start-ups face reduces their usual high failure rate. Lean start-ups redefine start-up as an enterprise aiming for scalable growth models, not the one that is determined to follow an established business strategy.

1.1 Learn to build a Lean Start-up

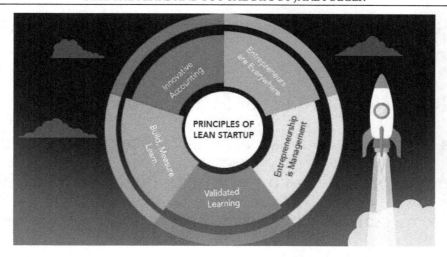

Do you know the 75 percent of all start-ups usually fail? You're likely to encounter obstacles, difficulties, and roadblocks of all sorts, no matter which type of company you're beginning to build. You could spend years on one business idea to fail if you've followed the conventional start-up formula of drafting a business plan, setting up to the investors, developing your product, & selling it. The Lean Startup Methodology is an inexpensive, fast, and less risky technique to carry your business concept to the market. Launching some form of business has always been risky. "Instead of using more traditional methods, the main distinction between building lean start-ups with Lean Start-ups Methodology is that entrepreneurs must ask themselves that "Should the products be built? "instead of "Can the products be built? It is about identifying a problem, validating the question, and creating a product that can fix the problem to create a lean start-up. When you create a lean start-up, you need to ensure that your product is consistently checked and verified, so your product's in the customer's hands as quick as possible. Subsequently, Lean Startups Methodology would help you optimize business growth. To begin creating a lean start-up, here are three moves entrepreneurs may take: Find, Execute, & Validate it.

Find the Business Idea

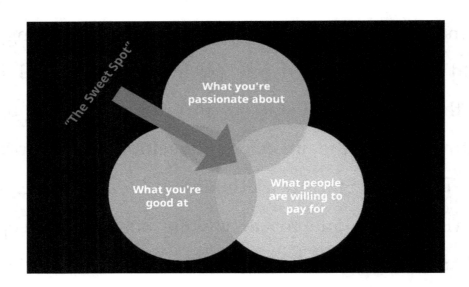

the big question is not: "could this be built?" or "Should this be built?" "It puts us in an extraordinary historical moment: the success of collective imaginations depends on our future prosperity. It's important to determine whether the product can fix is significant enough for clients to choose to buy it while selecting a company concept to pursue using the Lean Startup Approach. It can be easy to find a business idea, so it's essential to pay attention to the challenges people face daily. For the product to gain momentum, clients must be aggressively looking for solutions to a problem. It is time to execute the project after you settle on a business idea.

Execute the Business Idea

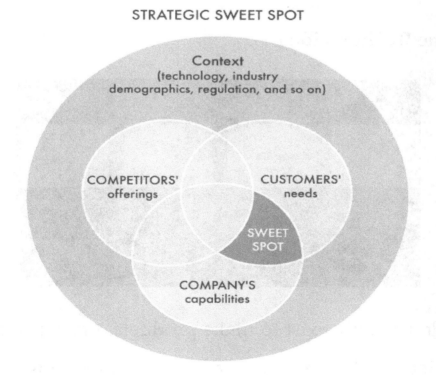

Next, you can create minimum viable products (MVP). MVP is a version of a product you plan to create, allowing the team to quickly gather as much knowledge as possible on your prospective consumers and their input on the product. Any Lean Start-up Philosophy advocates recommend that you take the "Kickstarter Approach" for your product, i.e., start selling the product before it's completed to build market value and drive demand in the product while collecting funds for the Lean Startup. It's time to validate the business plan once the business ideas are executed.

Validate the Business idea

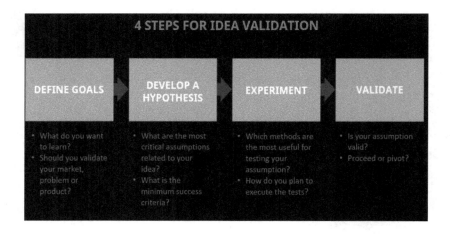

Start-ups do not only exist to make products, make profits, or even support clients. Their main target is to know how to create a profitable enterprise. By conducting multiple trials that allow the entrepreneurs to verify each aspect of the vision, this learning can be scientifically validated. Product validation's a crucial step in the development of profitable Lean Start-ups. In this phase, in the real world, it's time to play with the business idea. Early adopter or otherwise, test the MVP with actual consumers in the industry to see whether the product is feasible and to gain knowledge that you could study. Use this knowledge to determine if you can continue building your product, modifying the product, or pivoting your market plan. If the findings are mainly good from checking MVP in the marketplace, continue to develop your products using your initial approach while integrating tester input. If the outcomes of marketplace MVP research are favorable and unfavorable, tweak the product or business plan to make the product ideally suited to your consumers' desires and needs. If the findings are mainly disappointing from checking MVP in the industry, it's time for pivoting your product & business plan. To adapt vision to suit the desires and the needs of the clients would entail a radical change in your technique and work. Under certain circumstances, mainly unfavorable reviews would indicate that Lean Startup can fully quit the marketplace.

Why should one build a Lean Start-up?

Start-up's different way of seeing at the growth of innovative and new products, all at the same time highlighting rapid iteration & customer insights, huge vision & great ambition. Building a lean start-up is an ideal opportunity for entrepreneurs who need to start an inexpensive company and easily bring them to market. Building lean start-up essentially shortens product creation times and means that developers build products through experimentation & validated learning that satisfy consumer needs.

Example of Lean Startup

For instance, a healthy meal delivery service that targets busy, single twenty-somethings in the urban areas could learn that thirty-something wealthy mothers of newborns in the suburbs have a better market. The business could then alter its delivery schedule & the types of foods it serves to provide new mothers with optimal nutrition. It could also add options for spouses or partners & other children in the household for meals. The lean start-up approach is not intended to be used solely by start-ups. In developing countries where electricity is unreliable, companies such as General Electric have used the technique to develop a new battery for cell phone companies.

CHAPTER 2: Importance of Market Research

The method of evaluating a new product or service's feasibility through surveys carried out directly with prospective consumers is market research. Market analysis helps an organization discover the target market & collect customers' views and the other inputs on product or service participation. This form of research may be performed in-house through the organization itself or a 3rd party company specialising in market analysis. Through polls, product testing, & focus groups, it can be achieved. Usually, research subjects are compensated with the samples of goods or/and paid nominal stipends for the time. Market analysis is a vital aspect of new products or service's research and development (R&D).

The company uses market testing by engaging individuals with a prospective buyer to test its feasibility or service.

Companies will find out the target customers through market analysis and get customer reviews and input quickly.

This form of research may be performed in-house through the organization itself or an independent company specializing in the market analysis.

The study includes surveys, testing of products, & focus groups.

2.1 Develop an understanding of the Market Research

Figure 2.8 Proper Definition of the Marketing Research Problem

The market research aims to examine the market related to certain products or services to decide how the audience receives them. It will include the compilation of information for the market segmentation & product differentiation purposes that could be used to target promotional campaigns and assess what attributes are perceived as a concern by the customer. To complete the process of market analysis, an organization must participate in plenty of activities. Based on the business area being investigated, it needs to collect information. To assess the existence of certain trends or the related data point that it can use in decision-making, the organization needs to evaluate and understand the resulting data. Market research's a vital instrument for helping businesses identify what buyers expect, produce goods that people can use, & maintain a strategic edge over other businesses in their sector.

2.2 Collection of information through Market Research

The market analysis contains a mixture of the primary information, meaning what the organization or a person recruited by a company has collected, & secondary pieces of information, or what outside source has collected.

Primary Information

The Primary data is either compiled by the organization or gathered by an individual or a business contracted to do analysis. Generally speaking, this kind of knowledge falls into two categories: exploratory &/or specific research. Exploratory analysis is a less formal choice that works by many open-ended inquiries, resulting in the presentation of questions or challenges that might need to be answered by the enterprise. The relevant study seeks the solutions to questions previously understood that are mostly called to light by exploratory researches.

Secondary Information

Secondary data is data that has already been obtained from an external agency. It could include the demographic statistic from federal census results, research studies by trade groups, or research provided by the other organization working within the same business area.

Example of Market Research

Often firms use market analysis to evaluate potential ideas or gather customer knowledge on what types of products or the services they like and do not have at present. For instance, to test the feasibility of a product or service, a company considering going into the business might perform market research. If consumer interest is confirmed by market research, the company can proceed with the business plan confidently. If not, to make changes to the product to get it in line with consumer expectations, the organization should use market analysis findings.

Components of Market Research

The research of market involves the gathering of information about:

customers – for developing a customer profile

industry & market environment – for understanding factors that are external to the business

competitors – for developing competitor profiles.

Learn to research the industry and market environment

the business & market factors analysis will concentrate on knowledge regarding any legal, political, social, economic, and cultural problems or developments that may impact your organization. This external analysis will then be used to obtain knowledge about the composition of the target market, market differences, emerging market patterns, and where the new market prospects may lie. Research on the industry and business outlook could cover:

- Market size & trends
- Business regulations
- Marketing channels
- Market demographics (for example, age, gender, income)
- Sociographic (for example, beliefs & attitudes, lifestyle factors, interests).

Sources that can be used for collecting the data

- Pertinent business & industry associations
- Online trade journal
- Newspapers
- Council businesses support service
- Print media
- Television
- Industry expos along with trade shows

Regional councils & relevant state governmental departments (which is depending upon the industry)

consumer lists or Commercially sold marketing

search engines for Internet

Research the customers

To collect the relevant information about who your clients or future customers are, & what, where, when & how they shop, you can use consumer analysis.

Customer analysis will also provide you with useful insights into your consumers' perceptions towards your organization and your goods and services.

Research on customers may cover:

- Needs & expectations
- Social & lifestyle trends
- Attitude towards you
- Customer demographics (like age, income, gender)
- Attitudes towards your opponents.

Sources for researching customers

- Focus groups

- surveys & questionnaires for staff and customers

- Observations of the customer behavior

- Personal interviews

- Feedback on points-of-sale

- Sales staff

- Phone surveys

- Social media

- Development offices for local business (local council & independent)

Research the competitors

Your study into competitors will obtain data on current and future competitors. You will use your rival's data to gain knowledge such as the existing business advantages of your competitor, shortcomings in their sales tactics, & how their consumers view their goods and services. Analysis of competitors may cover:

- Present turnover & market shares

- Pricing structures and policies

- Products & services

- Branding, marketing, advertising

Sources for researching competitors

- Competitor marketing & advertising material, the price-lists

- Past clients

- Suppliers

- Official offices like licensing bodies

- Business directories

- Competitor stores, pages on social media, and websites

- Complaints blogs & chat sites

- Competitor print & lists of electronic mailing

- Personal & staff observations

CHAPTER 3: Digital Entrepreneurship

It is important to academic study to consider the conditions and reasons that promote digital entrepreneurship (DE) and to direct market practice and public policies aimed at promoting this development, given its positive impacts on job development and economic growth. Digital entrepreneurship is a concept that determines how entrepreneurship can evolve as digital technology begins to disrupt industry and culture. Digital entrepreneurship illustrates trends in the practice, philosophy, and curriculum of entrepreneurs. In a modern world, digital entrepreneurship encompasses everything new and distinct about entrepreneurship, including:

- New ways of locating customers for entrepreneurial ventures
- Innovative ways of designing and offering products and services
- Unconventional ways of generating revenue and reducing cost
- Identification of fresh opportunities to collaborate with platforms and partners

- New sources of opportunity, risk, and competitive advantage

Digital entrepreneurship opens up new opportunities on a realistic basis for someone dreaming about being an entrepreneur. Some possibilities are more technical, but many others are within reach for someone who learns the fundamental skills of digital entrepreneurship. Such specific skills include looking online for potential clients, prototyping new business concepts, and improving data-based business ideas. Digital entrepreneurship is all about new ways of thinking about entrepreneurship itself and learning new technological skills, which is another way of suggesting that it introduces new entrepreneurship theories. New questions about the policy, chance, and risk are opened up by digital entrepreneurship. Digital entrepreneurship unlocks new opportunities in terms of education to train the future generation of entrepreneurs. 'Doing it' is the perfect way to practice entrepreneurship and draw on the learning. In the normal world, beginning the latest company or releasing a new product is expensive and dangerous for beginners. Not only does the modern world reduce the hurdles to beginning something new, but it provides a range of routes to growth. Educationally, it's such a different environment from case studies, simulations, and business plans. There is also controversy over the precise concept of digital entrepreneurship, partly because it is early and partly because it is changing. What is fresh in digital entrepreneurship can change over time as digital technology progresses. Maybe one day, any business projects will be born digital,' and digital entrepreneurship will cease to exist as a separate topic. However, today, there is a strong need to help educate entrepreneurs for the modern world and offer a new route to entrepreneurship to more individuals.

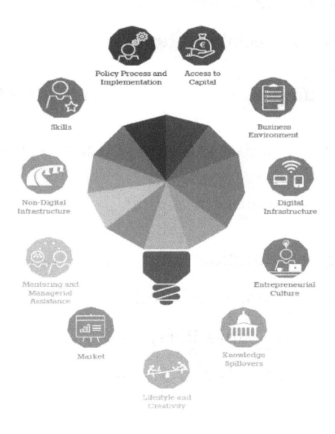

Simple Types of Digital Business Ideas

Digital marketers don't have a good sense of what is possible at the very beginning. It is advised that they begin with one of five basic forms to help beginners conceive of new digital business ideas:

A business offering knowledge on every specialized topic

It is possible to raise revenue through advertising, referrals, sponsorship, or merchandise

A neighborhood enterprise, hosting a vibrant and helpful discussion on every specialized topic

 The sales opportunities are close to the industry of information

An online marketplace that markets goods or services

The objects may be tangible or digital

A matchmaker corporation that puts together two sets of individuals. For instance, a product or service provider (for instance, prospective babysitters) and another group who will need their services are always one group (parents looking for a babysitter). Advertising income is a probability, but with good matches, a transaction fee may also be received.

A promotional organization that draws online clients to a market that already exists

A possible revenue stream here, or advertising, is fees per client referral

An ideal new business plan can be impossible to come up with right from the start, but everyone will easily develop a realistic idea among these five options. As long as they can conceive of a subject that could attract at least a few hundred other individuals, a product or service they want to market, groups of individuals that may support each other, or some small company who could use some promotional assistance, digital entrepreneurs will launch their journey from the beginning. These five basic forms often make it easy for a digital business concept to be shared. In this case, a new business concept is:

A content provider on [your subject]

A [your subject] neighborhood business

An online shop that sells [your product or service]

A matchmaking firm that connects [service providers/group A] to [service users/group B]

The promotion of an online business [a local business]

The options are nearly infinite, and they are still evolving

Digital Entrepreneurship in the face of the Pandemic

Small firms and start-ups have been struck hardest by the recent pandemic than any other area of the economy. To survive a disaster, small firms usually have few resources. Usually, small companies still have little background in the new world of becoming creative, which is now one of their best choices for weathering the storm. In this moment of recession, a variety of digital practices can be considered by small companies. The typical guidance involves applying for federal support, staying in contact with online buyers, and beginning existing products' sales using e-commerce. These are all positive moves, but studies on digital entrepreneurship suggest some additional solutions. For small companies and start-ups, here are three extra fields of digital opportunity.

New models for doing business

It's a smart idea to learn ways to market your current goods online but think about marketing your experience as a new online service. Many families have at least one person with increased time to develop new things or with an immediate need to discover new, more customized ways to entertain themselves. Another option is to offer digital products, such as online classes or digital how-to guides, depending on your expertise. However, digital entrepreneurship helps you pursue brand new areas of operation and offer similar new goods and services. The opportunity to pursue innovative business ideas at little or low cost is a major benefit of digital entrepreneurship. Your new digital company, for instance, may provide useful knowledge that lets customers make other buying choices. During this recession, internet traffic and investment are up and catch these emerging internet traffic sources' attention. Advertisers and marketers are involved and can pay for quality customer leads. Display advertisements, performance advertising, sponsorships, and commission fees from affiliate marketing transactions are new revenue possibilities. Another new potential for digital business is to become a matchmaker, connect individuals who need an online product or service with someone who can better provide it, and charge a purchase fee or percentage. What types of people do you meet already? During this crisis, what are their special needs? And where can you refer them to for assistance? Many of the world's major digital matchmakers, Airbnbs and Ubers, would need to be temporarily replaced by more local alternatives that fit local conditions and will be able to handle local constraints as they evolve.

Perfect the digital business process

An easy way to think about digital business is to see it as an ABC method with three steps: acquisition, behavior, and conversion. The acquisition adds new buyers through social media campaigns, search results, email, search, or social advertisement, among many other platforms to the digital sector. Behavior is what tourists do to fulfill their needs and help them reach their goals through their digital presence. Conversion is the task that each of your guests would like to do, whether it's finishing order, clicking on advertisements, calling for an appointment, or installing a menu. In each of these three critical regions, this problem is an incentive for the organization to develop its capability. Now is a perfect time to create digital marketing campaigns for the acquisition of consumers. When they are ready to buy again, this will make buyers and opportunities ready for it. By enhancing the digital consumer experience, behavior can be changed. To see which ones are more popular, improve interaction, try new features, new content, and new ways to organize and manage your online presence. Your friend, here is the analytics data supplied by your digital company. An integral digital business capability is to turn tourists into future or real customers. Use the time to try new calls to action. It would help if you also used this opportunity to tell clients to do something that would improve their engagement. Practice getting the guests to do easier things such as likes, comments, and shares. Then intensify the participation by signing up for updates and discounts, uploading their material, or scheduling a future appointment. Don't fail to remember how they all come together when you practice each of the digital business ABCs. With promises that can't be met or ambitions that you can't meet, it's easy to have new tourists. Acquire the right visitors who are happy and will convert.

Start experimenting

The freedom to innovate continuously is a key advantage of digital entrepreneurship. There are several fresh ideas to try in each part of the ABC process. Get familiar with the analytics data, which will be from Google Analytics for most digital entrepreneurs. It will provide you with reliable input on what works and what doesn't. It is still being practiced by major corporations, conducting hundreds or thousands of tests on their clients every day. If they continue to remain competitive, small firms would need to develop the skills of digital experimentation. Fortunately, the benefit of emerging start-ups is that they can hop on emerging developments that are not yet big enough to interest the big players. A crisis scenario is a hotbed of emerging developments in the quest, new hashtags, new memes, and new points for the conversation to be taken advantage of. Once digital marketers discover innovative business concepts that work with their first 100 to 1,000 visitors, it is fairly inexpensive and easy to scale up such ideas when trends take off. Be on the lookout for new 'nano trends' as these developments play out, and be ready to expand.

CHAPTER 4: The Best Business

It doesn't need to require a big investment to start a profitable company. You can start a company without spending much capital, or even purchasing inventory, with a great business concept and the right resources. Adapting to a growing economy requires finding new, smart ways to fulfill clients' needs. To find the answer to the following important questions, you have to analyze the market:

What sorts of goods or services will fulfill the new consumer demands?

As an entrepreneur, how can your skills better fulfill those demands?

Any of the money-making, small business ideas that need very little investment are provided below.

4.1 Start your own online Dropshipper business

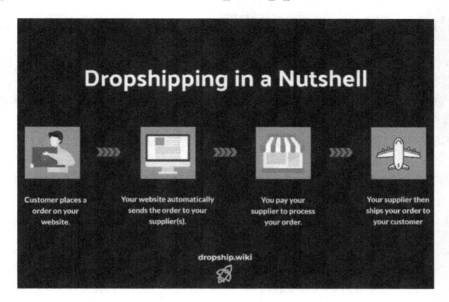

To sell online, you do not need to store inventory or spend a lot of money. You escape the expense of producing goods, handling inventory, and exporting with the dropshipping business by working with third-party vendors that do it all for you.

How it works

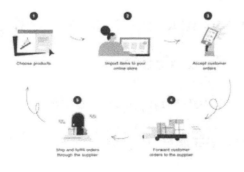

Dropshipping is a retail fulfillment technique where a retailer does not hold the items in storage that it offers. Instead, when a store sells a product using the dropshipping model, it orders the product from a third party and directly sends it to the consumer. As a consequence, the seller doesn't have to handle the items personally. The main contrast between dropshipping and the traditional retail model is that no product is held or controlled by the selling trader. Instead, to execute orders, the seller purchases inventory if appropriate from a third party, typically a wholesaler or retailer. You should start advertising your company using digital marketing tools to drive customers to your site once you're finished setting up your online store, and your site goes live. You'll get an order notice each time they make a transaction. They will complete it after the order is delivered to the supplier. You've just become the manager of your own e-commerce company. To get started with your dropshipping business, link your Wix account with Modalyst or Spocket. You can sell all kinds of great goods at your set prices after procuring products from millions of reliable suppliers. Just try to strike a balance with each sale between competitive prices and how much you earn.

Choose products to sell

You may need to select dropshipping items to sell before you launch your online business. Take the time for clarification of your brand and vision. To figure out what individuals are buying, do some market research. Before selling them in your store, determine the future demand, price, and profit margin of items. For an online shop, you will thrive by finding a way to stand out. Explore specialty items to source and market, and by offering a range, aim to stop placing all the eggs in one bowl. That said, to make your online store easier to browse, aim to organize your items into collections. Keep out of markets that are still saturated with stores. Take the time to set up marketing and advertising efforts to save you time and improve your revenue eventually.

Example: Trending work from home products

Think of what customers do at home to select the right business to establish with little investment. With equipment for living room workouts, open your online fitness shop. Open an adorable store selling puppy items for professionals working from home, such as quiet pet toys. It's all about feeling at ease in your home setting during COVID-19. It is why items such as sweatshirts, leggings, hoodies, slippers, and socks selling out everywhere. The athleisure trend has a moment. While people do not dress up at home as much, with cute pajama sets or multi-use makeup for a simple beauty routine, they may also look for ways to feel and look healthy. Your customers can also opt for at-the-home beauty items, such as grooming accessories or nail kits, with salons now less available.

As remote employees and students set up shop at home, home office products are also common. You have to dream of tech devices such as lap desks, laptop stands, desk organizers, keyboards, or home storage. The market has also spiked for ergonomic desk chairs that help posture and back alignment or convenient seat cushions. But not all of this is work and no play. As consumers search for new recreation ideas, gaming items have also become popular. As people look for things to do, at-home leisure products, such as game boards, trivia, or knitting equipment, sell well. Shoppers must spend more time cooking at home with restaurants closed. It suggests a spike in sales of kitchenware as well as online food and beverage items. Parents also need childcare and work-life to be tackled. So, consider adding quiet toys and play spaces to your dropshipping company, like the car park mats. Shoppers also like to video chat or watch Netflix with friends without holding their laptops all the time. In the dropshipping shop, try offering bedside mounts and table mounts.

Promote your online store

When you introduce items, it's time for your shop to be advertised. It Is where a strong approach for e-commerce marketing comes into play. Allow the best of the business software for the e-commerce website. Automate your email marketing promotions and client outreach to save time. Advertise your dropshipping business on Facebook and Instagram with paid campaigns. Work with influencers to support your brands and advertise them to their followers if it's important to your company. In promoting your online dropshipping business, your SEO strategy will also play a crucial role. It suggests the development of high-quality advertising and low-budget ads to improve the search engine results' exposure. Increase the visibility of your website with keyword optimization, for example. Let's presume you're selling home clothing for comfortable work. If you include the phrases "luxury comfort wear," "work from home," or "athleisure clothing" in your web copy, when people search for those keywords, you will have a better chance of ranking on Google.

Get creative with branded products designed by you

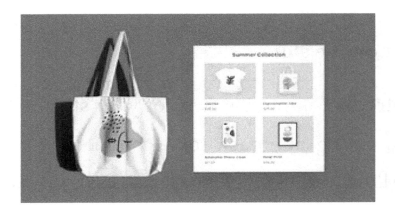

Now, let's take one step further with dropshipping. By linking Printful or Printify to your online shop, you add a personal touch with print on demand. You partner with print-on-demand businesses supplying the inventory, just like with dropshipping. Choose any customizable merchandise and introduce your creative touch, from t-shirts to phone cases, bags, and more. Go ahead and design graphics, quotations, or images to be printed on the chosen items. Start by choosing from thousands of different products to customize your online store and sell your designs. Start a business with funny quotes on a t-shirt. Add photos of your cat to Novelty Socks. Your logo or designs that match your brand create stickers—another cool option: selling goods made by you with original artwork. Yet, to market exclusive designs, you should not have to be a graphic artist. Hire and collaborate with freelance artists to create unique art for your products that are printed on-demand. You will distribute to over 90 places internationally when you receive an order. Forward your orders while managing everything from your Wix dashboard to your chosen supplier. Only think about it; shoppers would rock all over the world your exclusive creations.

Create digital video content

Now that individuals spend more time at home, by taking on new hobbies or returning to old ones, they're looking for ways to keep themselves occupied. Do you work in an industry, such as fitness, restaurants, or education, traditionally requires face-to-face interaction? Use this opportunity to create digital instruction videos, such as cooking demonstrations, workout routines, and more streamed online by people. The shutdown of schools and daycare services in 2021 means that parents have to spend a lot more time with their little ones at home. Moms and dads are searching for ways to keep their children busy, engaged, and learning. So if you are at home and temporarily out of a job, how can you apply your experience to satisfy this market demand? Especially now, family-friendly activities are always trendy. Get ahead of the competition by selling children-friendly video content. Create exercise videos for children if you're a fitness trainer. Promote the use of child-friendly content, such as workouts or classes for baby yoga. To help parents home-school their children, post daily lessons online. With your children, you can even create an entertaining cooking show. With digital video content, there are distinct pricing models to earn money. To give customers full access to exclusive content, you may charge a monthly channel subscription. You can monetize your content based on the number of viewers if you work with video hosting platforms like YouTube. Selling or renting your videos is another option. Over a 24-48-hour cycle, viewers may download the video or watch it on your site. To give clients an idea of your product and nudge them to make a purchase, consider offering some of your content for free. Zoom, Vimeo, and YouTube can also host live streaming or webinars.

Comprehend the Supply Chain of Dropshipping

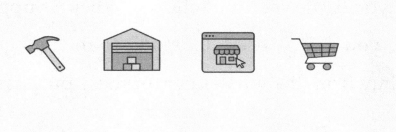

Supply chain's some fancy word that defines the journey a commodity takes to move from creation through manufacture and eventually into a customer's hands. If we are talking about suppliers of hard core chains gurus, they would insist that the supply chain stretches all towards mining products to make an object (like oil & rubber). But it's a bit intense. We do not need to be quite so specific. The three most important participants in the dropshipping supply chain must simply be understood: wholesalers, manufacturers, & retailers.

Manufacturers

Manufacturers produce the commodity, & most don't sell directly to the public. They sell bulks to wholesalers & dealers instead. The easiest way to buy goods for resale is to buy straight from the manufacturer, but most of them have minimum purchasing standards you'll desire to follow. When shipping them to consumers, you'll still need to store & re-ship goods. It's also cheaper to buy from the wholesaler for these purposes directly.

Wholesalers

Wholesalers purchase products from manufacturers in bulk, mark them up marginally and then market them to the retailers to sell them to the public. They're normally much smaller than those needed by a vendor if they have buying minimums. Wholesalers normally store goods from thousands of producers, if not a hundred, and prefer to work in a single field or drop shipping niche. Many operators are exclusively wholesalers. It means that they only sell to retailers & not direct to the general public.

Retailers

the retailer is anyone who sells the products directly to the public after adding his margin. If you are running a business that fulfills your orders through dropshipping suppliers, you are a retailer.

Dropshipping is a service, not a role

You will find that "drop shipper" is not one of the supply chain players. Each of the three will operate as drop shippers - manufacturer, wholesaler, and retailer. If the manufacturer is prepared to supply its supplies directly to your consumer, it's "dropshipping" for your sake. Similarly, a supermarket retailer will offer drop ship, but its price would not be as favorable as a wholesaler because the manufacturer does not buy it directly. It doesn't mean you're having bulk rates simply because someone declares to be a "drop shipper." It means that, for your sake, the company would ship goods. You desire to ensure that you deal exclusively with a reputable manufacturer or wholesaler to get the best prices.

The order process

Let us observe how the drop shipped order is processed so that you have understood the players involved. We would follow the order put with a theoretical shop, an online seller Phone Outlet, specializing in smartphone accessories, to demonstrate. Phone Outlet dropships all its items directly from the wholesaler that we will call Wholesale Accessories. Here's a sample of what the whole ordering process could look like:

Customer Places Order With Phone Outlet

Allen requires a case for the new smartphone and places an order through the Phone Outlet online store. A few things happen once an order has been approved:

Phone Outlet & Mr. Allen would receive an email of confirmation (likely alike) of new orders which store software automatically generates.

During the checkout process, the payment of Mr. Allen is captured and automatically placed into the bank account of Phone Outlet.

Phone Accessory Outlet Places the Order With Its Supplier

The step is generally as artless as sending the confirmation of an email order to a sales representative at Wholesale Accessories by Phone Outlet. Wholesale Accessories has a credit card from Phone Outlet on file & will charge it for wholesale goods, including handling fees or shipping. Some sophisticated drop shippers will support XML Automatic (a normal format for stock files) orders uploading or the ability to place orders manually online. Still, email is the most common method to place orders with dropshipping vendors because it is universal & easier to use.

Wholesale accessories ships the order

If items in the stock and wholesaler have positively charged the Phone Outlet card, the order will be boxed up and shipped directly to the customer by Wholesale Accessories. Although shipments come from the Wholesale Accessories, the name & address of the Phone Outlet would appear on the label of the return address, and the logo would appear on the invoice & packing slip. Wholesale Accessories would then email invoice & tracking numbers to the Phone Outlet once the shipment has been finalized.

Turnaround time is often quicker than you would think on dropshipped orders. In a few hours, most feature suppliers would be capable of getting the order outdoor, allowing merchants to publicize shipping on the same day when they use drop shipping suppliers.

Phone outlet alerts the customer of shipment

When this tracking number's collected, Phone Outlet gives the customer tracking information, potentially using an email interface built into the online store interface. The order and delivery process is complete with the order delivered, the invoice received, and a customer told. The benefit (or loss) of Phone Outlet is the contrast between what this costs Mr. Allen & what this paid for wholesale accessories.

Dropshippers are invisible

The drop shipper is invisible to the end buyer, despite its vital position in the ordering & fulfillment process. Just the Phone Outlet return address & signature would be on the shipment when the package is received. If Mr. Allen obtains the wrong case, he will call Phone Outlet, who would work with Wholesale

Accessories behind scenes and get the right item shipped out. To the ultimate buyer, the wholesaler does not exist. Stocking and shipping dropshipping products is the sole responsibility. The merchant is responsible for all else—website creation, marketing, customer support.

4.2 How to Find and Work with Reliable Dropshipping Suppliers

One of the most popular questions ambitious entrepreneurs pose is: What is my e-commerce store's best dropshipping supplier? Supplier directory for dropshipping is a distributor database grouped by niche, market, or commodity. Many of the directories employ a few scanning mechanisms to ensure that legitimate wholesalers are suppliers listed. Many are managed by for-the profit corporations who charge a fee to use their directories. While membership folders, particularly for brainstorming the ideas, may be useful, they're by no means essential. If you already know the commodity or drop shipping niche that you need to sell, you must locate the big suppliers in the market with a little bit of searching & the techniques mentioned above. Plus, you once start dropshipping company, unless you want to locate suppliers for the other things, you would probably not need to revisit the directory. That said, the supplier directory is an easy way to scan for or/and browse a vast range of suppliers in 1 location easily and is useful for brainstorming ideas for marketing goods or entering niches. If you are short of time and ready to spend cash, a helpful tool may be supplier directories. There is a range of different suppliers and businesses for dropshipping.

Best dropshipping suppliers

CJdropshipping

Oberlo

CROV

DropnShop

Supplymedirect

Modalyst

To make this easier to select best drop shipping companies for specific needs, we will focus on the following factor:

Location and shipping options

So, Where do the supplier's locations exist? How much time is consumed in producing the item after the customer has put orders?

Product types

Which kinds of products they dropship?

Recommended for

And Is the particular suppliers suited for experienced or beginner dropshippers?

Oberlo

Shopify. The Oberlo is dropshipping the platform, making it easier to find AliExpress items to sell in the Shopify store. It is the best online drop shipping supplier directory for Shopify. The platform provides over 30 thirty of the latest dropshipping goods from vendors across the globe in 60 plus niche categories. Oberlo has free registration, beginning at 29.9 dollars a month for paid plans.

Location & shipping options

In different places around the world, Oberlo links you with suppliers. Usually, each includes many delivery solutions for the clients to send products. On each commodity page in the Oberlo app, you will find what delivery methods the supplier uses. the Popular shipping method includes:

China Post. Affordable / Free shipping expenses. Delivery could take 20 to 50 days.

AliExpress Shipping. Affordable costs of shipping. Delivery can take up to 15 days.

ePacket. Affordable / Free shipping expenses. Delivery could take 15 to 30 days.

DHL/UPS/FedEx. Express the shipping expenses. Delivery could take between five to fifteen days.

Product types

So You may find anything that includes bracelets, antiques, car parts, wedding supplies, sunglasses, furniture, and much more.

Recommended for

It's recommended for the beginner & veteran drop shipper.

CJDropshipping

With fast delivery, it is the best dropshipping service. CJDropshipping is a marketplace that allows retailers to scale up the drop shipping business affordably. You can conveniently import goods directly from 1688 and Taobao marketplaces into the Shopify store, usually at a price lesser than on AliExpress. Along with other dropshipping applications like Oberlo, it's also a free Shopify application that you could add to the store.

Location & shipping options

To perform processing on the same-day for the store, CJDropshipping uses US-based warehouses. UPS, USPS, DHL, & FedEx work with it. The shipping line known as CJPacket will bring goods to the US in 7 to twelve days if you are shipping from China.

Product types

Independent designers & owners of small businesses in China are home to the 1668 and Taobao marketplaces. Via CJDropshipping, there are 100s of millions of listings you may browse, & products vary from mainstream goods to difficult-to-find items & even the virtual product. If the CJDropshipping app does not have a product, you can upload a request & CJDropshipping would list this once the best source is identified.

Recommended for

The retailer who needs a 1-stop location for all the things drop shipping, including inventory procurement, order preparation, distribution, and fast shipping to United States, is highly recommended.

SupplyMeDirect

It is the strongest dropshipping provider for the UK, US, & European markets for private labels. SupplyMeDirect is a wholesale provider that supports the size of dropshipping business. The app provides private labeling & secure sourcing. It's a free Shopify application that you could contact twenty-four 7, supported by dedicated support staff.

Location & shipping options

The SupplyMeDirect is different. The reason is that nearly 60 percent of the stock resides in the warehouses established in the United States, the UK, Canada, & Europe. It makes shipping reliable and fast. The shipping has an average time of delivery of 4 to 7 days.

Product types

Any product from apparel to kitchenware, the toys to the accessories, & more

Recommended for

It is best for the drop shippers who intend to sell in the whole world & want fast shipping.

CROV

For the multi-channel vendors, it is the strongest dropshipping provider. CROV links retailers from vetted lists of US vendors to a wide variety of items. It is yet another free-of-cost Shopify app to populate the store with products and automate orders.

Location & shipping options

In the 42 countries, shipping is available. Costs rely on vendors & their shipping processes, which can be found in a directory on every product detail page. To ship the domestic orders quicker, CROV has a US warehouse.

Product types

It offers extra than 35 thousand products in more than 20 other trending categories from the selected suppliers.

Recommended for

It is the best for eCommerce sellers. Especially for those who need to sell different products on Amazon, Shopify, & eBay.

Modalyst

It is the greatest supplier of dropshipping high-tickets for US apparel. For online retailers, Modalyst is an automatic dropshipping program. It is known for delivering items that customers would enjoy from the brand names such as DSquare, Calvin Klein, Dolce, and Gabbana, & other famous brands. For any target demographic, Modalyst often features a curated collection of independent & trendy brands. The website has an official API collaboration with AliExpress Dropshipping, allowing you to access the millions of items with a Google Chrome plugin to connect to your shop with one click.

Location & shipping options

The Modalyst has the own marketplace of US manufacturers and products that can offer domestic orders free of charge between six to eight days. Also available are UK dropshipping vendors & Australian drop shippers. Businesses, except countries in South America and Africa, will ship to more than 80 countries in the world

Product types

It generally emphasizes premium and fashionable products. Modalyst is part of the Booster Program of AliExpress also, offering an infinite catalog of items for drop shippers to browse.

Recommended for

It is recommended for users of Shopify who want their shops to add exclusive items. You will also market goods using Modalysts Private Label Software with your branding. You will take advantage of any of the luxury brands and vendors that Modalysts has to sell if you chose the Pro plan.

dropship

It is the best source of dropships for French goods. DropnShop is a dropshipping program for Shopify that provides online sales of French goods. It offers inventory from the top factories of French. It takes the requests from e-commerce partners to diversify product catalog and expand your business due to partnerships with thousands of producers. There's an availability-free plan.

Location & shipping information

To have worldwide delivery at a decent rate, DropnShop partners with numerous suppliers. Every product has different shipping information, but you may find anything you require to know on the product detail page of the app.

Product types

Would you like to sell France's best cosmetics products in your shop? With DropnShop, you may. The supplier also sells 1000s of SKUs, all 100 percent manufactured in France, across several categories, from children's toys to the hair & products of skincare.

Recommended for

It is the best for eCommerce stores. It is best, especially for those who desire to add the French product to the catalog.

Let us learn to find dropshipping suppliers

Suppliers are not always made equal, like most things in life. It is also more important to ensure that you are dealing with top-notch players in the dropshipping community. The supplier is a vital part of the dropshipping fulfillment operation.

Before you contact suppliers

Okay, so you've discovered a range of good suppliers & are prepared to go forward — great! Yet you would want to get all ducks in a row before you start approaching businesses.

It would help if you were legal

we discussed earlier, before authorizing you to register for some account, most amazing wholesalers would need confirmation that you are a legal entity. Most wholesalers report their prices to licensed consumers, but you will need to be legally authorized before seeing the type of pricing you will receive. Before contacting vendors, make sure you're lawfully integrated.

Don't be afraid of the phone

One of the strongest worries people have is picking up phone & making the call when it comes to vendors. It is a paralyzing prospect for many. For such problems, you may be capable of sending texts, but you'll have to pick the phone up more frequently than not to get the answers you need. The good news's that this isn't as terrifying as you would imagine. Suppliers, including novice entrepreneurs, are used to having the people calling them. You're going to get someone to answer questions who's polite and happier. Here's a trick to motivate you: just type your questions down in advance. When you have a list of already written questions for asking, it is surprising how easy it's to make the call.

Great vendors for dropshipping tends to have most of the following six characteristics:

Expert staff and industry focus

There are knowledgeable distribution agents from top-notch manufacturers who truly know the market and the product lines. It's invaluable to contact a representative with concerns, especially if you're starting a store in a niche you're not too familiar with anything.

Dedicated support representatives

individual sales agent responsible for taking good care of yourself & any concerns you have should assign you to quality drop shippers. Problems take even longer to fix because we generally must nag the people to take care of a crisis. Getting a single interaction with a supplier allows you to locate the entity responsible for fixing your problems which is very valuable.

Invest in technology

When there are many great suppliers with obsolete websites, suppliers that know the advantages of technology and spend extensively in it are typically a joy to deal with them. For online retailers, features like an inventory of real-time, a detailed online catalog, personalized data feeds & online searchable history of orders are pure pleasure & may help streamline the activities.

Can take orders via email

it may seem like a small challenge, but have to call in each order or put it manually on a website makes handling orders even more time-consuming.

Centrally located

It's helpful to use a centrally placed drop shipper in a big country like the United States since shipments can cover more than 90percent of the country within 2-3 business days. It may take an additional week for shipments to be delivered around the country where a retailer is based on one coast. Centrally placed vendors allow guaranteeing quicker turnaround times reliably, theoretically saving you cash on shipping costs.

Organized and efficient

few vendors have qualified personnel and outstanding processes that contribute to effective and often error-less fulfillment. Every 4th order will be botched by others & make you need to rip the hair out. But without ever using it, it's impossible to tell how a professional supplier is.

While it cannot give you the full picture, it will give you a better sense of how suppliers perform by placing a few small test orders. You can see:

How to order process is done

How rapidly things ship out

And How fast this follows with monitoring details and invoice

 quality of package when the product arrives

It is important to learn how to distinguish between genuine suppliers of wholesale & retail stores acting as wholesale suppliers when looking for suppliers. A real wholesaler buys straight from the producer & will usually offer you even better prices.

How to spot fake dropshipping companies

You will come across a significant number of " fake" wholesalers based on where you're looking. Unfortunately, historically, legal wholesalers are bad at selling and appear to be more difficult to find. It results in non-genuine wholesalers showing more often in searches, usually only intermediaries, so you'll need to be careful. Following dropshipping tips would help you decide whether it is a legal wholesale supplier.

They want ongoing fees

Real wholesalers don't charge their clients monthly fees for the luxury of doing a business & buying from them. It's usually not legitimate if a retailer asks for a monthly subscription or a service fee. It's necessary to distinguish between the suppliers and directories of suppliers here. Supplier directories are bulk supplier directories grouped by commodity categories or sector & screened to ensure suppliers' authenticity. Many directories, either 1 -time or continuous, can charge a fee, but you do not take it as an indication that the directory itself's unlawful.

They sell to the public

You would need to register for a wholesale account to get real wholesale rates, demonstrate you are a legal entity, and be accepted before making your first order. So Any wholesale seller selling goods at "wholesale" to the general public is the only retailer offering the items at inflated rates. However, here are a few legal dropshipping charges that you would possibly encounter:

Per-order fees

Depending on the size and complexity of the goods being dispatched, certain drop shippers would charge a dropshipping fee per shipment that can vary from 2-5 dollars or more. As the prices of packaging and delivering individual order is much greater than shipping bulk order, this is common in the industry.

Minimum order sizes

There would be a minimum beginning order size for certain wholesalers, which is the lowest sum you may have to buy for your 1st order. They perform this to weed out window shopping vendors with questions & minor orders that will not translate into real sales and will waste their resources. If you're dropshipping, some problems may be caused. For starters, what would you might do if you have a minimum order of $500 from a supplier, but your mean order size takes about $100? Only for the privilege of making a dropshipping account do you not want to pre-order $500 of the stuff. It's best to make an offer to pay the seller $500 in advance, in this case, to create a loan with them to apply for the drop shipping orders. It helps you fulfill the retailer's minimum purchase obligation (as you are committed to buying a product at least 500 dollars in product) without having to position a single big order without accompanying any customer requests.

Tips for working with dropshipping wholesalers

It's time to start looking for vendors now you can detect a scam from the actual deal! There are a variety of different techniques that you may use, some more successful than others. In order of usefulness and choice, the ways below are enlisted, with the preferred methods enlisted first.

Contact the manufacturer

It may be the ideal way for legal bulk vendors to be conveniently identified. Contact the manufacturer to inquire about their wholesale dealers' list if you know the product(s) you intend to dropship. To observe if they dropship and ask about setting an account up, you may then email these wholesalers. Because most wholesalers carry goods from several manufacturers within the niche, you are pursuing, and this strategy would permit you to source a range of items easily. You'll easily be able to find the leading wholesalers in that market after making few calls to leading producers in some niche.

Use Oberlo

Oberlo helps you quickly import goods straight into the Shopify store from vendors and directly send them to your consumers, all in some clicks.

Features

Products can be imported from suppliers

Product customization

Orders are fulfilled automatically

Inventory & price automatic updates

Pricing automation

Search using Google

You may use Google to fetch high-quality suppliers. It is quite obvious, yet there are some factors to keep in mind:

You have to search extensively

Wholesales are not good at marketing & promotion. Furthermore, they aren't going to cover the top search results related to "wholesale suppliers for some product X." You will have to do all the research yourself.

Don't judge by their website

Wholesales are now infamous for making '90s-style websites. Although a quality site can suggest a successful supplier in some instances, many legal wholesalers have cringe-worthy website homepages. Don't let you get turned off by the bad design.

Attend a trade show

trade show helps you to engage in a niche with all key manufacturers & wholesalers. It's a perfect method to make friends, all in one place, and research the commodities and suppliers. It only applies if the niche &/or product has already been chosen, and it is not possible for everybody. But it's a perfect method to know vendors and the suppliers in the region if you have the time and resources to participate.

Ways to pay dropshipping suppliers and companies

A large number of suppliers shall accept payments in 1 of 2 ways:

Credit card

Many suppliers will ask you to make the payment by credit card as you're starting. Paying with credit cards is always the better choice after you've developed a flourishing business. Not only are they easy (no requirement to constantly write checks), but lots of loyalty frequent flier/ points miles can be racked up. You will rack up a high number of sales with your credit card without requiring to pay any real out-of-the-pocket costs when you are purchasing a product for a client who has already paid for it on your website.

Net terms

"Net terms" on invoices are the most typical method to pay the suppliers. It assumes that you have certain days for paying the retailer with the items you have ordered. So if you're on the "net 30" term, you have exactly 30 days to pay the supplier for the items from the purchase date you ordered by bank draw or check. Usually, before providing net payment terms, a supplier would make you have credit references, so it's lending you money. It is a normal procedure, but if you have to provide any documentation while paying on net terms, do not be alarmed.

Usually, before providing net payment terms, a supplier would make you have credit references, so it's lending you the money. It's a normal procedure, but if you need to provide any documentation while paying on the net terms, do not be alarmed.Bottom of Form

Top of Form

Bottom of Form

FAQs about dropshipping suppliers

Given below are some of the frequently asked questions, along with answers about the dropshipping suppliers.

How do I find dropshipping suppliers?

On directory vetted such as Oberlo, you can find dropshipping suppliers, colleagues' suggestions, or look the suppliers for the products for brands you like. You may also find several excellent alternatives with some research work.

What are the best dropshipping suppliers in 2021?

Some top suppliers for dropshipping are Worldwide Labels, Doba, SaleHoo, AliExpress, Alibaba, Wholesale Central, & CDS.

Is dropshipping still profitable in 2021?

In 2021, dropshipping also represents a viable market opportunity. Since you don't need to spend on the inventory or incur holding expenses, it's a sustainable business model.

Which platform is best for dropshipping?

Combined with the Oberlo, Shopify allows for a streamlined setup for dropshipping. On Oberlo, you can check for vendors and make items available on the branded Shopify website for sale. You make the sales, & your drop shipping supplier will do the rest.

Common questions about dropshipping

We have compiled a list of questions that could be posed by anyone planning to start a new drop shipper business.

How much do I need to invest in starting dropshipping?

While it is difficult to predict exact prices for any individual company, to get started, there are few things on which each drop shipping company would need to be spending money. Here's a short rundown of the critical expenditures.

Online store

Estimated price: ~29 dollars per month

To establish & host an online shop, you'll need to find an e-commerce site. We suggest launching a shop at Shopify. You will be capable of syncing source items with Oberlo marketplace conveniently, and you will get access to a full range of themes & free branding software so that you can quickly get your company up & running.

Domain name

Estimated price: $5 to 20 per year

Without the domain name, it's difficult to develop trust with clients. Although there is a range of top-leveled domains available (example, example. co example. shop), if one is available, we recommend searching for the .com which suits the brand.

Test orders

Estimated price: Varies

While dropshipping helps you to have limited interference in managing your total product catalog, that you can set aside, also little of the time, cash to test the items you want to sell. You threaten listing products with too many flaws or faults if you don't, which will lead to disappointed consumers and a lot of the time wasted coping with refunds.

Online advertising

Estimated price: the Scales with the business; It is recommended to start budgeting with a minimum of $500

Each e-commerce organization must look for ways of reducing the average cost of acquiring a client across organic networks such as SEO, content marketing, & word of mouth. But advertising is typically an important medium for many product-based firms to start every company. Search engine marketing (the SEM), displays advertising, social media advertising, and smartphone ads are among the most common channels.

How do drop shippers make money?

Dropshipping businesses act like product curators, choosing the best dropshipping products for market to the customers; remember that marketing costs you incur, into both time & money, help the potential customers find, explain, & buy the right products. You will also have to include the cost of supporting customers whenever there is a product or a shipping problem. Last but not least is the original price for which the supplier sells a product. With all these prices to be accountable for, the dropshipping business mark up the individual products in exchange for the distribution. It's why the suppliers are okay with having drop shippers markets the products for those people — dropshipping stores also drive extra sales, which supplier would've missed out otherwise. it is good to find out how much this costs to "acquire" customer, & price the products with it in mind.

Is dropshipping a legitimate business?

Dropshipping is essentially a fulfillment model, one used with many global distributors, and is completely legitimate. Satisfying consumer needs and creating brands that resonate with the right demographic is also vital for long-term growth, as with any company. Owing to a misconception of how dropshipping works, this question generally occurs. The bulk of discount shops at which you shop are most likely not to sell items they directly make. Dropshipping takes the curated approach & converts it into an online company-fit distribution model. of course, you must do more simple things to operate your business lawfully. To guarantee that you are doing business lawfully in your country, find a lawyer who has specialized in these matters.

Benefits of dropshipping

For emerging entrepreneurs, dropshipping is a perfect business model to start with because it's accessible. You can easily test multiple business concepts with a small drawback with dropshipping, which helps you learn a lot about picking and selling in-demand goods. In 2021, dropshipping is still a viable market opportunity. Since you don't need to spend in inventory or incur holding expenses, it's a sustainable business model. Combined with Oberlo, Shopify allows for a streamlined setup for dropshipping. On Oberlo, you can check for vendors and make items available on your branded Shopify site for sale. You make purchases, and your drop shipping provider will do the rest.

Less capital is required

Stocking a warehouse takes a lot of money. By using dropshipping, you can eliminate the possibility of falling into debt to start your company. You can launch a dropshipping company with zero inventory instead of buying an extensive inventory and hoping it sells and start making money immediately. Perhaps the greatest bonus of dropshipping is that an e-commerce website can be opened without having to spend thousands of dollars in stock upfront. Traditionally, manufacturers have had to bind up large quantities of inventory with capital investments. For the dropshipping model, unless you have already made the sale and have been paid by the consumer, you do not have to buy a product. It is possible to start sourcing goods without substantial up-front inventory investments and begin a profitable dropshipping company with very little capital. And because you're not dedicated to selling, as in a typical retail company, there's less danger involved in launching a dropshipping shop without any inventory bought upfront.

Easy to get started

Managing an e-commerce business is much easier as you don't have to deal with physical products. With drop shipping, you won't have to worry about:

Warehouse cost and management

Handling returns and inbound shipments

Packing and shipping of your orders

Keeping track of inventory for accounting purposes

Perpetually ordering products

Continuously managing stock level

Low cost of inventory

If you own and warehouse stock, inventory is one of the biggest costs you would have. You can end up with old inventory, causing you to find ways to reduce your inventory, or you may end up with very little inventory, resulting in stockouts and missed sales. Dropshipping lets you escape these challenges and concentrate on increasing your client base and developing your brand.

Low Order Fulfillment Costs

Usually, order fulfillment requires you to store, organize, label, select and carry and ship your inventory. Dropshipping lets all of it be taken care of by a third party. In this arrangement, the sole job is to ensure that they receive customer requests. They will do all the rest.

Low overhead

Your operating rates are minimal because you don't have to do with buying inventory or maintaining a warehouse. In reality, many popular dropshipping stores are managed as home-based enterprises, needing nothing more to run than a laptop and a few recurring costs. These costs are likely to escalate as you expand, but they will still be low relative to those of conventional brick-and-mortar companies.

Flexible location

From just about anywhere with an internet connection, a drop shipping company can be managed. You can run and handle your company as long as you can effectively connect with vendors and clients.

A wide selection of products to sell

Without the limitations of a physical inventory and the associated costs, dropshipping allows you to rapidly, comfortably, and cheaply upgrade your inventory. You will instantly deliver it to your customers without waiting for it to arrive in your factory if you know that a product is doing well for another store or reseller. Without the risk of bringing old products, dropshipping helps you to try new products. You're paying just for what you offer. Since you don't have to pre-purchase the items you sell, you can show your future buyers various trending products. If suppliers store an item, you can list it for sale at no added cost at your online store.

Easier to test

Dropshipping is a valuable form of fulfillment for both the opening of a new store and for company owners looking to measure consumers' demand for additional types of items, such as shoes or whole new product ranges. Again, the primary advantage of dropshipping is the opportunity to list and likely sell goods before committing to purchasing a significant quantity of stock.

Easier to scale

For a typical retail organization, you would typically need to do three times as much work if you get three times the orders. By leveraging dropshipping vendors, suppliers will be responsible for most of the work to handle extra orders, helping you to improve with fewer growing pains and less gradual work. Sales growth can often bring extra labor, especially customer service, but companies that use dropshipping scale particularly well compared to conventional e-commerce companies

Conclusion

Digital entrepreneurship may be clearly described as entrepreneurial businesses which are carried through a digital medium. Most studies proved that entrepreneurship a crucial driver for economic development & also for the reduction of unemployment. I's really important to grasp all the principles relevant to entrepreneurship. For meeting market competition & achieve the business target, every entrepreneur must be up to date with changes that arise in the customer's tastes & desires and even in the market. It is often important to use certain new digital technology & softwares to connect with the consumers and increase quality demand. As today's environment is largely dependent on national & global technology, it is important to have the sector's technologies. In this way, digital entrepreneurship plays a critical role in enabling the entrepreneur to conduct all the tasks accurately and efficiently. Using software apps allows any entrepreneur to increase the market demand for his or her product & grow the business both technologically and traditionally. As the Information & communication technologies (ICT) skills are crucial elements of digital enterprise success, it's significant to learn how it allows people to improve their business so that you can use the same for creating your own successful business. It will allow any person who engages in the business to learn about digital entrepreneurship in the Present world, changing dramatically in all fields, particularly in information & communication technology (ICT). In this case, the exponential growth of emerging technology with new creative functionalities is changing competitive environment, modifying the general market strategies, systems, and the procedure. For example, on networked economy motorized by new technologies, many businesses or company is becoming tinier with just one person where the partnerships are evolving. Digital Innovative technologies, including big data, social media, and mobile & cloud platforms, are giving rise to new ways of collaborating, exploiting capital, service/product design, creation, and deployments over the open standards & collaborative technologies. They're, in turn, impacting the market activities through generating job opportunities. Like, Alibaba.com is digital technology that allowed millions of Chinese people to be entrepreneurs. It is also responsible for the creation of employment.

Even digital technologies generate vast job opportunities. They're creating several challenges also. Emerging technologies are modernizing the labor market. Several countries are facing several obstacles, such as Australia, to face economic competition. To face the obstacles and eliminate the barriers, countries are recommended for taking over digital entrepreneurship & achieve an acceptable role. Digital entrepreneurship increases jobs across ICTs like Facebook, social computing, mobile technology, and digital channels. Many firms began digital businesses by selling the products online to meet competition in the industry. As this becomes necessary, focusing on how a business venture must be started is rising with utmost significance. People who need to start a digital company should know the differences between digital versus conventional opportunities, downfalls, entrepreneurship, and digital entrepreneurship challenges. The people need a format or digital entrepreneurship system that consists all information about the new digital enterprise, including its features and objectives.

Deducting | The Right Way

Untangling Small Business Accounting and Taxes Based on Online Activities

By

Jake Folger

Table of Contents

Introduction 499

Chapter: 1 Online Business and its importance? 500

  1.1 The importance of eCommerce 501

Chapter: 2 Accounting and Its Purpose 512

  2.1 Why is Accounting Important? 512

  2.2 What Is the Purpose of Accounting? 512

Chapter: 3 Why Is Accounting Useful for Small Business Owners?
....517

Chapter: 4 Accounting basics How to Run a Successful Online
Business 519

Chapter: 5 Common Accounting Mistakes and How to Avoid
Them 532

Chapter: 6 Business Challenges & Solutions....................536

Chapter: 7 Key Accounting Terms...................................552

Chapter: 8 Common Accounting Reports 555

  8.1 Profit & Loss Statement 555

  8.2 Balance Sheet 556

8.2 Cash Flow Statement...557

Chapter: 9 Taxation 559

9.1 What is Taxation 559

9.2 Purposes of Taxation...559

9.2 Classes of Taxes..560

Chapter: 10 Small Business Tax Return 567

Chapter: 11 How to Audit Your E-commerce Business 573

11.1 Review your current vision......................................573

11.2 Be critical 574

11.3 Use tools to source the accurate data you need 576

11.4 Get into auditing to maximize the value of your business .577

Chapter: 12 The impact of Covid-19 on eCommerce......................579

12.1 Six% eCommerce revenue decreased during the lockdown
....580

12.2 Online profit margin increased by 38%...............................581

12.3 The impact of Covid-19 on the workforce 582

12.4 Measurements for physical retailers....................................583

12.5 Shifted strategies 584

12.6 Financial consequences 585

Chapter: 13 What is the Future for Online Business? 586

Conclusion 590

Introduction

You'll definitely have to do a lot of day-to-day daily duties, including accounting, when you first launch your small online business. Knowing how to track and forecast your business's income and expenses is a valuable skill for growth, so familiarise yourself with the basics of accounting.

And if you're willing to outsource your accounting and bookkeeping right now, learning the fundamentals can help you appreciate your finance professional's findings and correctly evaluate your company's financial wellbeing.

We've broken down all you need to understand about small online business accounting, including how to monitor and evaluate your business's main financial indicators, in the parts below.

Chapter: 1 Online Business and its importance?

There has never been a better or easier time in history to start your own business than now. Everyone is connected now, regardless of their income status or geographic location, thanks to the development and growth of easy-to-use website creation tools and social media.

Whether you are rich and powerful or impoverished, you can now freely share your abilities and connect with people around the world. It can also be very inexpensive and simple to get started for those looking to start an online business.

Many people have started online businesses for less than 200 dollars. (the cost purchasing a domain name, hosting service and professional theme).

You can start a business if you can connect with others and fill a need.

In fact, there are numerous advantages to starting and owning your own online business, ranging from increased income and freedom to assisting others in achieving their own personal goals;

however, in order to keep things simple and to the point, I will only go over seven of the many advantages to starting and owning your own online business.

1.1 The importance of eCommerce

1. eCommerce Helps You Reduce Your Costs

To make your online store, it isn't essential that you have every one of your items introduced in an actual space. There're various organizations that work online where they just demonstrate all their stock through their electronic business.

This suggests not just saving by not requiring a purchase or rental of premises, yet besides all that includes electric power, the internet, and so forth or then again in the event that you need to have one, so clients have an actual space, it doesn't need to be just about as extensive as all that you offer. Regardless, you'll reduce your expenses.

2. eCommerce Helps Businesses Go Global

Straightforwardly identified with the previous point, this reality permits you to put your items available to be purchased anywhere on the planet. They won't have the express need to venture out to where you're to perceive what you've to bring to the table.

If you're running an actual store, it'll be restricted by the geological zone that you can support, yet possessing an eCommerce site will offer you the chance to expand your effort. It will offer your items and administrations to clients around the entire world, paying little heed to the time zone and distance.

Besides, this wipes out a wide range of topographical and etymological tango hindrances. Your online business converted into various dialects will permit them to purchase from various nations.

With eCommerce & mobile business also, the whole world is your jungle gym. Your services and products are accessible for many clients sitting on another edge of the world.

In this way, if you need to develop your online business worldwide, it is a good thought to begin making your online store & localize it in various dialects.

3. eCommerce Can Also Be Done through Fewer Overheads and Fewer Risk

Beginning an online store might mean essentially bring down expenses of a start-up contrasted with a physical retailer. The retailer or the online entrepreneur does not need to think about the shop rent high costs, employing a sales associate to facilitate the client, efforts, service charges, safety, and so forth. This, can empower you to sell them at good costs. Moreover, an online shop allows you to grasp expanded productivity with less danger.

4. eCommerce Can Broaden Your Brand & Expand the Business

Having some eCommerce store can be used to widen the scope of items or administrations available to be purchased, extending your business, bringing you a huge number of customers, and broadening your deals. It is the ideal method to take a personal brand from a conventional block & mortar store to a novice, all-around adored one.

With eCommerce, there's no compelling reason to have more than one branch, only one particular online store permitting you to completely arrive at clients without agonizing over moving areas; you can deal with your online business from home.

It's imperative to specify that eCommerce will be useful for Both B2B & B2C businesses to help personal brand mindfulness in the online market.

5. eCommerce Offers Better Marketing Opportunities

Your eCommerce website is the best advertising device that you could at any point have. On a web account, anybody can advertise via online apparatuses such as web-based media advertising, email promoting, web search tool advertising, pay per click advertisements, and SEO assists you in constructing valuable connections & contacts.

For instance, with great SEO, your online store will show up in the top searches of SERPs. Likewise, online media organizations will give you a stage to draw in and construct trust with your clients through audits and appraisals, just as keeping them acknowledged with normal posts about your items and offers.

6. Your Online Store Will Stay Open 24*7/365:

Additionally, one of the incredible significances of eCommerce that eCommerce merchants can appreciate is store timings are currently all day, every day/365 as the eCommerce stores are working 24 hours per day, 7 days per week, contrasted with the customary stores.

Along these lines, merchants can expand their deals by boosting the number of requests. Nonetheless, it's additionally useful for clients when they can buy items and administrations at whatever point they need, whether it's early morning/midnight.

7. eCommerce Is Easier & More Convenient

Individuals' lives are rushed; getting to an actual store implies taking a ton of time and exertion. In this way, beginning an online store implies you can find a way into your client's bustling lives, making the items they need available when they need them.

The agreeable thing about eCommerce is purchasing those choices that are fast, simple, helpful, and simple in understanding with the capability to move supports on the web.

"In web-based shopping, your product is consistently a single tick away instead of actual shopping where you might be compelled to hang tight for quite a long time or months before a product you requested is accessible," says Heritage House, who sell kid suits on the web.

On account of eCommerce's accommodation, shoppers can save heaps of time, endeavors just as cash via looking for their items effectively and making buying on the web.

8. Personalize Your Shopping Experience

In the event that there is one of the unmistakable favorable circumstances of having an online store, you will have the option to know what your buyer does. Genuinely, it would be entirely awkward for a likely purchaser to enter your store, and you were constantly behind him, inquiring what he needs or for what valid reason he doesn't accept your item.

Web-based business permits you, for instance, to know when in the process you left the buy midway and even recall that you left it in the center by sending an email. This, also, can assist you with improving your shopping experience for other events: shortening the means to finish the request or offering those purchaser items with comparable attributes.

9. Improve the Image of Your Business

Among the benefits of having some online store, there's no uncertainty that it likewise incorporates improving the picture of your organization. Offering a decent online deals stage to clients will give your organization an extraordinary corporate appearance.

Not exclusively will it end up being state-of-the-art; however, it will likewise show interest in encouraging buyer buys. For instance, it keeps you from making a trip to the actual spot of offer and permits you to analyze costs from home. Likewise, because of what we have referenced as devotion or input, you can even actualize upgrades in your items that clients will esteem emphatically

10. Easily Receive Feedback on Products

Have you generally needed to understand consumers' opinions about what you are selling to offer more or make it greater?

Indeed, the online store will permit you to get that input to actualize enhancements in the business, through star appraisals, with the chance of leaving remarks.

Also, the client will feel heard after their buy. There could be no greater method to thank you for your trust in buying your organization's items. Besides, in the event that you offer the quality, you'll have nothing to stress over. Empowering an immediate channel where others notice what they can anticipate from the given resource is an extraordinary public illustration of trust in online business.

11. Maximum Security of Transactions

Today, working on the internet is practically more secure and dependable than doing this in an actual store. From home, without anybody watching on your mysterious number or Mastercard. The eCommerce site should have an SSL endorsement.

This testament not just permits safe perusing on the website. What's more, it keeps the information scrambled to be protected to add keys & passwords. This won't just be important for the client's business account yet to utilize much more touchy information, for example, Mastercard data with complete, true serenity.

It merits referencing that 33% of eCommerce specialists distinguished security, versatile installments, and portable applications as the main interests in 2019. Security will keep on being one of the best spotlights on eCommerce.

With changes in innovation, client practices, and shopping designs, dealers should give arrangements guaranteeing the trust and security of shopping measures.

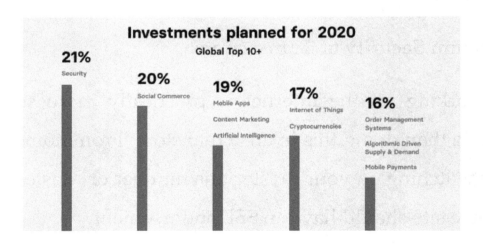

12 Ready for the Trade of the Future

It's another significant detail considering the long haul of the business. Search customer spending and patterns, the headway of innovation, and the most recent insights gauge that by 2040, 95 percent of buys will be executed through the web.

Along these lines, it's not just discussing a pattern of the present yet additionally about what the business relations of things to come will be. Furthermore, similarly, as though you are not on the internet, you don't exist; if your business doesn't sell on the web, it is monstrously restricting its deals.

13. Increase in Sales

Everything mentioned previously is centered around a certain thing: having the option to build your deals. At the end of the day, the business relies on selling more, and in this way, what it will be based on.

All the past focuses add to the way that the 10th and last bit of leeway are that there's an expansion in the acquisition of your items. Arriving at more clients, improving your items on account of remarks, or being accessible 24 hours daily will without a doubt add to the entirety of this.

As a rule, it's normally beautifully simple, with minimal risk and cost to begin an eCommerce business. As you choose your benefits/items incisively, have a suitable plan, got the right partner to help you construct your store, there is very much potential for automated revenue & high ROI.

Chapter: 2 Accounting and Its Purpose

Accounting is the structured method of defining, tracking, assessing, classifying, checking, and transmitting financial records. It shows a company's profit or loss over a specified time, as well as the value and quality of its assets and liabilities, as well as its shareholders' equity.

2.1 Why is Accounting Important?

Accounting is very important and necessary for small business owners because it requires owners, administrators, investors, and other stakeholders to determine the company's financial results. Accounting provides key facts regarding profit & loss, costs & earnings, assets & liabilities for decision-making, scheduling, and risk management within an organization.

Accounting's main goal is to document financial transactions in books of records in order to recognize, calculate, and transmit economic results. Furthermore, tax reporting authorities mandate you to maintain simple books that track profits and expenditures.

2.2 What Is the Purpose of Accounting?

Accounting is regarded as the "Language of Business." It is a system of communicating financial information to multiple uses for decision-making purposes. The major objects of accounting are:

1. Recording transactions

Accounting's primary purpose is to control a systematic, accurate, and full record of a company's financial activities. The accounting system's backbone is made up of these reports. When appropriate, company owners should be able to review and evaluate transactions.

2. Budgeting and planning

Business owners must prepare how they can distribute their limited resources, such as workers, cash, machinery and equipment to meet the company's goals.

Budgeting and planning, an integral aspect of business management, enable companies to prepare accordingly by forecasting requirements and resources. This assists in the coordination of multiple corporate segments.

3. Decision making

Accounting assists in a variety of decision-making processes and facilitates business owners in developing policies to improve business process efficiency. The price to be charged for products and services, the resources required to produce these products and services, as well as financing and business opportunities are all examples of decisions based on accounting information.

4. Business performance

Business owners may use financial records to assess how good their organization is doing. Financial reports provide a credible tool to evaluate important performance indicators, encouraging business owners to compare their output to that of their rivals as well as their past performance.

5. Financial position

The financial statements issued at the end of the accounting period represent a company's financial position at the time. It displays the amount of capital invested, the number of funds utilized by the company, the profit and loss, as well as the number of assets and liabilities.

6. Liquidity

Mismanagement of funds is a common cause of small business failure. Accounting assists in assessing a company's liquidity, which is characterized as the cash and other liquid capital available to pay off debts. Via the identification of bottlenecks, the information lowers the risk of bankruptcy.

7. Financing

Accounting assists business owners in the preparation of historical financial records and also financial forecasts that may be utilized while preparing for a loan or securing investment.

8. Control

Accounting assists in avoiding losses attributable to stealing, fraud, mistakes, injury, obsolescence, and mismanagement by enforcing different checks within the company. Internal monitoring secures the company's finances to eliminate long-term risks.

9. Legal requirements

Businesses must retain correct financial statements of their activities and disclose those records with shareholders, tax officials, and regulators, according to the statute. The financial statements and details are often needed for the filing of indirect and direct taxes.

Chapter: 3 Why Is Accounting Useful for Small Business Owners?

One of the most common causes of small business failure, especially in the first year, is poor financial management. Accounting plays a critical role in providing information that assists small companies in their growth and advancement when they have a restricted budget and other resources.

Accounting is important for small business owners for the following reasons:

➢ Maintain a careful watch on the cash balance. You should enforce strategies for effective record-keeping and a solid financial strategy to prevent the company cash flow from running dry.

➢ Cost management may help small business owners grasp the principles of fixed expenses, variable costs, and how to correctly cost a project. This way, you won't waste funds on a project you felt would be profitable.

➤ Accounting helps you to have a clearer view of the company's health. Learn to interpret a balance sheet, financial statement, and cash flow statement to do this.

➤ It helps you in identifying and avoiding consumer, employee, and supplier bribery and stealing.

➤ You'll be more able to tackle investigations if you grasp corporate accounts and transactions.

➤ When working with corporate leaders who have a strong grip on the company's finances and are mindful of the financial consequences, bankers are more comfortable.

If you're a sole proprietor or have workers, the trick to expanding your small company is to monitor your financial records on a routine basis and build a comprehensive budget that helps you to recognize operating inefficiencies. Saving a little money on a few things will add up to a lot of money in the long run.

Chapter: 4 Accounting basics How to Run a Successful Online Business

A painful task is accounting. It is the dull side of the business. But you can't ignore it if you want your business to grow. You could try to dump all your receipts into a drawer and hand them over to a stranger. Yet you are going to give them financial power. That means losing your business's future. You will hand them a sweet slice of change to do it all for you, too. I guarantee it isn't as hard as you may be afraid of, though. And, for day-to-day operations, you shouldn't require an accountant. You should still know the fundamentals yourself, even though you are paying for guidance. You may acknowledge and challenge what someone is talking to you in this context. It's your business at stake, after all.

The following accounting fundamentals help you need to know to grasp your money.

1. Get Accounting Software

Don't bother using excel or a calculator to piece it all together. Do yourself a favor and get software for accounting. FreshBooks are sold to clients that operate e-commerce businesses. Or there are a variety of accounting software apps you should get right in their app store if you use Shopify. Your business and interests would rely on the right choice. Make sure you choose a bookkeeping system while you're shopping in the app store. Look for software to monitor revenue, expenditures, and inventory. Keep away from programs that generate invoices only or include reports only. You want a tool that's able to do everything for you. Select one that can sync directly to your e-commerce store, whether you want apps like Shopify or go for something different. It would make things even better.

2. Monitor Cash Flow

Get one if you don't have a separate bank account with your business yet. You need to realize that making money is your job. And watching the cash balance is the best way to see this. When you've got more coming in than heading out, you actually do well, don't you? The timing of money going out and coming back can also be monitored. After all, what if, tomorrow, all your bills are due? When you have one million rolling's in next month, it won't mean a whole lot if you can't pay the workers by then. Bear in mind any investments on your accounts that you have. What ways of payment do you give your clients? Are some of them putting a grip on the money? From the moment a consumer spends to the time the money is in your accounts, is there a five-day delay? When you're finding out when you have resources to spare, you ought to remember this. For monitoring currency, Shopify offers a free template. With Excel, you can quickly build your own.

Per week, monitor what you plan to spend. Track the money that you plan per week to come in. You realize you're going to have a challenge if what you need to pay is more than the new bank balance and what's coming in. To improve to boost your cash flow, adopt these tips:

- Do not spend anything sooner than you have got to. If it is due within thirty days, compensate it within thirty days.

- To ensure revenue stays through, suggest selling recurring payment contracts or subscriptions to consumers.

- Hold a reserve 'just in case' in your company bank account.

- Do not overcomplicate yourself. You do not require massive statements of cash balance.

3. Determine how inventory should be counted

Ignore this step if you're selling a service. Inventory is the product that you sell or all the materials that you use to make that item. Do not forget to include any costs for your product being wrapped or packaged. Decide what minimum inventory volume you want to have on hand, and make sure you are tracking inventory before you pass this point so you can reorder. The last thing you want is for inventory to run out and lose sales.

Why does inventory form part of the basics of accounting?

Money equals inventory.

It is the money you spent buying that stuff. You will not make any money back until you sell your product. And while it is sitting in your warehouse, the money tied to your inventory can change (or store, or apartment).

If I purchase 50 items for 100 dollars each, and the price rises up to 150 dollars tomorrow, then immediately, my inventory is worth more.

So, if tomorrow's price falls to 50 dollars, the worth of my inventory is less.

And beware of 'shrinkage'!

That's why, unexpectedly, you have fewer inventory than you should have.

You know you've purchased 50 items. You understand that you sold and delivered 40. You should be left 10 items, right? What if you have only 8 left? This is shrinkage. Perhaps an item was misplaced, or robbed, or destroyed and had to be discarded away. There are plenty of explanations for why this happens. When you don't have a physical department location, the positive thing is the shrinkage is smaller. Currently, factory shrinkage is pretty poor. Less than 1% of the overall product is a normal shrinkage. It's also less probable that you will have shrinkage if you're running a business out of your house. After all, if you're the only person around it, you are less likely to see anyone rob the inventory. Compared with a large warehouse, it's also a lot tougher to lose stock in an apartment. Having said that, shrinkage will happen to everyone. This is why it's necessary to routinely physically count inventory. If you have missed 100 dollars worth of goods and factor it into your accounting, you ought to know.

CGS, which means cost of goods sold, is an expense directly linked to the goods sold by you. This is inventory sold, and also how much it costs to produce that inventory. Suppose say there is one widget you sell. The cost of goods sold for that widget should be whatever it costs you for the parts and also whatever it costs to build it. If the widget parts cost 60 dollars, the packaging cost is 15 dollars, and you paid someone 15 to put it together, that the total cost of the widget will 90 dollars.

MATERIAL COST	60$
PACKAGING COST	15$

LABOUR COST	15$
TOTAL COST OF GOODS SOLD	90 $

4. Calculate all Expenses

You already understand that the costs are directly tied to the volume of sales. Next, you need to know how much it costs you for anything else. Any costs that do not grow as you sell more or drop when you sell fewer are known as 'fixed costs.' Let's say If you pay a monthly rent, for instance, the price is set. If you sell one widget or a million, it won't shift. Such costs are not part of the cost of the goods sold, and the profit margin is not compensated for. However, they do control your earnings and your cash flow.

Some Common fixed expenses are

➢ Utilities

➢ Rent

➤ Interest on loan payments

➤ Property Tax

➤ Wages

These expenses are considered a fixed expense because even though you sell nothing next month, you have to reimburse them. Do not confuse this with an expense where every month is the very same amount. An expense such as electricity may be more than one month longer than the next. Or maybe there's more to it in winter than in summer. In accounting standards, it is always a fixed expense. You will use an average for budgeting if expenses change month to month.

5. Find out Break-Even Sales

Budgeting and planning are essential aspects of operating a business. Next, you are not only going to want to know if last month you made a profit, you are going to want to know if this month and next you want to earn more.

Your break-even sales amount is the amount of sales dollars you need to earn to cover all your costs.

Let's assume, for instance, all the fixed costs add up to 5,000 dollars a month. This ensures that you have to sell enough of the product to meet the cost of producing it (including labor cost) and also an additional 5,000 dollars only to break-even (no profit, no loss).

Break-Even Sale = ___Fixed Cost___

Revenue per unit-Variable cost per unit

$$= \quad \underline{Fixed\ Cost}$$

Unit Margin

If your break-even number of units are 5,000 and you sell only 3000, then you are in problem. And if break-even 5000 and you sell 7000, then you are in a good position.

6. Schedule your right tax rates for customers

Here is the aspect for which most citizens groan: taxation. Taxes are necessary, and they may become very complex. At this point, you may want to contact a tax consultant specialist, if you sell a number of various goods & services to a lot of people around the world. Thankfully, systems these days are fairly smart. For you, the software can take control of much of this.

7. Prepare your Tax Payments

Now, if you are properly set up to collect tax, you also need to make sure you are ready to pay it. Your tax laws will rely on where you are located, actually. At a minimum, believe that as much tax as you have earned must be submitted. This suggests that it is necessary to consider that money of tax is set aside. If not, then when you submit tax return, you face some hurdles. Many online shopping platforms allow you to pay tax on your purchase price, such as Shopify.

For example, if you buy a product that price is 100 dollars and the tax rate is 20%, then you will pay the amount included tax.

Product Cost	100 $
Tax Rate (15%)	15 $
Total amount included Tax	**115 $**

8. Balance Sheet

At the end, you must understand your balance sheet. We have already addressed all as well as cash balance on the income statement. The balance sheet is the final thing to cover. This is what helps you watch the long-term performance of your business and see how your business is performing in general. An income statement is a timely overview. The broader image is a balance sheet. Assets, liabilities, and equity make up the balance sheet.

BUSINESS CONSULTING COMPANY
BALANCE SHEET
As at December 31, 2015

Assets		$	Liabilities & Stockholders' equity		$
Current assets:			Liabilities:		
Cash		85,550	Notes payable		5,000
Accounts receivable		4,700	Accounts payable		1,600
Prepaid building rent		1,500	Salaries payable		2,000
Unexpired insurance		3,600	Income tax payable		3,000
Supplies		250	Unearned service revenue		4,400
Total current assets		95,600	Total liabilities		16,000
Non-current assets:			Stockholders' equity:		
Equipment	9,000		Capital stock	50,000	
Acc. dep. - Equipment	3,600	5,400	Retained earnings	35,000	85,000
Total assets		101,000	Total liabilities & stockholders' equity		101,000

I have finally discussed all the accounting basics you should be practicing day to day and month to month. Start with simple accounting software. It can make your life a lot easier.

Then, note that cash is king, and keep a grip on your cash flow. You should be doing this on a frequent basis unless you have a large cash reserve built.

Next, you ought to consider the revenue, expenditures, and earnings. This is your income statement, which lets you know whether you are earning money per week, month or year.

Do not neglect to schedule for taxation. Set up the e-commerce platform to receive them if you need to. Place the money together to reimburse them should you need to.

Finally, construct the balance sheet. Or let the accounting software do it for you. This will help you exactly how 'healthy' the business is long term. It's a simple way to know if you have so much debt.

There are plenty of other accounting rules and methods that will help you save money at tax time.

There will also be reporting options that can be addressed whether you're seeking to get investors or a loan for growth.

But for running your company, don't get pulled into the complicated laws. It will only distract you from your crucial day job of operating your business.

An accountant will assist you with something beyond and above the fundamentals if you require to.

Chapter: 5 Common Accounting Mistakes and How to Avoid Them

Numerous new business visionaries handle their bookkeeping and accounting when they are beginning. Here are how to stay away from some normal DIY bookkeeping ruins.

When numerous business visionaries first begin, they attempt to deal with their bookkeeping to set aside cash. Notwithstanding, following each penny of pay, costs, charges, and seller installments are messy and tedious. Errors can happen effectively & they can charge your huge business loads of cash.

To help you forestall these monetary blunders, the absolute most regular bookkeeping ruins are below that entrepreneurs make and — all the more significantly — how to keep away from them.

1. Lack of organization

Accounting requires extraordinary association abilities. You'll need to record each exchange, digitize or store receipts for future reference, figure duties, and the sky is the limit from there. In case you're not appropriately following or putting away data, you'll probably miss a significant exchange or lose a receipt, which could get you into difficulty come season of tax.

2. Not following a regular accounting schedule

With the wide range of various duties, you have as an entrepreneur, refreshing your books may tumble to the lower part of your plan for the day. Notwithstanding, it's imperative to set a normal timetable for including late payments and costs. While every day refreshes are ideal, you ought to, in any event, enter your exchanges consistently.

3. Failing to reconcile accounts

While you are recording monetary information and income in your books, you need to routinely return and guarantee your ledger mirrors that equivalent equilibrium. In the event that there's a difference between the two, there's likely a mistake that requires quick thoughtfulness regarding keep the issue from deteriorating. Consistently exploring your business financial balances against your books can likewise help you get any fake exchanges that may have happened.

4. Ignoring small transactions

It's not difficult to disregard that little thank you blessing you sent to a customer or the ream of printer paper you got on your way back to the workplace. Regardless of how immaterial the exchange is, it's critical to record it & get some receipt. In case of an assessment review, you should have the option to give the IRS records of all your costs of doing business, even the little ones.

5. Not backing up your data

Envision if the gadget on which you put away your business' monetary data was lost, hacked, or taken — and you did not have it upheld up anyplace. These problems can emerge whenever, and you should be set up to reestablish your books. Luckily, there are numerous reinforcement alternatives accessible that will empower you to keep an extra, state-of-the-art duplicate of the business financials.

6. Not using an accounting software

In case you're monitoring your business funds in an Excel bookkeeping page or a paper record, you might need to consider moving up to programming. Putting resources into the correct bookkeeping programming can assist you with maintaining a strategic distance from botches and, at last, make it simpler to deal with your accounts.

Most bookkeeping programmings incorporate the financial balance, meaning less manual work. These projects likewise make it simple to back up your information if there should be an occurrence of a crisis. Also, if you wind up expecting to recruit a bookkeeping administration for your business, having unified programming will guarantee the bookkeeper has all the recorded information they require to deal with your books, finance, and assessments.

Regardless of whether you're taking care of your bookkeeping or moving to an expert, accounting mix-ups can cause significant issues for your business. It is ideal to forestall & face these problems.

Chapter: 6 Business Challenges & Solutions

Small enterprises experience a number of obstacles throughout their first few years of operation. Others are more challenging to resolve than others, and according to the U.S. Bureau of Labour Statistics, about 20% of small companies collapse during their first year. Fifty percent go under by the close of their fifth year, and that figure increases to 80 percent by the tenth year.

With so poor survival rates, it's clear to see why people are worried for their first few years of the company. In fact, though, many common market issues and problems are actually fixable. You can notice several moments when you need to take a step back, make an effort to understand the pressure points that you experience and re-think your plan.

Each small business faces some problems here, including some tactical tips about how to solve them.

1. Find the Customers

2. Increasing Brand Awareness

3. Designing Email List

4. Lead Generation

5. Delighting the Customers

6. Hiring Talented People

7. Managing Workflow

8. Financial Strategy

9. Scaling

1. Find Customers

This first one is not just an issue for small enterprises. Marketers of well-known firms such as Toyota, Apple, KFC, and McDonald's are not yet waiting for the leads to come in: Also, the largest, most popular firms have employees working tirelessly to attract new customers every single day.

Finding consumers may be especially challenging for small companies that are not well-known. It seems, for instance, like there are too many platforms you may choose to concentrate on. How do you decide what to prioritize and where money can be allocated?

How to solve it:

Seeking consumers begins by deciding who the target consumer is. It does not work for everyone to spray and pray — you need to ensure you distribute the message to the correct people.

By designing buyer personas, you will get a feel of what your potential buyers are like, what they are doing, and where they spend some time online.

It will significantly boost the market outcomes by producing very particular ones. When you have developed your buyer personas, you can start developing content and reaching out to your potential buyers in areas where they invest time online and with ads that appeal to them.

2. Brand Awareness

Customers can not purchase from you if they don't know who you are. Often it may seem like the largest brands of today seem to have sprung up from nowhere. When did it turn into a household name? Why did they continue to spread so quickly? Is it feasible for your organization to expand in the same way?

Of note, the hard work, mistakes, and rejections of each of these businesses existed behind the scenes. But there are tactics how you can begin right away to spread the word about your company and create a strong reputation.

How to solve it:

There are several approaches to increase brand awareness, but concentrate on three in this book about public relations, blogging & co-marketing.

- **Public Relations**

Public relations are less about competing for a place on a news site and more about concentrating your message on the consumer and discovering your location. I suggest reading First Round Capital's excellent research about what entrepreneurs and small companies often get wrong regarding public relations, which also provides some useful guidance about how to find out who reports the industry, develop relationships, and communicate with reporters.

- **Blogging**

Running a high-quality blog on a daily basis can also help you create brand recognition. A blog not only helps push traffic to your website and turn the traffic into leads, but that also helps you to build authority and confidence among your prospects in your industry. It will also assist you in the creation of an email list, which takes us to our next step.

- **C0-marketing**

Collaborating with another brand allows you to inherit some of their name and credibility while still producing brand evangelists outside of your immediate radius. It's an ideal opportunity to complement the organic marketing activities by acquiring a wide range of potential connections. More details about how to get acquainted with co-marketing can be found in our ebook.

3. Designing Email List

You must create confidence by being top-of-mind and continually delivering value to drive prospects down their buyer's path to finally becoming your client.

The first move is to link prospects to your email list.

As if creating an email list is not complicated enough, the typical marketing account degraded by 22.5 percent last year. That means you'll need to expand your email list by nearly a quarter just to hold it up to date, let alone develop it. Seeking opportunities to continuously introduce fresh, different email addresses to the lists is the task of the marketing staff.

Yet what many people term "making an email list" is simply purchasing an email list, and it is never a smart idea to purchase an email list. I repeat not a good idea. It is not only a waste of resources, but it'll also damage your email deliverability and I.P. credibility. If purchasing or renting email lists is your new plan, then it's time to rebuild and find appropriate ways to position certain tools.

How to solve it:

Develop opt-in email lists instead of purchasing or renting lists. Subscribers who willingly give you their email address so that you can send them updates make up an opt-in email list.

The process of opting in needs the accessibility of the website that catches their email address. This can be accomplished with a shape builder or other method to transform (more on that later).

Creating a market is the other part of the puzzle. Through making excellent blog posts, you will do this and make it convenient for people to subscribe, which can help you improve your web visibility, build up search credibility, and develop evangelists from your content at the same time.

Create an informative opt-in message and email it to your old list, inviting contacts to re-opt-in and pledging to delete any contacts that don't reply.

Rising your email list does not often mean growing your sales-qualified lead list, which leads me to my next stage.

4. Lead Generation

Lead generation is another concern most small companies share, namely, creating sufficient leads to maintain the sales staff satisfied.

However, the most critical goal of a marketing team is to produce high-quality leads in vast amounts. A decent lead generation engine transforms website users into future buyers and maintains a constant stream of sales leads flowing in as you sleep.

How to solve it:

To make the lead generation method function for your business, you must first increase the conversion rate of your current website. The most critical asset you have for converting opportunities into clients is your website. Look and question yourself from your website:

Do visitors specifically direct each of the webpages to take some action, or do they leave them uncertain what to do next?

Can you use a program, like HubSpot's free lead generation tool, that instantly pulls the inputs from your forms and brings them into your communication database?

For any single campaign that you manage, can you build custom landing pages?

Do you have CTAs for any of your blog posts for lead generation? (Have you got a blog at all?)

First, prioritize the most major blogs on your website. The homepage, "About" page, "Contact Us" page, and probably one or two of the most famous blog posts are usually the sites that pull in the bulk of visitors for most companies. Learn how to decide which sites to prioritize and how to customize them in this topic.

Then, utilizing conversion applications such as:

- Hello bars, hello

- Pop-up windows

- Diaposit-ins

Finally, free lead generation tools and applications for startups can be used. It is a huge obstacle in and of itself to afford ads in general, but it can be a game-changer to identify and incorporate the most effective free marketing methods.

5. Delighting the Customers

A perfect target is consumer loyalty, but much greater is customer delight. After all, the ones who purchase from you again, write expert opinions and accept case studies, and recommend you to others they trust, are delighted consumers.

You have to transcend standards and offer an unmatched service in order to gain true consumer delight such that your consumers become promoters of your brand.

How to solve it:

For your customer, it takes effort to begin solving in a fashion that converts them into crazed fans. Here are few moves that will bring you into the proper mindset:

- ➢ Realize why you were picked by your customers and what they want and need

- ➢ At the beginning of the commitment, set clear goals

- ➢ Deliver on certain requirements (and serve the wishes of your customers)

➢ Dream of innovative approaches to include unique extras that go beyond and above the call of duty.

➢ Continue to monitor consumer loyalty and allow changes.

6. Hiring talented workers

Without a great team who knows your mission and encourages your actions, none of the above will happen at large.

Hiring is one of the most challenging tasks for small companies, particularly when small corporate leaders are often under-resourced to start with. Hiring new hires is a huge deal and a difficult operation, and most businesses invest about 4,000 dollars per new hire on onboarding. Employee attrition can be very costly if you do not recruit properly.

Still, as Howard Bernstein, CEO of 2020 On-site Optometry, says, it is hard to recognize anything on your own. That's why it is crucial to identify and recruit the best people and others who are genuinely passionate about what you are doing.

How to solve it:

For a short-term recruiting approach, it is simple to send out a work description, screen candidates, and make a decision. However, owing to the high expenses of recruiting the incorrect employee, it's essential to dedicate a considerable amount of time to the hiring phase. When you may locate excellent workers, do not settle for decent staff, even though it takes more time. Good workers are what can drive the business to the next stage.

And when you build customer personas for your employers, for your career seekers, create nominee personas. For each new job you recruit for, the personas must be different, but they may share certain basic characteristics across the culture of the business.

Next, take care in drawing applicants to the name of your company and making them involved in knowing more. This would assist you in creating a recruitment pipeline that will have the same certainty in hiring as it does in revenue. Then translate certain opportunities into applicants.

7. Managing the Workflow

When you have the staff in position to make the magic possible, handling operations as you scale is the next obstacle. You want to make sure the staff has the procedures and resources they need to perform successful work fast.

Around the same moment, as a corporate owner, you will not be everywhere at once. So, how can you remain centered on the market but still ensuring that everybody in the organization gets everything they require?

How to solve it:

By providing opportunities for them to get suggestions, the only approach to diagnose the barriers the team encounters and improve productivity is to build ways to identify them. It is possible to do this via:

➢ Surveys on employee satisfaction

➢ Frequent discussions of immediate reports one-on-one

➢ Assuring the success of your direct reports Hold one-on-one conferences for their direct reports

➢ Occasionally, skip-level meetings are conducted.

➢ Asking regarding group risks and the things that cause them the most "pain" in their positions

➢ Seeking the similarities & the bottlenecks in the reviews you get

8. Financial Strategy

More capital (whether staff, resources or time) can ideally improve productivity and output. Providing all of the support you can to the staff is the first move in maintaining smooth operations.

In principle, it seems easy, but have you realized the caveat, everything. Can you? Unfortunately, corporate owners have revenue-based and margin-based spending constraints.

It becomes a struggle then to maximise productivity when operating under such limits, investing in the company without going overboard. By making sound choices focused on strong financial planning, this is solved.

How to solve it:

Each business is going to be different, so by remaining in front of invoices and bookkeeping, you'll need to use business credit carefully, reduce expenses where possible, and control cash flow. You will be assisted by corporate accountants and investment planners who evaluate the financial condition and help you to make sound choices.

9. Scaling

According to Nick Rellas, Drizly's co-founder and CEO, "There's this balance of creating power efficiency early, versus doing just what you have to do to get it all completed."

This is a complicated one, especially because every scenario is different. This topic can be seen in any aspect of the industry, including product growth, promotion, and content design, recruiting, and so on.

Most business leaders, for instance, would drive production at all costs. However, if you develop your business too fast, you'll find yourself trying to recruit staff quickly. Since preparation requires time, this can overwhelm the more seasoned team members. And if you wouldn't adequately prepare your staff, it might backfire.

How to solve it:

There's no right solution here, sadly. "The scale can tip one way or the other based on where you are in your business' lifecycle," Rellas says, "although I do agree you need both at various times."

Not obsessing about every aspect, but obsessing about the correct specifics, is what it comes right down to. For example, obsessing over product excellence may be less relevant than obsessing over customer care. It is easier to set away your worries and introduce a product that is not flawless so it can be changed and enhanced at all times. After all, you will understand a lot more easily what's effective and what isn't until the goods are in possession of your consumers.

Chapter: 7 Key Accounting Terms

The following are some standard accounting terminology that any small business owner should be acquainted with:

1. GAAP (Generally Agreed Accounting Standards)

2. Cash basis accounting

3. Accrual basis accounting

4. Accounts payable

5. Accounts receivable

1. Generally Agreed Accounting Standards (GAAP)

GAAP is a series of standard accounting principles that most American corporations are expected to follow. These guidelines detail how to keep track of, calculate, and report on the company's assets to third parties.

2. Cash basis accounting

Cash basis accounting is one of the two most popular accounting techniques, as it involves recording revenue and expenditures where they are earned and charged. Small companies like this approach because it is easy, despite the fact that it can offer a false impression of your cash flow (e.g., if you receive payment for a bill the month after you issued it).

3. Accrual basis accounting

Accrual basis accounting is needed for companies with a turnover of more than $25 million. You must log revenue as you charge it, rather than when it is paid, which implies you might be paying taxes on the money you haven't even received. However, opposed to cash basis accounting, it offers a more reliable long-term perspective of the finances.

4. Accounts payable

Accounts payable contains all unpaid payments for goods and services that you owe to suppliers. To accurately forecast cash flow, these liabilities must be considered against the company's assets and income.

5. Accounts receivable

Any of the money owing to the company by its consumers or clients is paid for in the accounts receivable. These accounts are normally monitored by invoices, which specify payment conditions (e.g., within a specified number of days of receipt) so you know when to expect incoming funds.

Chapter: 8 Common Accounting Reports

As part of their financial accounting procedures, every business must learn how to prepare a few main financial reports. Outside participants, such as owners, suppliers, and creditors, can use these documents to record the business's profits and expenses.

8.1 Profit & Loss Statement

When it is time to file your company returns with the IRS, accountants and tax preparers would most certainly ask for a (P&L) statement, but you will still need to share it with lenders if you apply for financing. Your profit and loss statement (P&L) outlines profitability of your company by listing gross margin, profit, sales, cost of goods sold and other primary indicators over a specific time period (monthly, quarterly and annually).

Profit and Loss Statement Template

[Company Name]

[Street Address], [City, ST ZIP Code]
[Phone: 555-555-55555] [Fax: 123-123-123456]
[abc@example.com]

Profit & Loss Statement

For the Period Ended _____

Income	$	$
Sales	0000000	
Services	00000000	
Other Income	00000	
Total Income		**0000000**
Expenses		
Accounting	0000000	
Advertising	000000	
Assets Small	000000	
Bank Charges	000000	
Cost of Goods Sold	00000	
Total Expenses		**00000000**
Profit/Loss		**00000000**

8.2 Balance Sheet

Balance sheet is a "snapshot" of the company's financial condition at any specific point in time. It includes a summary of the company's capital, assets & liabilities, both of which may be used to assess the valuation of your company.

ACCOUNT FORMAT

BUSINESS CONSULTING COMPANY
BALANCE SHEET
As at Date_____

Assets	$	Liabilities & Stockholders' equity	$
Current assets:		Liabilities:	
Cash		Notes payable	
Accounts receivable		Accounts payable	
Prepaid building rent		Salaries payable	
Unexpired insurance		Income tax payable	
Supplies		Unearned service revenue	
Total current assets		Total liabilities	
Non-current assets:		Stockholders' quity:	
Equipment		Capital stock	
Acc. Deal - Equipment		Retained earnings	
Total assets	101,000	Total Liabilities & Stockholders' equity	101,000

8.2 Cash Flow Statement

A cash flow statement is a financial statement that records and categorises each actual cost and revenue line by line, helping you to maintain track of the company's financial operation. About any line item in the cash flow statement would be identified as an operation, investment, or financing task.

You will also be liable for making a stockholders' equity statement whether the business includes shareholders or partners with equity in the company. This declaration, which is part of your balance sheet, outlines all adjustments in the valuation of the stockholders' equity rights over time, normally from the beginning of the end of the year.

Example Corporation		
Statement of Cash Flows		All numbers in thousands
Operating Activities	$	**10,100**
Net Income from Operations	$	10,000
Add: Depreciation Expense	$	100
Investing Activities	$	**(500)**
Purchase of Equipment	$	(1,000)
Sale of used equipment	$	500
Financing Activities	$	**4,500**
Increase in Long Term Debt	$	2,500
Issuance of Stock	$	5,000
Dividends Paid	$	(3,000)
Net Change in Cash Flow	$	**14,100**

Chapter: 9 Taxation

Taxation is the method of enforcing or levying a tax on individuals and corporate companies through a government or the taxing authority. Taxation applies at all levels, from corporate tax (GST) to goods and services tax.

9.1 What is Taxation

The federal and state governments have a major influence on how taxes are set around the country. The state and federal governments have enacted numerous policy changes in recent years to streamline the taxation mechanism and maintain accountability in the region. The Goods and Services Tax (GST) was one such reform that eased the tax system relating to the selling and distribution of goods and services in the world.

9.2 Purposes of Taxation

In the nineteenth century, the common assumption was that taxation could be used solely to support the nation. Governments have used taxes for more than just fiscal reasons in the past, and they do so again today. The differentiation between wealth sharing, income inequality, and economic prosperity is a valuable way to look at the function of taxes, according to American economist Richard A. Musgrave. (Sometimes global growth or progress and foreign competition are identified as distinct priorities, but they can be absorbed under the other three in general.) The first target, resource distribution, is reinforced if tax policy does not intervene with economic allocations in the absence of a legitimate justification for intervention, such as the need to minimize emissions. The second aim, wage redistribution, is intended to reduce income and wealth inequality disparities. The aim of stabilization is to sustain high jobs and market stability, which is achieved by tax reform, monetary policy, government budget policy & debt management.

9.2 Classes of Taxes

Taxes have been categorized in different forms in the theory of public finance, based on who pays for them, who carries the ultimate responsibility of them, the degree to which the burden may be transferred, and other considerations. Taxes are more generally categorized as either direct or indirect, such as the income tax of the former category and the sales tax of the latter. The requirements for discriminating between direct and indirect taxes are contested by economists, and it is uncertain which group such taxes, such as property tax or corporate income tax, should fall under. A direct tax is generally said to be one that cannot be transferred from the individual to anyone else, although it can be an indirect tax.

1. Direct Taxes

2. Indirect Taxes

Now we learn about direct and Indirect Taxes

1. Direct Taxes

Direct taxes are mainly imposed on individual citizens and are generally dependent on the taxpayer's capacity to compensate as determined by revenue, spending, or net worth. The following is a list of the most popular forms of direct taxes.

Individual income taxes are usually based on the taxpayer's gross personal net income (that might be an individual, couple, or family) that reaches a specified level. The conditions surrounding the capacity to pay, such as marital status, amount and age of the child, and financial pressures arising from sickness, are more widely tailored to take into consideration. Taxes are often charged at phased scales, which ensures that rates rise as income increases. A taxpayer's and family's personal exemptions can produce a range of income that is entitled to a zero-tax rate.

Net worth taxes are imposed on a person's overall net worth, which is proportional to value of assets less his liabilities. As in income tax, the taxpayer's specific situation should be taken into account.

Personal or direct consumption taxes (also referred to as taxes on spending or taxes on expenditure) are essentially imposed on all receipts that are not channeled into savings. In comparison to indirect spending taxes like the sales tax, a direct consumption tax may be customized to a person's financial circumstance by taking into account considerations like age, marital status, family status, and so on. This tax method has been implemented in only two nations, India & Sri Lanka, although it has long been appealing to theorists; both cases were short and ineffective. The "flat tax," which produces economic results close to those of the direct consumption tax by exempting many capital gains, came to be regarded favorably by tax analysts at the end of the 20th century. No nation has introduced a flat-rate tax base, while many have just one rate of income tax.

Inheritance taxation, in which the taxable object is the bequest earned by the individual inheriting, and estate taxes, of which the taxable object is the cumulative estate inherited by the deceased, are the two kinds of taxes imposed upon death. Inheritance taxes also take into account the taxpayer's specific conditions, such as the connection of the taxpayer to the beneficiary and his net wealth when the bequest is received. Estate payments, on the other hand, are normally phased depending on the value of the estate, although in certain nations, they include tax-free transfers to the partner and account for the number of heirs. Tax regimes which include a tax on gifts in excess of a certain threshold rendered by living individuals in order to avoid death duty from being circumvented by an exchange of property prior to death (see gift tax). Transfer taxes usually do not raise any money, if only because substantial tax collections can be prevented conveniently by estate planning.

2. Indirect Taxes

Indirect taxes, including imports and exports, are imposed on the output or sale of products and services or on transactions. Examples include general and limited excise taxes, VAT, taxes on some aspect of production or manufacturing, taxes on lawful purchases, and customs or import duties.

General sales taxes are levies that cover a large amount of consumer spending. The same tax rate may be extended to all taxable items, or separate rates can be applied to different products (such as food or clothing). Single-stage taxation may be levied at the retail level, like some states in the United States do, or at a pre-retail level (such as production or wholesale), as some developed countries do. At each point in the production-distribution process, multistage taxes are introduced. VAT, which grew in prominence during the second half of the 20th century, is usually collected by enabling the taxpayer to exclude from the sales debt the tax credit charged on transactions. At each point of the manufacturing and delivery process, the VAT has effectively substituted the turnover levy-a tax, with no tax relief charged at previous levels. Tax cascading, or the combined impact of the turnover tax, distorts economic decisions.

While they are usually applicable on a wide variety of items, sales taxes often exclude low-income families from the obligation to lower their tax burden. Excises, by contrast, are imposed only on individual products or facilities. Although almost all, including basics such as beef, flour, and salt, to non-essentials such as food, beer, cigarettes, coffee, and tea, to luxuries such as jewels and furs, taxes on a small category of goods, tobacco items, motor fuel, and alcoholic drinks, place excises and customs duties on most nations. Taxes on customer durables were extended on luxury items such as carriages, saddle horses, pianos, and billiard tables in earlier centuries. The car is currently a primary luxury tax item, primarily because registration regulations promote tax administration. Any nations also tax gaming & state-run jackpots have similar consequences as excises, with "take" of the government being, in essence, a gambling tax. Taxes on raw products, intermediate commodities (e.g., natural oil, alcohol), and equipment are imposed by certain nations.

Some excise duties and customs duties are particular, i.e., they are assessed on the grounds of the quantity, weight, duration, volume, or other particular features of the taxable product or service. Such excerpts, such as income taxes, are ad valorem, as determined by the price, depending on the valuation of the item. Legal transaction taxes are charged on the issue of bonds, on the selling (or transfer) of houses and land, and on sales on the stock market. They sometimes take the form of stamp duties for administrative reasons; that is, the legal or commercial paper is stamped to signify payment of the fee. Stamp taxes are regarded as an annoyance tax by many tax analysts; they are more often seen in less-developed countries & slow down the transactions on which they are applicable.

Chapter: 10 Small Business Tax Return

Most people are dreaming of holiday shopping, celebrations, and holidays as the year draws to an end. You're already worried about your 2017 tax return as a small business owner. Filing taxes, mostly as a small company, can be perplexing, daunting, and even cause you want to rip your hair out. It won't be too terrible if you take your time to make sure you have everything you need. Here's a short guide to filing a small business tax return in five easy measures.

1. Determine how to file

2. Collect all the documents

3. Find what forms you need

4. Make sure you are getting the deductions you deserve

5. Recheck your work with the help of a CPA

1. Determine how to file

The first step in planning for tax season as a small business owner is to know what sort of business you have. It would have an effect on the way you prepare your taxes. Are you a single proprietorship, an LLC, an S company, a general partnership, or a C corporation? When setting up your company, this should have already been known, but now it comes into play again. Different company forms have various criteria for tax returns, so it is necessary to consider what sort of business you are in order to understand what would be needed.

2. Collect all the documents

You've already learned that filing taxes needs a bunch of documentation, and this is true. Your documentation can be made up of real documents, or the documents might be digital. In any scenario, be-ensure you have them.

"The IRS says, "The company with which you are affects the kind of documents you need to maintain for federal tax purposes when it comes to what sort of documentation you can obtain. A list of your company activities should be included in your recordkeeping method.

Payroll, sales slips, bank slips, bounced checks, invoices, certificates, and cash register recordings are also exampling documents. Don't forget to keep track of travel costs, any sales, and records of items you buy and are using in your company, such as furniture or machinery. Last but not least, job documents are needed. Do the utmost to maintain track of these items during the year, instead of struggling throughout the tax season, to make it easy on yourself.

3. Find what forms you need

It's an unfair fact that while filing the taxes, there would be some filling-out of paperwork. The kind of small company you have may influence the forms to fill out, as described earlier. Every state may have its own types and specifications, so here's a short rundown on some of the federal income tax measures:

Form 1120 U.S. Business Income Tax Return-Form 1120 is for tax reports submitted by C companies. C businesses are organizations where the shareholders do not incur taxes on individual reports themselves.

Form 1120 S U.S. Income Tax Return – For S Companies, this is the form to use. S Company owners, unlike C Companies, pay income tax on their corporate income tax reports. As a consequence, each shareholder is expected to complete a Schedule K-1 Method.

Form 1065 U.S. Relationship Benefit Tax- You would need to plan one of these types if your small corporation is set up as a collaboration. Since partnerships do not incur income tax, this type is just for information purposes. Every participant may also need to fill out a Schedule K-1 Form if you are part of a relationship, which goes into specifics regarding the profits, dividends, and losses of each particular partner.

Form 1099 MISC-This is a form that is processed and issued as part of the tax return to any independent contractors you might have employed, and it is often submitted to the IRS.

You may still need to complete separate documents for the boss, such as Form W-2 Pay and Tax Declaration.

4. Make sure you are getting the deductions you deserve

Deductions are the one aspect of paying the taxes that may be deemed pleasant.

Taxes are not all about the government having its due, Drew Hendricks of Forbes points out. Some tax laws are loopholes that provide for deductions – which are simply opportunities for the government to get you and your company to use money the way it wants."

You have put in a lot of time this year because operating a small company is an expensive activity. Making the best of the tax deductions, but be mindful of what is and is not an appropriate deduction. The Internal Revenue Service (IRS) offers certain basic guidance in this regard. The deductible business cost must be "usual and essential." Supplies, car costs, corporate transport, contract labor, staff compensation, pensions, employee benefits, and employee investment systems are some of the most typical ones on a small business tax return. Be vigilant not to combine personal expenditures with work expenses and be mindful of what company costs are 100% deductible versus a lower percentage.

5. Recheck your work with the help of a CPA

It may be confusing to submit a tax return as a private citizen, and filing as a small businessman is much, much harder. It's important to consider the measures involved in processing a small business tax return, as well as the criteria. It is advised, however, that you enlist the assistance of a licensed CPA to ensure that everything is properly and accurately filled out, particularly if this is your first filing as a small business. A CPA will help you manage all the forms, locate deductions, and advise you what reports and documentation to gather are required.

Chapter: 11 How to Audit Your E-commerce Business

E-commerce is one of the fastest-growing business markets nowadays, so make sure you are prepared with an online business audit to help you develop the site. To boost traffic, make profits, and create a long-term consumer community, e-commerce companies need great material.

> How is the content performing?

> Is there anything that you should be doing?

> What was the last period you performed a comprehensive e-commerce audit?

It is important to take a step back and audit the material on a daily basis and ensure that it is fulfilling your company objectives. Continue reading to learn how to audit (and improve) your e-commerce material.

11.1 Review your current vision

Before you start your e-commerce business audit, you can do some deep thinking. This involves having a good, hard look at the new plan and finding some places that you might be falling short.

Do you really have any editorial calendar for the company's site and social network, for example? An editorial calendar is an important and basic function that many e-commerce company owners ignore.

> Take into consideration if the material is advertised. Are you making the best out of your email & social network accounts?

> Do the landing pages have well-defined objectives?

Prior to implementing some modifications or improving your approach after an e-commerce market analysis, you must first recognize existing issue areas that need to be resolved. You are already mindful of where (and why) you've been deficient in strategic guidance. Tackle certain places with passion, and bid farewell to your strategy-poor past.

11.2 Be critical

Now it's time to get back to work for the content auditing.

Create a list of every website on the e-commerce platform, beginning with the home & landing pages and making your way down to specific blog posts and product pages. Now go to each page and ask yourself the following questions:

- ➢ Is the website producing as it promises? Are your headings in line with your text? Do the call-to-actions execute on their promises?

- ➢ Is anything current? Since search engines don't value old material as much, it's crucial that the connections, items, and material are accurate and up-to-date.

- ➢ Is there a conceptual framework for each piece? Examine the organization on the website. It should sound normal and not haphazardly placed together.

- ➢ Is it easy to find? Internal links should be plentiful in your material, linking it all together. It's not just SEO-friendly, but it's still user-friendly.

- ➢ Is it efficient? Using the site analytics to see if any specific piece of material gets a tonne of traffic or converts. Don't forget these metrics if you want to expand your e-commerce business.

When undertaking an e-commerce company audit, don't be delicate with yourself: a stern eye on each material feature can sound harsh, but it will deliver the best outcomes.

11.3 Use tools to source the accurate data you need

Since an e-commerce company audit involves effort and time, it's a smart idea to use one of the numerous free or low-cost tools available to assist you to organize and quantify data easily. You have access to a wide variety of content resources, each of which is customized to a particular target.

➤ **Google Analytics:**

Google Analytics is helpful for finding issue areas and assessing the success of content by indicators.

➤ **Screaming Frog:**

Screaming Frog is an SEO tool that crawls your site and returns valuable (and actionable) details.

➤ **Site Analyzer:**

Site Analyzer offers a thorough review of the site, as well as an overall rating dependent on criteria such as speed, style, and copy.

> **Yoast:**

Yoast, a wonderful WordPress SEO plugin that offers a fast rundown of keyword targeting for blog posts and websites.

But be careful: with so many auditing tools at your hands, it's possible to get too dependent on them. To get the best out of the e-commerce quality audit, invest just in a handful and use them wisely. Don't get paralyzed by research paralysis. There are many resources that will assist you.

11.4 Get into auditing to maximize the value of your business

Finally, don't feel too cozy. Auditing is a constant phase that necessitates daily focus. Your content isn't a stand-alone entity; it's up against a slew of other products in a saturated sector, and standing away requires effort.

A content audit is a valuable practice that will help you keep on top of things. It's also a particularly rewarding talent to practice.

Flipping websites is a popular route for aspiring entrepreneurs, and a content audit will make it simple for you to acquire an online company, transform it around, and then market it for a profit — it's a talent that can pay off again and again. It all comes down to providing outstanding web content in terms of profitability, performance, and market resale value.

Chapter: 12 The impact of Covid-19 on eCommerce

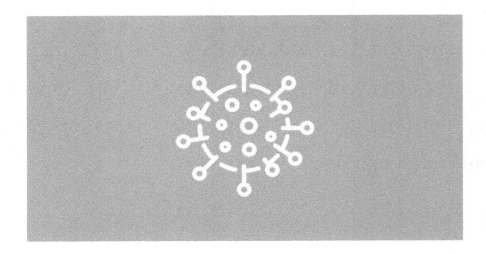

2020 was a difficult year for almost all individuals. Simultaneously, the online business developed more than ever. What would we be able to anticipate from 2021? SearchNode distributed another report on the most recent web-based business patterns and the effect of Covid-19.

A year ago, SearchNode distributed a report on online business patterns in 2020. Obviously, in those days, there was mostly secret about the Covid that would spread all over the globe. In the overview, there were loads of discussions with Magento, an improved spotlight on personalization and natural manageability.

2020 was, of course, all about Covid-19.

What has changed in a year? You should discover, as the Lithuanian tech organization distributed another report on online business patterns. In October 2020, the organization interrogated 100 internet business leaders from Europe and North America.

12.1 Six% eCommerce revenue decreased during the lockdown

There were inquiries concerning Covid-19. It appears to be that most web-based business organizations saw their online income increment during the worldwide lockdown in the spring of 2020. As per the study, 90% of organizations saw their online deals increment at any rate a piece, with 50% of respondents asserting it developed by more than 100%. Yet, 6% say their online business income diminished during Covid lockdown.

After the lockdown was finished, numerous purchasers began shopping at physical retailers once more. 86% of respondents say that their online incomes expanded, and just 4% say it diminished.

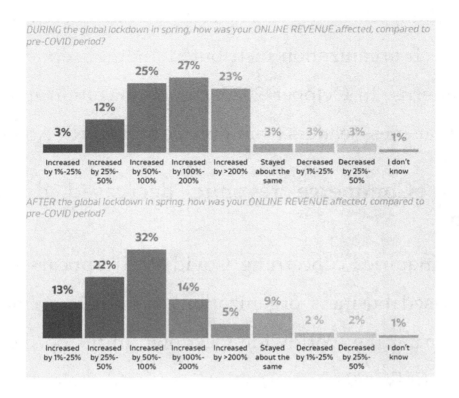

12.2 Online profit margin increased by 38%

Producing on the web deals is a certain something; the entire Covid-19 circumstance has additionally prompted things like disturbed inventory chains, inadequately staffed client assistance, and the sky is the limit from there. This straightforwardly influences the online net revenue. It appears to be that for 38% of internet business leaders, their online net revenue developed during the worldwide lockdown, while for a comparative rate

(40%), the circumstance expressed about the equivalent. Just 15% asserted that it diminished.

12.3 The impact of Covid-19 on the workforce

The pandemic has, obviously, additionally prompted a few changes in organizations' labor force. Around 44% said they needed to move staff, while three out of ten recruited more individuals. The opposite side of the coin is that 26% needed to terminate a few groups, and 15 percent say they needed to lessen their workers' pay rates. Also, perhaps somewhat amazing for a few, yet 5 percent figured out how to expand compensations. What's more, much astonishing: 21% of organizations didn't change their labor force by any means.

21% of organizations didn't change their labor force.

23% of omnichannel players observed disconnected deals increment

Another intriguing finding from the investigation is that for retailers on the offline and online stores, 23% say their disconnected deals expanded, and 16 percent figured out how to keep it comparative. Lamentably, for 43%, their disconnected deals endured a shot.

12.4 Measurements for physical retailers

Numerous physical retailers needed to change their business on the off chance that they needed to maintain a strategic distance from to leave the business. In this way, numerous new practices were presented a year ago. Among the members, 31% presented in-store pickup, while 26% decided to present home conveyance. Sadly, around one of every five needed to close down some actual stores for great.

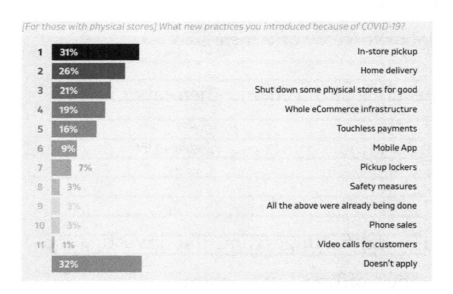

Covid has vigorously affected online retailers on various levels. Among the fundamental difficulties for internet business organizations, upset stockpile chains and satisfying interest for items were the, for the most part, referenced ones. Yet, restricted tasks because of the lockdown, overseeing stock, and the general absence of representatives were likewise vital difficulties for online retailers. What's more, 17% said it was testing since they need to shut down their actual stores.

An upset store network was the primary test for some online retailers in Europe.

12.5 Shifted strategies

A year ago, numerous respondents said they would generally execute, improve or change personalization, site-search and omnichannel. This year, the essential vision has moved because of Covid-19. The majority of the organizations (45%) will presently have more spotlight on the advanced piece of their business by changing the combination, putting resources into new online business programming or emphasizing additionally on internet advertising channels.

One of every five said they would increase activities, which means they need to execute their methodologies and act quicker. One out of ten says they are currently centered around actual store changes, and 8 percent went for inventory network changes, from minor ones to new store networks or coordination's.

12.6 Financial consequences

Notwithstanding all the terrible things occurring because of the flare-up of the Covid, monetarily 2020 wasn't so awful for some web-based business organizations. The greater part of them (63%) say the year (up to October) was effective. Furthermore, 28% case their web-based business was progressing nicely, while their actual stores didn't. What's more, an astounding 2% said the inverse!

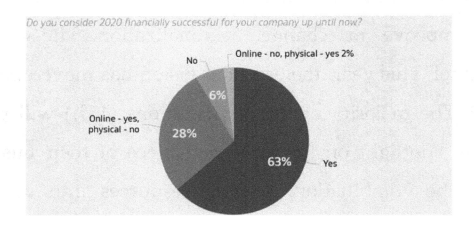

Chapter: 13 What is the Future for Online Business?

With the online world changing apparently from one day to another and an expanding number of sites (today, there are just about 2 billion sites out there), the future for organizations working on the web consistently appears to be unsure. From the finish of unhindered internet to the limitations on YouTube adaptation to progressing computerized innovation and that's just the beginning, the inquiry is the thing that patterns will be generally noticeable for online organizations within a reasonable time-frame.

Right now, with the US economy extending, it appears to be that the not-so-distant future for online organizations is splendid gratitude to more noteworthy customer certainty and ways of managing money. What follows are new patterns in online business that have all the earmarks of growing as buyer propensities change over the following, not many years, which will significantly affect how web-based advertising is being performed.

Expansion of Cryptocurrency

While there has been impressive information about the inconveniences related to bitcoin, digital money itself has all the earmarks of being extending quickly and turning out to be standard. With more organizations and governments going to cryptographic money as an alternative, the exchanges will turn out to be solidly advanced. This implies an adjustment in the manner purchasers purchase across all business sectors, which implies that online organizations should be set up to acknowledge this type of cash soon.

The advent of Machine Learning

This type of innovation is ready to venture into deals and client service, implying that how organizations work with clients will be improved. AI will be through utilizing discourse examination, which better aids client assistance divisions in how to react to every one of their clients. This improves connection which means assembling a more grounded brand and enduring fewer misfortunes because of mistaken assumptions.

Increased Security Spending

In light of ongoing hacks and break-ins that have uncovered the individual data of millions of clients, more organizations are venturing up their security conventions to keep it from happening to them. This has implied a move in accentuation from avoidance towards recognizing interruptions and reacting in like manner. Better security implies more costs, which may tremendously affect the monetary situation of little and medium-sized online organizations.

Personalized Marketing

With such countless online organizations attempting to arrive at similar clients, it can get hard to get over the clamor. This is why individual promoting patterns have been developing and will keep on extending as more organizations spring up around the planet. Effective online organizations will zero in on brilliant showcasing that arrives at the individual, not simply the ideal buyer gathering. On account of new advanced innovation, specific Artificial Intelligence (AI) (web-based business organizations are now confronting this test), the progressions are now occurring and will keep on developing.

Rise of the Sharing Economy

The blend of the sharing economy, which is most broadly addressed by ride-sharing administrations like Uber. It has additionally dug into retail with monsters, for example, Google and Amazon getting into this pattern. For online organizations, the sharing economy addresses an incredible pattern ready to attack medical care and monetary administrations, which may change how numerous online organizations work.

For online entrepreneurs, the extension of the web to world business sectors implies a new wilderness of clients just as contenders. The individuals who succeed will be adaptable to the inescapable change that happens and finds a way to remain one stride ahead to guarantee their future.

Conclusion

Accounting is described as "the processing, review, and systematic documentation of numerical business transactions, the preparation of financial reports, and the examination and evaluation of these reports for management's knowledge and guidance."

Accounting is an accounting mechanism that observes, tracks, and communicates an economic entity's monetary activities.

It is the method of defining, evaluating, and communicating economic data in order for consumers of the data to make educated choices and decisions. Human life is evolving in this ever-changing environment.

Accounting has taken on a different form as a consequence of technical advances, such as holding records mechanically.

With the widespread usage of electronic accounting tasks, a modern arena has arisen. As a consequence, it is obvious that the concept of accounting will evolve in the coming years.

CPSIA information can be obtained
at www.ICGtesting.com
Printed in the USA
LVHW061451040621
689358LV00005B/436